Praise for

*Aid Under Fire: Nation Building and the Vietnam War*

"Elkind's excellent book makes an important contribution to the literature on early US involvement in Vietnam, offering an engaging and well-researched social history of the American aid workers responsible for implementing the US nation-building project. Her analysis is astute, and she ably situates the grassroots efforts of the aid workers within the broader context of US policy."

—Scott Laderman, coeditor of *Four Decades On: Vietnam, the United States, and the Legacies of the Second Indochina War*

"A thought-provoking and cogently argued study of US nation-building programs in Vietnam. Elkind's ground-level analysis highlights the enormous, perhaps insurmountable, obstacles that hampered the American aid effort."

—Philip E. Catton, author of *Diem's Final Failure: Prelude to America's War in Vietnam*

"*Aid Under Fire* is an important book that expands our understanding of the US effort to 'modernize' South Vietnam by revealing the critical role played by aid workers on the ground."

—Amanda Kay McVety, author of *Enlightened Aid: U.S. Development as Foreign Policy in Ethiopia*

# Aid Under Fire

# AID UNDER FIRE

## *Nation Building*
### and the
## *Vietnam War*

JESSICA ELKIND

UNIVERSITY PRESS OF KENTUCKY

Copyright © 2016 by The University Press of Kentucky

Scholarly publisher for the Commonwealth,
serving Bellarmine University, Berea College, Centre College of Kentucky, Eastern
Kentucky University, The Filson Historical Society, Georgetown College,
Kentucky Historical Society, Kentucky State University, Morehead State University,
Murray State University, Northern Kentucky University, Transylvania University,
University of Kentucky, University of Louisville, and Western Kentucky University.
All rights reserved.

*Editorial and Sales Offices:* The University Press of Kentucky
663 South Limestone Street, Lexington, Kentucky 40508-4008
www.kentuckypress.com

Library of Congress Cataloging-in-Publication Data

Names: Elkind, Jessica Breiteneicher, 1976- author.
Title: Aid under fire : nation building and the Vietnam War / Jessica Elkind.
Description: Lexington, Kentucky : University Press of Kentucky, [2016] |
  Series: Studies in conflict, diplomacy and peace | Includes
  bibliographical references and index.
Identifiers: LCCN 2016011182| ISBN 9780813165837 (hardcover : alk. paper) |
  ISBN 9780813167176 (pdf) | ISBN 9780813167169 (epub)
Subjects: LCSH: Vietnam (Republic)—Politics and government. |
  Nation-building—Vietnam (Republic) | Technical assistance,
  American—Vietnam (Republic) | United States. Operations Mission to
  Vietnam. | Intercultural communication—Vietnam (Republic)—Case studies.
  | Military assistance, American—Vietnam (Republic) | Economic assistance,
  American—Vietnam (Republic) | Vietnam (Republic)—Economic conditions. |
  United States—Foreign relations—Vietnam (Republic) | Vietnam
  (Republic)—Foreign relations—United States.
Classification: LCC DS556.9 .E55 2016 | DDC 959.704/31—dc23
LC record available at http://lccn.loc.gov/2016011182

For Ethan

And Caleb, Maya, and Sadie

# Contents

# Abbreviations

| | |
|---|---|
| ARVN | Army of the Republic of Vietnam |
| COMIGAL | Commissariat General for Refugees |
| DNE | Department of National Education |
| DRV | Democratic Republic of Vietnam |
| GVN | Government of Vietnam |
| ICA | International Cooperation Administration |
| IVS | International Voluntary Services |
| MAAG | Military Assistance and Advisory Group |
| MSU | Michigan State University |
| NIA | National Institute of Administration |
| NLF | National Liberation Front |
| PAD | USOM Public Administration Division |
| PAVN | People's Army of Vietnam |
| PSD | USOM Public Safety Division |
| RVN | Republic of Vietnam |
| USAID | US Agency for International Development |
| USOM | US Operations Mission |
| VBI | Vietnamese Bureau of Investigation |
| VWP | Vietnamese Workers' Party |

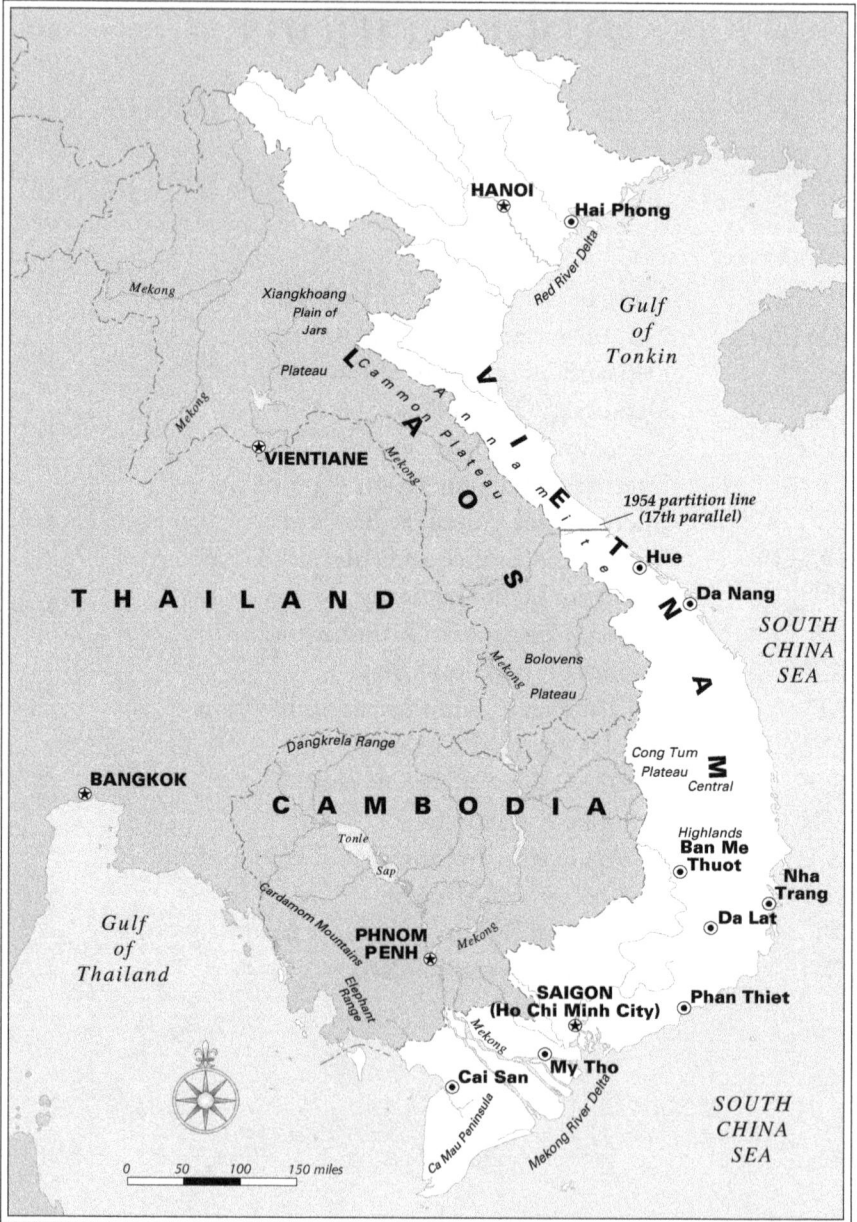

Mainland Southeast Asia. Map by Dick Gilbreath, University of Kentucky Cartography Lab.

Introduction

# Building South Vietnam

On a humid day in October 1956, a small group of Americans traveled from Saigon deep into the Mekong delta of southern Vietnam. The group consisted of several prominent figures, including Leland Barrows, the director of the US aid program in South Vietnam, and Allen Ellender, a Democratic senator from Louisiana. The Americans had ventured nearly two hundred kilometers southwest from Saigon on an observation tour of Cai San, an area being developed as a resettlement site for northerners who had fled their homes following the partition of Vietnam two years earlier. As the visit by these high-ranking officials indicated, Cai San was an important showpiece of modernization efforts in South Vietnam. The newly arrived aid workers, along with high-level policy makers in both Washington, DC, and Saigon, believed that introducing American-style institutions and developmental models in projects like Cai San would accelerate South Vietnam's transition to modernity. In the process, American aid workers would bolster a separate, non-Communist state that would be friendly to the political, economic, and strategic interests of the United States in Southeast Asia. South Vietnam, they hoped, might eventually serve as a model for other nations in the decolonizing world.

But, as the Americans approached a ferry terminal to cross the river at Long Xuyen, the sound of gunshots and explosions shattered the serenity of this delta outpost. Three minutes before the Americans reached the ferry boarding, insurgents ambushed a jeep carrying South Vietnamese army troops. The attackers threw grenades and trained small arms on the vehicle, injuring several of the Vietnamese soldiers in the process.

The Americans narrowly escaped the attack. Although South Vietnamese President Ngo Dinh Diem suggested that the insurgents had intended to hit the American aid workers, US and South Vietnamese officials were never able to confirm conclusively the identity of the attackers or their intended target.[1]

This incident demonstrates the deep hostility and serious challenges that Diem's government faced from its inception. More importantly, it suggests that, as a result of their support for the Saigon regime and their involvement in nation-building efforts, American aid workers would be implicated in the burgeoning civil war. Over the following decade, those aid workers would find themselves not only at the front lines of the fighting in the countryside but also at the center of many of the debates and conflicts that shaped the partnership between the United States and South Vietnam. Even by 1956, the fates of the two nations had become hopelessly intertwined. Indeed, many Vietnamese commonly, and derisively, referred to the Saigon regime as "My-Diem," or "American-Diem." This dynamic would define and ultimately hamper any efforts by American nation builders to assist the South Vietnamese government or people in the coming years.

As Americans soon came to learn in horrific fashion, the 1956 attack near Long Xuyen was not an isolated incident. Violent assaults on South Vietnamese officials, military personnel, and infrastructure became increasingly commonplace as the decade wore on. By the early 1960s, antigovernment insurgents also routinely targeted Americans, including civilians, for their role in supporting the unpopular and authoritarian Government of Vietnam (GVN). However, instead of reexamining their core assumptions or altering their approach as the violence escalated, US policy makers and aid workers only strengthened their commitment to nation building while attempting to link explicitly their development goals with counterinsurgency efforts. Even after many aid workers later became outspoken critics of the very policies they had once helped craft and implement, American officials refused to heed their advice. Ultimately, the joint American and South Vietnamese nation-building experiment proved such a failure during the decade following Vietnam's partition in 1954 that, in a last-ditch effort to save South Vietnam, American policy makers felt compelled to authorize direct military intervention.

# The American Mission in Vietnam

In the mid-1950s, modernizing South Vietnam through ambitious nation-building policies seemed like a win-win proposition to US officials as well as to the aid workers they enlisted. The South Vietnamese people would enjoy a higher living standard and enhanced security, while the United States would cultivate an important anti-Communist ally in the region. Yet a significant number of South Vietnamese decisively rejected this vision and eschewed offers of material assistance from the United States, ultimately expelling the Americans entirely. Why did US policy makers become so heavily invested in pursuit of these nation-building and modernization goals in South Vietnam? How did the role of civilians in this endeavor shape its implementation? And why did South Vietnamese and American modernization efforts in the 1950s and early 1960s fail so spectacularly to create a stable anti-Communist state that US officials eventually resorted to a disastrous war? This book, which is based on American and Vietnamese archival sources as well as interviews with a number of aid workers, tells the story of how nation-building programs functioned on the ground in South Vietnam. It demonstrates the important role played by nonstate actors in advancing US policies and reveals in stark terms the limits on American power and influence in the period widely considered the apex of US supremacy in the world.

The nation-building effort in South Vietnam failed because it was fundamentally a campaign to achieve a geopolitical outcome that the majority of the Vietnamese people did not support. Far from being an unconditional offer of assistance for whatever the Vietnamese people needed, the aid programs advanced the American political goal of creating a stable, separate, and non-Communist nation in southern Vietnam. However, most Vietnamese, including GVN officials, wanted an independent state that reflected their economic, social, and cultural values—not those of a foreign power. As a result of their Cold War priorities, American nation builders supported a repressive regime in South Vietnam that routinely subverted the will of the people. This support caused many Vietnamese to view American aid workers as accomplices to harsh policies and hold them responsible for keeping Vietnam subject to foreign intrusion and control. By helping design and execute those policies, civilian aid workers unwittingly contributed to increased political polarization and the subsequent military intervention. To make matters worse, because Americans introduced nation-building programs to further their foreign policy goals and not in response to local needs, the South Vietnamese people sometimes proved reluctant to accept assistance. Even when they did, US aid programs rarely translated into political support for the GVN. By the mid-1960s, the overtly political goals that tainted every aspect of the nation-building endeavor, from conception to implementation, turned the aid workers and their programs as well as the Vietnamese people affected by them into the first casualties of the deeply flawed US course in Vietnam.

## Scholarship on the United States and Vietnam

Despite the important role of civilian aid workers and the implications of their shortcomings, which led directly to military escalation, historians have only recently begun to devote significant attention to the nonmilitary aspects of early US intervention in Vietnam or the ways in which nation-building efforts played out on the ground. Instead, most studies focus on the diplomatic and military facets of American involvement. A majority of scholars frame the Vietnam War as essentially a proxy war among the Cold War superpowers, and recent literature emphasizes the international dimensions of the conflict.[2] Within this framework, scholars contend that the United States became involved in Vietnam largely as a result of American relationships with the Soviet Union, China, and other countries in Europe and Asia during the Cold War.[3] Conventional arguments also emphasize American decision making in the early to mid-1960s, focusing heavily on officials in the Kennedy and Johnson administrations.

However, Lyndon Johnson's decision to send ground troops to Vietnam in 1965 was a direct outgrowth of earlier American involvement and experiences, notably the failure of nation building. As this study demonstrates, specific historical, political, and social conditions within Vietnam as well as Americans' reactions to them largely determined the outcomes of nation-building policies. Civilian aid workers played a critical role because they served as the key conduit for shaping and delivering those policies on the ground, and, as a result, they saw firsthand the effects of American intervention. By predominately emphasizing the geopolitical and military dimensions of American involvement in Vietnam and the post-1965 period, many historians have underestimated one of the major factors that precipitated the US decision to go to war in Vietnam: the failed American and South Vietnamese modernization efforts.

In addition to several excellent studies of early US intervention that were published in the 1980s, there has been a welcome and recent trend among scholars to reexamine the period from 1954 to 1965 in both northern and southern Vietnam.[4] During the last few years, a number of books by historians such as Edward Miller, Jessica Chapman, and Philip Catton have explored the US-GVN partnership and some aspects of nation building. Relying on previously unavailable Vietnamese sources, these studies offer compelling new descriptions of the complex and often contentious relationship between American and South Vietnamese officials. They also challenge the conventional view of Ngo Dinh Diem as a puppet of the United States.[5] Other scholars such as James Carter, William Rosenau, and John Ernst consider state building from a more US-centered perspective and shed new light on specific projects, especially those designed to support American military and counterinsurgency efforts.[6]

Although recent scholarship devotes more attention to the pre-1965 period and the US-GVN partnership, most studies still focus on the interactions of high-ranking officials, policy formulation, and the discourse of nation building.[7] Catton's and Miller's work, in particular, reveals the deep-seated conflicts—most of them ideological and philosophical—between American and GVN policy makers. But the extant scholarship largely focuses on how officials conceived of nation-building schemes and differences among policy makers rather than the disconnect between policy goals and political, social, and cultural developments outside Saigon and Washington, DC. Yet it is impossible to understand fully how modernization projects functioned and why those efforts failed without looking closely at the ways in which development programs were implemented or without considering the central position of civilian aid workers. This study builds on and complements recent scholarship but also departs from the existing literature in its emphasis on previously understudied actors and its bottom-up approach to examining nation building on the ground in Vietnam.

## Decolonization, the Cold War, and Modernization

The flawed American policy to bolster South Vietnam grew out of deeply held assumptions about the US ability and responsibility to modernize the world, particularly in the aftermath of the Second World War. The United States emerged from that conflict with unparalleled wealth and preponderant power as well as a monopoly on atomic weapons. But the war and the international depression that preceded it had a profoundly destabilizing effect on the established world order. As European empires crumbled, nationalist leaders throughout the colonized world struggled for independence while asserting their vision for how their societies might develop. American policy makers expressed growing concern as many of those nationalist leaders looked to Marxism-Leninism and Maoism for inspiration and as many anticolonial revolutions, including the one in Vietnam, became increasingly radical.

Meanwhile, the economic, political, and ideological rivalry between the United States and the Soviet Union, which had its roots in the early twentieth century but had been temporarily suspended as a result of the wartime alliance, reemerged as a dominant feature of American foreign relations. The post-1945 contest between the superpowers largely manifested as a competition over resources, allegiance, and influence in newly independent nations. As one scholar writes: "The most important aspects of the Cold War were neither military nor strategic, nor Europe-centered but connected to political and social development in the Third World."[8] According to the historian David Ekbladh: "Both sides sought transformation in new states as a way to demonstrate that their ideologies were best suited to deliver the benefits of modern life."[9]

In the face of tremendous instability in the decolonizing world and the renewed rivalry with the Soviet Union, US policy makers looked for new diplomatic tools to meet what they saw as unprecedented challenges to American economic interests, international political stability, and national security. Many officials believed that they had found a panacea as well as an alternative to formal colonialism in modernization theory. American modernization theorists argued that historical development occurs along a linear trajectory and that political, economic, and social transformations are integrated.[10] They considered underdeveloped or poor societies to be particularly vulnerable to radicalism and susceptible to Communist ideology. As Michael Latham explains, US officials were attracted by the "perceived potential to link the promotion of development with the achievement of security."[11] According to modernization theorists, more advanced nations, such as the United States and other liberal, capitalist democracies, could hasten the transition from traditional to modern in "backward" societies by exporting American institutions and models. Traditional, underdeveloped societies would benefit from higher living standards, greater security, economic opportunities, and eventually expanded political freedoms.

As recent scholarship has convincingly demonstrated, modernization and nation-building efforts during the Cold War had antecedents in earlier periods and domestic policies. Early attempts at modernization and foreign aid occurred within the borders of the United States as the Bureau of Indian Affairs introduced educational-, political-, and economic-development programs to Native American communities.[12] At the same time, American leaders also sought to expand US influence abroad, particularly through colonial expansion in the Pacific and the Caribbean, cultural and educational exchange in Europe, and the opening of markets all over the world.[13] The historian Jeremi Suri argues for a direct historical link between building the American nation and US efforts overseas, tracing case studies from the founding of the United States to Reconstruction, the American colonial project in the Philippines, and the post-1945 American occupation of Germany.[14] And David Ekbladh, Nick Cullather, and Michael Adas have all emphasized the connections between New Deal policies in the United States, particularly massive infrastructure projects such as the Tennessee Valley Authority, and development aid abroad.[15] As Ekbladh explains: "Modernization ideas worked their way into Cold War policies, they were not created by them."[16] By the mid-twentieth century, scholars from a number of academic disciplines embraced the modernization framework, and the historian Nils Gilman has described modernization as "the highest flowering of American intellectual life."[17]

Modernization theory was not simply an intellectual exercise—it had important practical applications and powerful implications for international relations. The logic of modernization dictated active and interventionist foreign policies, especially in the decolonizing world. For example, during the 1950s and the early 1960s, US policy makers justified interventions in South Korea, Guatemala, Iran, and Indonesia as necessary to bring development and progress to those backward and unstable societies. As the historian Michael Latham explains, modernization theory grew out of a "long-standing conviction that the United States could fundamentally direct and accelerate the historical course of the postcolonial world."[18] Nick Cullather explores this process in postcolonial Asia, arguing: "Asians, at the moment of their emancipation, ceased to be colonial subjects only to become developmental subjects, mobilized, sterilized, and enlightened by foreign experts."[19]

But modernization efforts, which lay at the heart of the US mission in the world, were not based entirely on a pure impulse to improve the human condition.[20] In fact, in most cases, these "enlightened aid" projects amounted to little more than thinly veiled attempts to promote and protect short-term American interests overseas.[21] And many policy makers found modernization theory appealing precisely because it served concrete objectives and enhanced American influence while avoiding military commitments. For example, Cullather suggests that nation building, and in particular rural-development projects, gave Americans "a degree of authority over resources, territory, and people that colonial empires never had."[22] And as Ekbladh explains: "Modernization is deeply implicated in what has more aptly been described as the establishment of American global hegemony."[23]

Although modernization endeavors were closely linked with the establishment of US hegemony, American policy makers went to great lengths to distinguish their modernizing efforts from imperial projects. They drew on the ideas and experiences of their predecessors while emphasizing American exceptionalism. For example, during the Second World War, President Franklin D. Roosevelt employed Woodrow Wilson's rhetoric of self-determination and expanded on it, calling for an end to imperialism and independence for colonies. At the same time, the United States struggled to assert its influence over the decolonizing world and rarely allowed true self-determination. In fact, the superpower competition in the Third World functioned as both a continuation of and a break from earlier colonial interventions. According to the historian Odd Arne Westad: "Different from the European expansion that started in the early modern period, Moscow's and Washington's objectives were not exploitation and subjugation, but control and improvement."[24] However, as my study demonstrates, many aspects of American nation-building efforts in South Vietnam closely resembled and were informed by earlier imperial projects. And many Vietnamese, from officials in Saigon to peasants in the countryside, viewed US-sponsored programs as a continuation of previous attempts by foreign powers to assert their influence in Vietnam.

Despite the widespread appeal of modernization theory among US policy makers at the height of the Cold War, not everyone involved in nation building accepted the theory wholesale. In fact, some aid workers consciously rejected the centralization, standardization, and bureaucratization that accompanied large modernizing projects. These men and women offered what the historian Daniel Immerwahr refers to as a "rival inclination" that emphasized community development and small-scale institutions. As Immerwahr explains, these people "sought development—but development without modernization."[25] Many of the aid workers examined in this study, especially those working on agricultural-development in Vietnam, subscribed to this alternative worldview, which emphasized grassroots assistance and focused on programs oriented around one village or community.[26]

Nation building in South Vietnam was an ambitious and multifaceted undertaking that consisted of top-down and bottom-up efforts simultaneously. Aid workers brought a variety of approaches to and perspectives on development to Vietnam, and many promoted small, community programs rather than grand, state-building exercises or capital-intensive infrastructure projects. However, despite the diversity of aid workers' views and approaches, Americans in Vietnam generally subscribed to the broad aims of US policies and displayed a healthy (if not brash) enthusiasm about their ability to transform Vietnamese society. They also accepted the core ideological tenets of what the scholar Emily Rosenberg describes as "liberal developmentalism," which included a belief in the universal applicability of American models.[27] In other words, even when they rejected modernization theory and offered alternative approaches, civilian aid workers in Vietnam proved to be willing partners and active participants in carrying out and reinforcing development efforts on the ground. Furthermore, they had a distinct political orientation and presented their programs as an alternative to communism. As Latham explains, American nation builders claimed to be supporting "the right kind of revolution" in the decolonizing world.[28] Policy makers and aid workers agreed that Vietnam might serve as a prime test case for applying their theories and expertise to policy.

Proponents of nation building maintained that foreign aid and development projects offered a solution to some of the world's most intractable problems while securing American interests. They also had compelling reasons to feel confident in the efficacy of their approach. On the basis of the apparent successes of the Marshall Plan in Western Europe and the postwar reconstruction of Japan, American policy makers adopted a strategy of using foreign assistance, in the form of military and civilian development programs, to prevent the spread of communism.[29] Following the victory of anti-Communist factions in Greece and Turkey, in part as a result of American assistance, President Harry Truman's administration was emboldened to dedicate resources to the developing world and rely on foreign aid as an important weapon in the US diplomatic arsenal. With a focus on containment in the decolonizing world, Truman announced the Point Four Program in his 1949 inaugural address.[30]

Perhaps no intervention was more influential at shaping the aid programs in Vietnam than the recent conflict and nation-building endeavor on the Korean Peninsula. This experience strongly affirmed for US policy makers the connections between modernization and containment and became a model for development assistance in South Vietnam. Although the Korean War produced no significant military or political gains for either side, American officials celebrated US involvement as a decisive factor in South Korea's defiance of Communist aggression. At the same time, policy makers in Dwight Eisenhower's administration vowed not to become embroiled in another ground war in Asia, and they looked to modernization and nation building as less costly methods for countering Communist expansion.

Following the cessation of fighting in Korea, the United States continued to engage in nation-building activities and provide large amounts of foreign aid to South Korea. As the historian Gregg Brazinsky has shown, those efforts, combined with Korean participation in nation building, translated into economic development and political stability and made South Korea an important American partner during the Cold War.[31] Yet, at the time, American policy makers largely ignored the critical involvement of the Koreans and instead emphasized their own contributions to Korean development while assuming that they could exert similar influence in Vietnam. Perhaps as important for American officials, the preservation of a divided Korea, along with the post–World War II partition of Germany, set the precedent for a two-state solution in contests between Communist and anti-Communist forces. American policy makers sought to replicate the German and Korean models in Vietnam.

But policy makers overlooked important differences among the populations they sought to modernize and instead assumed that a uniform approach to development could apply to societies with a diverse range of histories, cultures, and political landscapes. Because most nation builders emphasized the universal applicability of American-style development, they downplayed the inherently political and self-serving nature of their recommendations. As a result, aid workers rarely conceded that development efforts faced serious limitations in instances in which US objectives did not align with the foreign aid recipients' concerns. In South Vietnam, this limitation—the lack of agreement between US foreign policy goals and local interests—represented a fundamental flaw that contributed to the shortcomings of nation-building programs.

## Vietnamese Resistance

American policy makers and aid workers encountered a different cultural, social, and political environment in South Vietnam during the mid-1950s than what they had experienced to date in their modernization efforts. The anticolonial, nationalist movement in Vietnam was more developed and organized than similar movements in other parts of Asia. And their recent battlefield successes against the technologically superior French military forces had left many Vietnamese emboldened and committed to full independence from foreign influence. For their part, American aid workers were also operating with a healthy dose of hubris, and they felt certain that they could accomplish their geopolitical goals through modernization in Vietnam. Yet they were completely unprepared for the resistance they would confront from Vietnamese revolutionaries as well as from independent-minded leaders in Saigon.

Throughout its history, Vietnam had been invaded and colonized by foreign powers. Beginning with their defeat of the occupying Chinese forces in the late tenth century, the Vietnamese people had repeatedly repelled attacks by outside powers and had contested foreign domination. Although the Vietnamese expanded their own territory and power at the expense of other societies, most notably the Chams and the Khmers, many developed a sense that they were perpetual underdogs who had managed to preserve their identity and autonomy in the face of an onslaught of nearly continuous outside aggression. When in the late nineteenth century the French seized Indochina as part of their overseas empire, in part as a result of cooperation from members of the Vietnamese court, a powerful anticolonial movement emerged in response. Vietnamese nationalists demanded not only their autonomy but also rectification for specific abuses inflicted by colonial administrators and their local collaborators.[32] The Japanese invasion of Southeast Asia in the early 1940s, which temporarily bolstered the French colonial authorities because of the wartime alliance between the Vichy and the Tokyo governments, only contributed to the grievances and determination of Vietnamese nationalists.[33]

By the time US officials took an active interest in Vietnam, anticolonial resistance had coalesced under the leadership of the Viet Nam Doc Lap Dong Minh Hoi (known as the Viet Minh). Founded in 1941, the Viet Minh was ostensibly an umbrella for various nationalist groups that opposed continued French colonization in Indochina. However, it operated as a classic front organization, and its upper echelons consisted primarily of members of the Indochinese Communist Party. Ho Chi Minh and other leaders of the Viet Minh believed that Marxism-Leninism offered the best model for how the Vietnamese could escape the yoke of colonialism as well as the exploitation of capitalism.[34] As Ho explained when asked about his strategy for gaining independence from France: "One also needs . . . a set of beliefs, a gospel, a practical analysis, you might even say a bible. Marxism-Leninism gave me that framework."[35] By the 1950s, the Viet Minh had developed an intricate organizational structure throughout the country—particularly in the northern provinces—and a sophisticated propaganda machine as well as effective recruitment and training methods. More significantly, as a result of its military achievements during the First Indochina War, the group enjoyed tremendous popular support, with many Vietnamese crediting Ho for delivering independence.

## A Misguided Commitment to Ngo Dinh Diem

To counter the popularity of indigenous revolutionary groups like the Viet Minh, the United States supported policies and governments that it believed could weaken or defeat them. Beginning in 1950, Truman's administration openly assisted France, an important European ally of the United States, over Vietnamese nationalists fighting for their independence from the French Empire. According to the records of the US Joint

Chiefs of Staff, between June 1950 and June 1954, the US government contributed $2.7 billion to France's military pursuits in Indochina.[36] By the final years of the First Indochina War, the United States provided nearly 80 percent of the funding for the French war effort. Following the decisive Viet Minh victory at Dien Bien Phu in the spring of 1954, American officials looked for a way to prevent Vietnam from falling under the control of the Communist-led Viet Minh. They found a solution in the Geneva Agreement, which established an armistice and delineated Vietnam's transition to independence. The agreement called for a temporary partitioning of the country along the seventeenth parallel and a three-hundred-day cooling-off period during which combatants could return to their homes on either side of the demilitarized zone. It also called for national elections to be held within two years, at which time the country would be reunified. However, it did not clearly define the process for uniting the northern and southern halves of the country. As a result of this ambiguity and their assumption that reunification would bring Vietnamese Communists to power, US policy makers treated the partition of Vietnam as a permanent arrangement, over the objections of many local people in both the northern and the southern regions. American officials immediately launched an active campaign to help Emperor Bao Dai and his new prime minister, Ngo Dinh Diem, maintain a separate, anti-Communist state in southern Vietnam.[37]

In many ways, Ngo Dinh Diem represented the lynchpin of early US nation-building efforts in South Vietnam. From the perspective of many Vietnamese people, ranging from disaffected intellectuals in Saigon to Buddhist and other non-Catholic religious leaders to impoverished peasants who had been displaced from their homes during the First Indochina War, Diem was ill suited to lead the country. Because of his absence from Vietnam during a significant portion of the war against the French, he lacked the nationalist credentials that others such as Ho Chi Minh or Vo Nguyen Giap commanded as a result of their contributions to the armed struggle for liberation. Furthermore, as a devout Catholic, he did not share a common religious or cultural background with most of the people he would represent. Finally, his close relationship with American officials and his regime's financial dependence on US aid enraged a population eager for independence from foreign intrusion.

In June 1954, Diem returned to Vietnam after years of self-imposed exile.[38] During his exile, he had traveled to Japan, where in the summer of 1950 he met Wesley Fishel, a young American political scientist who was conducting field research and teaching English and would later become a leading American aid worker in South Vietnam.[39] Diem spent the majority of his time overseas in the United States, living at Maryknoll Seminary in New Jersey. While he was in the United States, he met a number of influential Americans, including congressmen, university presidents, religious leaders, and government officials. In the following years, these Americans, known as the Vietnam Lobby, became some of his staunchest allies and advocates.[40] On returning to his homeland, Diem briefly served as prime minister in Bao Dai's administration. In October 1955, with the help of his American patrons, he staged a referendum on Bao Dai's continued rule. As a result of his electoral victory, he then replaced the emperor as the Republic of Vietnam's head of state.[41] Despite their support for Diem's presidency, many US policy makers at the time recognized the fraudulence of the referendum and expressed concern over Diem's legitimacy. As Miller explains: "Many U.S. leaders in Saigon and Washington were deeply skeptical of the 'Diem experiment' when it began."[42]

As recent studies by Miller, Catton, and Matthew Masur demonstrate, Diem and his inner circle of advisers, which consisted primarily of his brothers and other trusted acquaintances, had a strong vision of how Vietnam might modernize through economic and political development.[43] But Diem also proved to be a stubborn and independent-minded leader. He demonstrated little tolerance for different viewpoints, whether those challenges came from his American allies or from fellow Vietnamese. The South Vietnamese president resisted opposition to his policies, ideas, or worldview, even from close advisers or loyal confidantes, and his regime routinely stifled any dissent. As a result of his distrust of outsiders, Diem surrounded himself with family members and others who either shared his vision for how to govern the country or restrained from questioning official policies.[44]

From the inception of his presidency, Diem demonstrated that he was more interested in ensuring his own political survival than in building democratic institutions.[45] A staunch anti-Communist himself, he astutely recognized his American patrons' fixation on potential subversion by Communists and other leftists. He labeled all political rivals *Communists,* and he launched a "Denunciation of Communists Campaign." That draconian campaign encouraged public confessions and invited individuals to inform on their neighbors while meting out harsh punishments for those accused of supporting the Communist movement. The Vietnamese president relied on his army and secret police to deliver suspected adversaries to South Vietnam's notorious political reeducation centers.[46] By the late 1950s, tens of thousands of people had been sent to those centers, where forced labor and torture were commonplace. According to the US Defense Department's analysis in *The Pentagon Papers,* most Vietnamese observers believed that the majority of those imprisoned were not Communists.[47]

In addition to the Diem regime's overt attempts to extinguish political opposition, the GVN implemented a number of other harsh policies to control South Vietnamese society. As a result of popular pressure to deal with the problems stemming from high rents in rural areas and the uneven distribution of agricultural plots in South Vietnam, Diem enacted a failed land-reform program that served to further aggravate impoverished peasants.[48] In 1956, he abolished the locally elected village councils and began appointing outsiders, mostly Catholics from northern Vietnam, to lead administrative bodies in the villages.[49] This decision outraged many villagers who had historically been accustomed to a significant degree of local autonomy.[50] In his efforts to strengthen control over the population, Diem also specifically targeted Chinese and other ethnic minority groups.[51] For example, in September 1956, he issued Ordinance 53, which restricted foreigners and foreign nationals from participating in many industries.[52] He attempted to assimilate ethnic minority communities by eradicating their traditional agricultural techniques and cultural practices in order to integrate the upland areas into the central state.[53] Finally, and perhaps most importantly, South Vietnam's inhabitants, many of whom practiced some form of Buddhism, viewed his preferential treatment of Catholics and his persecution of Buddhists as particularly egregious.[54]

For eight years, US policy makers tolerated—and in many cases even encouraged—Diem's repressive and authoritarian policies because their desire to preserve an anti-Communist nation in South Vietnam outweighed any commitment to promote democracy or address the concerns of Vietnam's people. In doing so, American policy makers and aid workers discounted local political dynamics and exhibited overconfidence in their ability to impose their vision rather than contend seriously with the legacy of colonialism or the nature of the ongoing revolution in Vietnam. This approach was part of a long pattern: during the early years of the nation-building period, Americans routinely ignored warnings from their French allies, despite the fact that the French had firsthand knowledge of the Vietnamese resistance and a better understanding of the political situation in Vietnam. As Kathryn Statler argues: "American views of France as an unreliable and weak ally led the Eisenhower administration to reject the lessons that the French experience in Indochina had to offer."[55]

But the problem was not only American obstinance in the face of French advice. It was also that the Americans involved—from high-ranking policy makers in Washington to low-level aid workers on the ground in Vietnam—believed that they knew what was best for Vietnam and could solve the country's problems through military aid, technical assistance, and economic development. They also consistently abandoned democracy in favor of political stability and anti-Communist leadership while effectively turning a blind eye to South Vietnamese leaders' use of brutal and authoritarian tactics. As a result, the United States embarked on an expensive and ultimately destructive path to preserve the autonomy of South Vietnam even though many Vietnamese displayed strong objections to that goal.

## Nation Builders in South Vietnam

Into this complex and challenging environment, US policy makers sent an army of civilian aid workers. American nation builders in Vietnam comprised a diverse group of men and women who were motivated by a range of issues, including an altruistic desire to improve the world, religious conviction, staunch anticommunism, and an interest in sharing their professional knowledge. Convinced of the righteousness of their cause and the applicability of their expertise, American aid workers— many of whom were nonstate actors—played a vital role in spearheading nation building in Vietnam. They continuously reinforced US policies by implementing development programs, and, in many cases, they served as key contacts with the local population.

However, like the government officials who recruited them, most aid workers lacked a basic knowledge and understanding of Vietnamese culture, history, and politics. As a result, they attempted to replicate political, economic, and military systems modeled on their own experiences while displaying a willful blindness to the conditions and attitudes in Vietnam. In many cases, their unresponsiveness and inflexibility limited their ability to implement specific projects. Their obstinacy also made it challenging to alter policies once it became clear that they were having negative consequences. From minor problems communicating in a language that few Americans learned to fundamental misreadings of the GVN's ability to garner popular support and legitimacy, ignorance about Vietnam and its people caused difficulties for policy makers and aid workers alike.

At the most basic level, the nation builders sought to develop institutions to advance the US political goal of bolstering the South Vietnamese government. They believed that supportive institutions, which might include political, economic, financial, and social associations, served as the foundation for modern nation-states.[56] But in South Vietnam this process did not involve merely building an American-style administrative state or, as some scholars have suggested, constructing identity.[57] Nation builders in Vietnam had more ambitious goals, which consisted simultaneously of top-down institution building and bottom-up development efforts. They were attempting to transform and modernize Vietnam by exporting American values, technologies, methods, even lifestyles. Although aid workers, US policy makers, and South Vietnamese officials often disagreed on many of the specific details of nation-building projects, they generally shared a vision for the ultimate goals of modernization—democratization and more efficient public administration, agrarian reform for basic social and economic transformations in rural life, and the creation of effective military and civilian security forces, all in service of the regime.[58]

The key American players in nation-building efforts hailed from the government's aid agency as well as private organizations, many of which had contractual relationships with the government.[59] During the Cold War, the US Agency for International Development and its predecessor agencies awarded the largest aid packages to countries that American officials deemed important sites for containing communism. Throughout the late 1950s and the early 1960s, South Korea and South Vietnam received the two largest aid packages. In 1957, for example, South Korea received 20 percent and South Vietnam 17 percent of total US foreign aid expenditures.[60]

The US Operations Mission (USOM), which was the official American in-country civilian aid team, coordinated and oversaw technical assistance and development work on the ground in Vietnam. USOM personnel were government employees who worked directly with Vietnamese officials as well as the general population. Members of the USOM country team also cooperated closely with other Americans in Vietnam, including embassy staff, military advisers, and aid workers from nongovernment organizations. Among the nonstate actors, a group of scholars and police advisers from Michigan State University (MSU) and volunteers from International Voluntary Services (IVS) were some of USOM's most important partners in South Vietnam.

MSU's involvement in Vietnam stemmed in large part from the ambitions of two men, John Hannah and Wesley Fishel. John Hannah, the president of MSU from 1941 to 1969, sought to elevate the university's national reputation in part by putting it at the service of the US government.[61] He believed that universities could contribute to the public interest by providing technical assistance overseas, and he offered President Truman "full cooperation" in carrying out the Point Four Program in the developing world.[62] Although Hannah and other administrators in the university's Office of International Programs actively sought out opportunities for MSU to engage in technical assistance, the direct impetus for the Vietnam Project's creation was the personal relationship between Wesley Fishel, a young political scientist, and Ngo Dinh Diem. After completing his doctorate in 1948, Fishel traveled to Japan to conduct field research and teach American servicemen stationed there. While in Japan, Fishel met Diem, who was living there under self-imposed exile, and the two immediately struck up a friendship.[63] After Fishel returned to the United States in 1951 as an assistant professor at MSU, the two stayed in touch, and Fishel encouraged Diem to pursue his aspirations for political leadership in Vietnam.[64]

Once in office, Diem requested Fishel as an unofficial adviser, and Fishel worked closely with Diem during the first few years of his presidency.[65] In a plan that he drafted with Fishel's help, Diem requested technical assistance in public and police administration from an American university group. MSU was well suited for this task as the university boasted some of the country's most highly regarded academic departments in these fields. In early 1955, MSU sent four university representatives to

During his visit to Saigon, Michigan State University president John Hannah meets South Vietnamese president Ngo Dinh Diem. Courtesy Michigan State University Archives and Historical Collections Vietnam Project, Records (UA 2.9.5.5), Photograph File Drawer.

Saigon to ascertain whether they might be able to aid Diem's fledgling regime.[66] The Americans returned to East Lansing with a mixed sense of concern and optimism. They expressed alarm over the current atmosphere of crisis in Vietnam while conveying hope for the role MSU could play in helping Diem "save the country from Communism." They also argued that the very existence of South Vietnam depended on American assistance.[67] After several months of negotiating, the university reached a joint agreement with the US and South Vietnamese governments.[68] In addition to providing technical assistance in public and police administration, the MSU group advised various GVN ministries, contributed to Diem's refugee-resettlement efforts, and selected Vietnamese bureaucrats to participate in training programs in the United States and other countries.

While MSU provided advisers to the GVN and worked primarily with Vietnamese elites, IVS offered grassroots assistance to South Vietnam's people, especially those living in rural areas. Founded in 1953 by several influential leaders from the American "Peace Churches," a loose coalition that included the Quaker and Mennonite congregations, IVS aimed to provide economic and humanitarian aid to the people of developing nations through grassroots projects.[69] At the height of the Cold War, the organization selected the sites for its programs with attention to how those programs might promote official US interests in the world. The chief of party for IVS's mission in Laos described this approach when he wrote of the IVS program: "It is a possible laboratory for Free World ideas and actions."[70] All IVS missions received significant financing from the US government, but the Vietnam contingent relied exclusively on public funding. In addition to their financial dependence, many volunteers had an ideological affinity with American policy makers, and they explicitly supported official policy goals. An internal history of the organization in Vietnam explains that the rationale of the IVS mission was to "execute the objectives of U.S. foreign policy." And, as one IVS report stated, the volunteers "accepted the purposes of U.S. government assistance to Vietnam as set forth in the Truman Doctrine."[71]

IVS recruited volunteers at college campuses and offered these young men and women a unique opportunity to spend several years living and working overseas.[72] For the most part, the volunteers, or IVSers as they called themselves, were idealistic and optimistic about their ability to improve the lives of people in developing countries, which they considered to be traditional or backward. According to the organization's literature, IVS volunteers sought to work with "limited, even primitive people" who desired development in the midst of the "winds of change that blow all about [them]."[73] IVS sent its first group of volunteers to Vietnam in December 1956 to assist with refugee-resettlement efforts.[74] The original volunteers were male agricultural specialists, and they quickly shifted their attention to agricultural-development initiatives. In 1962, IVS introduced an education team that included both male and female volunteers who taught English, science, and other subjects at schools throughout Vietnam. The organization also added a small public health group, which distributed medications and first aid kits, provided basic instruction in sanitation and health, and promoted malaria eradication programs.

Although MSU and IVS were not government agencies, aid workers from the two organizations functioned as appendages of the official American foreign policy machinery in Vietnam. They worked closely with USOM and relied on the US government for financial and logistic support.

# Nation Building on the Ground

American nation builders implemented and contributed significantly to modernization efforts in South Vietnam. Almost everyone involved, including mid- and low-level aid workers, accepted and advanced the basic course of action and shaped the outcome of the policies. The activities of American aid workers as well as their interactions with local people reflect basic flaws in the US approach to Vietnam and show how mistakes in execution only compounded the negative effects of a poorly conceived approach.

At the beginning of their tenure, most aid workers assumed that their models for development had universal appeal and could be applied to Vietnam with few modifications. As a result, they expected the Vietnamese leadership and people to accept their assistance with open arms. Their perceived success in working with the GVN and refugees from North Vietnam during their first few years in the country only reinforced the aid workers' early sense of optimism and faith in their vision for Vietnam.

But the American aid workers quickly discovered that nation building was a complicated and hotly contested process. In many cases, they found themselves confronted with an audience in Vietnam that was unreceptive or, in some cases, openly hostile to their endeavors. GVN officials demonstrated their willingness to challenge or disagree with their American patrons whenever they felt that their needs or interests demanded it.[75] The Vietnamese people also thwarted the efforts of American aid workers or were reluctant to adopt programs that were too closely associated with either the United States or the regime in Saigon. In conversations with aid workers, and in publications from the time, many Vietnamese cited the neocolonial dimensions of US aid as one of the key reasons for their defiance. As a Vietnamese student who worked closely with IVS volunteers explained: "People in a deplorable situation unhesitatingly received the help, but bitter experiences the French left behind still keep them suspecting the good will of another 'civilized' country from the West."[76] Given the unpopularity of Diem's government and the widespread antagonism toward foreign interference, it is difficult to imagine how any amount of financial support or technical assistance from the United States could have altered the political dynamics in Vietnam or made the GVN self-sufficient.

Aid workers also faced challenges from American officials in Washington and Saigon. Although policy makers and aid workers shared a vision regarding the broad outlines and value of nation-building aims, they rarely agreed on the best ways to accomplish those goals. Aside from a few important exceptions, much of the scholarship on US foreign policy and development during the Cold War emphasizes consensus on the American side.[77] However, as my study reveals, any consensus that may have existed broke down as aid workers strove to execute development projects and especially as security concerns intensified in South Vietnam. Officials, aid workers, and advisers engaged in heated disputes over specific policies and approaches. Often those contests pitted nonstate actors against policy makers, though sometimes bitter debates erupted within the government bureaucracy or between administrators at different agencies.

As aid workers became more familiar with the political situation in Vietnam and the challenges to their influence, their initial confidence was tempered. Most realized that, despite their best intentions, they would be unable to accomplish many of their objectives. This proved especially true for members of the MSU and IVS teams. Differences with American and South Vietnamese officials over how to implement particular projects, the failure of aid programs to generate political support for the GVN, and escalating political violence in the countryside limited the effectiveness of their endeavors. Many aid workers became demoralized not only about their own activities but also about US involvement in Vietnam more generally. Although they had once been some of Diem's most vocal boosters, many MSU and IVS participants came to doubt the wisdom of unwavering American support for the authoritarian Saigon regime. Similarly, despite their contributions to the very polarization that led to civil war, a majority of aid workers eventually questioned the appropriateness of the increasing US reliance on counterinsurgency methods and military solutions for Vietnam's political and economic problems.

American military intervention in Vietnam was not inevitable, even given the failed nation-building experiment. The experiences of American aid workers offered a potential source of knowledge and perspective that US policy makers could have used to inform their decisions and modify their approach in Vietnam and elsewhere. Their unique position also meant that the aid workers were often among the first Americans to recognize firsthand the negative effects of nation-building programs and US intervention generally. However, in the instances when USOM, MSU, or IVS participants confronted South Vietnamese or American policy makers directly, leaders of both governments refused to heed their advice.

Despite their increasing disillusionment with official policies, which had taken on a life and an inertia of their own, American aid workers were powerless to alter the fundamental mission of their institutions. Because they were not responsible for formulating policy, they lacked the authority to challenge the bureaucratic and political momentum. Ultimately, the organizations' dependence on the two governments for financial, material, and logistic support rendered them incapable of deviating from official aims. By the time these men and women came to appreciate fully the flawed underpinnings of American policies and began advocating for changes in the basic US approach in Vietnam, it was too late. At that point, civilian aid workers had already contributed significantly to American intervention and could do little to slow the path of military escalation.

## Aid Under Fire

Each chapter of the book focuses on one type of development program and illuminates a key aspect of American aid workers' efforts. Chapter 1, "'The Virgin Mary Is Going South,'" examines US involvement in refugee-resettlement schemes between 1954 and 1956 and argues that this experience created a misplaced sense of optimism and contributed to aid workers' naïveté about the possibility for successful nation building in Vietnam. Chapter 2, "Civil Servants and Cold Warriors," focuses on the misguided efforts by scholars from MSU to shore up the South Vietnamese state by improving public administration. Chapter 3, "Sowing the Seeds of Discontent," examines American agricultural-development programs and provides some explanations for why they did not result in a general improvement in peasants' living standard or in widespread support for the South Vietnamese government. Chapter 4, "Policing the Insurgency," details American nation builders' attempts to bolster South Vietnam by modernizing its police force despite American and South Vietnamese policy makers' insistence on employing military solutions at the expense of civilian law enforcement. Finally, chapter 5, "Teaching Loyalty," considers efforts to develop South Vietnam's education system and simultaneously to advance counterinsurgency aims in the country, showing how modernization efforts ultimately bore little connection to humanitarian or economic development but rather accelerated military escalation in Vietnam.

By exploring how and why American development programs in South Vietnam functioned and ultimately collapsed, this story reveals the profound limitations of nation-building and modernization efforts at the policy-making level and especially in the process of implementation. It sheds light on Americans' deeply held belief in their mission to change and improve the world in their image. Many of the same mistakes in judgment and execution that policy makers and aid workers committed during the first decade of US intervention were later repeated during the years of full-scale military intervention, with far-reaching and devastating consequences.

1

# "The Virgin Mary
# Is Going South"

## Refugee Resettlement in South Vietnam

Most striking of all, perhaps, has been the rehabilitation of more
than three quarters of a million refugees from the North.
—John F. Kennedy (1956)

When American aid workers began arriving in Saigon in late 1954 and
early 1955, they saw large groups of people sleeping in doorways, camp-
ing in parks, and sprawling on sidewalks. These were recent arrivals from
the northern provinces, and many of them arrived in the South without
any idea where they would settle. With nearly five thousand northerners
descending on South Vietnam each day, this was, as one American aid
worker put it, "a critical situation." Saigon bore much of the strain created by the flood of new arrivals. Because its port served as one of the
primary entry points for the northerners, its population burgeoned dramatically. According to Walter Mode, an adviser from Michigan State
University (MSU), between one and two thousand people slept in the
Saigon Assembly Building each night until the South Vietnamese government began building effective refugee centers. All other public spaces
in the city swelled with refugees, and no buildings remained vacant once
the northerners began arriving.[1] Although the Government of Vietnam
(GVN) and its American supporters had contributed to this exodus,

they were unprepared for the many challenges posed by the influx of northerners.

American aid workers' first major responsibility involved helping South Vietnamese officials resettle nearly one million refugees who fled from northern Vietnam between 1954 and 1956. Vietnamese and American policy makers believed that the refugee crisis was occurring at a crucial time for the fledgling state of South Vietnam. As a result, they became heavily invested in securing a positive outcome. These men understood that, without a successful resolution to the crisis, the entire nation-building experiment in South Vietnam might fail before it even had a chance to get off the ground. Perhaps as importantly, they saw the situation as a chance to prove South Vietnamese prime minister Ngo Dinh Diem's credentials as a leader and confirm the wisdom of supporting his government. For these reasons, refugee-resettlement efforts became one of the most important and defining features of early US aid to South Vietnam. American and Vietnamese officials seized the opportunity to solidify their partnership and demonstrate the effectiveness of the GVN by instituting an ambitious policy of refugee resettlement. The ultimate goal of this policy was to make the northern émigrés self-sufficient and fully integrated into the society of southern Vietnam.

Diem and other South Vietnamese officials as well as their American patrons claimed that refugee resettlement was effective, and they celebrated the endeavor as a resounding achievement.[2] US policy makers praised the South Vietnamese government for its accomplishments and argued that his successful handling of this crisis and others proved that Diem deserved continued American assistance. In fact, as the refugee crisis wound down, many Americans expressed a renewed sense of confidence in him, the "Tough Miracle Man of Vietnam," as a 1957 article in *Life* magazine referred to him, and in the role that future US aid projects could play in supporting his government.[3]

A more comprehensive examination of the implementation of refugee programs, however, reveals that resettlement efforts were not the overwhelming success that policy makers at the time and many scholars since then have made them out to be. First of all, US and South Vietnamese policies appear to have played a smaller role in driving the southern migration than has been widely assumed. As recent scholarship by Peter Hansen suggests, many northerners emigrated because of deep-seated concerns about their economic future as well as their political and religious freedom, not in response to encouragement or pressure from American and South Vietnamese officials.[4] Following the 1954 victory over French forces, leaders of the Vietnamese Workers' Party (VWP) in Hanoi shifted their attention from national liberation to promoting socialist transformation in the North. Many people feared the effect such policies might have on their livelihood and cultural practices as well as their survival.[5] Although Americans played a vital role in supporting the exodus— mainly by transporting the northerners and contributing to resettlement efforts—they did not create the refugee crisis. And, once the northerners arrived in the South, political aims—namely, bolstering Diem's anti-Communist constituency—guided American involvement, making this episode a classic example of how broad US foreign policy goals shaped the implementation of aid programs.

In addition, refugee-resettlement efforts exposed significant cleavages between the positions of US and GVN officials and, as a result, contributed to tensions within the partnership. American and South Vietnamese policy makers generally agreed on the need to integrate northerners into society and the basic contours of refugee assistance. However, they frequently offered different prescriptions for how best to implement those goals. For example, Vietnamese and American nation builders presented conflicting views regarding resettlement versus land redistribution as appropriate avenues for dealing with the refugees' poverty and landlessness. Such conflicts, which both sides downplayed at the time, presaged future, more serious ruptures in the alliance.

Most importantly, the shortcomings of the refugee episode suggest that the Diem government's weaknesses were endemic and predated the escalation of the insurgency later in the decade. Although nearly one million people were absorbed into South Vietnam without causing major social or economic disruptions, there is little evidence that they were integrated into their communities or that they enhanced Diem's legitimacy and popularity. In fact, much of the evidence suggests that resettlement efforts instead polarized Vietnamese society and cost Diem political support, owing to the northerners' failure to assimilate and the favors they received from the Diem regime. In some extreme cases, resettled northerners became the targets of antigovernment violence and attacks. While the refugee program achieved the immediate goal of relocating a large number of northerners, it fell short of satisfying many of the other critical objectives laid out by GVN and US officials, such as enlarging Diem's political base or increasing the chances of South Vietnam's ability to survive without substantial outside assistance.

American officials and aid workers overlooked the deficiencies of refugee efforts because of overconfidence in their methods as well as a profound desire to see Diem's government succeed. As a result, they chose to allow the short-term accomplishments of resettlement programs to mask the long-term flaws in their policy of maintaining a divided Vietnam and supporting an unpopular and authoritarian leader in the South. The refugee-resettlement period therefore represented a missed opportunity for Americans to notice some of the warning signs about the vulnerability and instability of their new partners in Southeast Asia as well as the limits of their influence on Vietnamese society and politics. Ultimately, the significant shortcomings of resettlement efforts—and the tendency of American policy makers to ignore them—not only undermined political support for the GVN but also foreshadowed many of the conflicts that would haunt the US–South Vietnamese partnership in later years.

## The High Stakes of the Refugee Crisis

In June 1954, Diem returned to Vietnam following several years of self-imposed exile. Bao Dai, the former emperor who served as chief of the State of Vietnam beginning in 1949, had appointed Diem as his prime minister. Although Bao Dai and Diem claimed authority over the entire country, the State of Vietnam derived most of its support from southern provinces, while the Democratic Republic of Vietnam (DRV) held power in the North. Diem served as prime minister of the State of Vietnam for over a year, until he launched a referendum that ended Bao Dai's rule.[6] Following his victory in the October 1955 referendum, Diem became president of the newly created Republic of Vietnam. Both before and after the referendum, Diem's government faced significant challenges from domestic political rivals, many of whom were also non-Communist and opposed to national reunification under the leadership of the VWP. Diem relied heavily on foreign assistance in his efforts to weaken political opposition and consolidate his hold on power in the South.[7]

At first glance, the exodus of northerners appeared perfectly designed to suit both American and South Vietnamese political aims. US and Vietnamese officials embraced the possibility that the northerners' arrival might provide the fledgling government in Saigon with a chance to demonstrate its abilities. Despite the challenges posed by the influx of refugees, those officials believed that the situation presented Ngo Dinh Diem, a Catholic leader in a predominately Buddhist country, with an opportunity for political gain. Not only would the northern transplants increase South Vietnam's Catholic population to nearly 10 percent; they might also dramatically enhance Diem's anti-Communist constituency.[8] Furthermore, the effective management of the refugee situation would lend legitimacy to the southern government, which was simultaneously involved in efforts to suppress rival political factions, including the Hoa Hao and Cao Dai organizations. Reflecting the high stakes that American policy makers placed on ensuring a favorable outcome to the refugee crisis, the US government provided Saigon with a large amount of financial, material, and technical assistance for resettlement efforts. Between 1954 and 1956, the United States dedicated $93 million to refugee resettlement, an amount that represented about $4.40 for every person in the country and just over 50 percent of the total nonmilitary aid package to South Vietnam in those years.[9]

## The Crisis and Southern Migration

The immediate impetus for the migration was the termination of the First Indochina War and the partition of Vietnam. The ceasefire agreement between Vietnamese nationalists and the French provided for a temporary regrouping period when, for three hundred days, combatants and civilians could cross the "provisional military demarcation line" at the seventeenth parallel.[10] According to the July 1954 Geneva Accords, this division would allow combatants on both sides of the demilitarized zone to return to their homes and provide time to prepare for free and open national elections. The Viet Minh signatories of the ceasefire agreement never intended a permanent separation of the country. As the historian Pierre Asselin argues: "[They] resolved to abide by the accords because Ho Chi Minh and other key leaders thought they would likely eventuate in peaceful national reunification under their governance."[11] However, the partition remained, and nationwide elections never happened, in large part owing to the GVN and US policy of neglecting the temporary nature of partition and preventing the scheduled elections from occurring.[12]

In fact, the American and South Vietnamese decision to refer to those who moved south as *refugees* was an attempt to render a permanent political boundary at the seventeenth parallel and define the two Vietnams as separate states indefinitely. This terminology also suggests that the northerners who moved south were compelled to do so because of their political, economic, or religious affiliations. In keeping with Vietnamese history and the spirit of the Geneva Accords, the United Nations did not consider the northern émigrés to be refugees because they were not technically leaving their country or society of origin.[13]

Following the Geneva settlement, hundreds of thousands of Vietnamese migrated from one side of the partition line to the other. In September 1954, the Politburo of the VWP in Hanoi insisted that all Viet Minh military personnel south of the seventeenth parallel regroup to the North, to the dismay of southern militants who hoped to continue the armed struggle for the establishment of a unified socialist state. Although the GVN attempted to discourage emigration, somewhere between 150,000 and 250,000 Viet Minh cadres and their families moved north during the regroupment period.[14] Far greater numbers of former combatants and civilians fled south beginning in the late summer of 1954. During the following year, nearly 900,000 civilians migrated from North to South Vietnam.[15]

The United States and the GVN actively encouraged and supported this southward migration through propaganda efforts and, more importantly, by providing physical assistance in transporting those people who wanted to leave their homes in the North. As early as August 1954, a mere month after the conclusion of the Geneva Conference, high-level figures in Dwight Eisenhower's administration committed to a policy of supporting mass migration into South Vietnam. In a document dated August 20, 1954, the National Security Council agreed to "aid emigration from North Vietnam and resettlement of peoples unwilling to remain under Communist rule."[16] American policy makers hoped that successful resettlement of northern refugees might shore up Diem's credentials and serve as an important propaganda victory for his fledgling government.

Many of the transplants were Catholics from the Red River delta region, and their arrival in South Vietnam offered a potential boon to

Diem's power base of staunchly anti-Communist Catholics. According to US Department of Defense (DOD) estimates conducted at the time, approximately 600,000 of the refugees were Catholics.[17] The arrival of these émigrés instantly doubled South Vietnam's Catholic population to approximately 1.17 million, which represented nearly two-thirds of all Catholics in Vietnam at the time.[18]

Before the partition, Catholics had occupied a tenuous position in Vietnamese society. In the eighteenth and nineteenth centuries, tensions between Catholics and non-Catholics ran high and frequently resulted in violence. Although the French attempted to end official persecution of Catholics, the underlying hostility and mutual distrust between Catholic and non-Catholic Vietnamese communities remained. As Hansen explains: "While the advent of French colonial rule led to suppression of physical attacks, it seemed to exacerbate resentment against a Catholic minority that was widely viewed as an ally of the colonial oppressors."[19] And, although most northern Catholics were poor subsistence farmers like their Buddhist compatriots, Catholics did constitute a disproportionately high percentage of the commercial, professional, and intellectual elite of Vietnam's northern provinces during the French colonial period.[20] After the French defeat, those Vietnamese who had served in the colonial administration or military found themselves in an uncomfortable situation. Despite Ho Chi Minh's numerous appeals for national unity and his government's guarantee of private property rights for loyal Vietnamese citizens, many Catholics worried about reprisals as a result of their religious or political affiliations.[21]

As Hansen has shown, northerners chose to move south for a host of reasons, including their fear of religious persecution—for which there was historical precedent, especially in the North—concern about their connections to the French military, anticipation of land confiscation, and the expectation of employment and other economic opportunities in the South. But, according to Hansen, for Catholic refugees at least "decisions about migration were shaped above all by the words and deeds of their parish clergy."[22] And Kahin writes: "Whether or not they feared Viet Minh reprisals, most of these priests presumably felt they would have greater scope to practice their religion in a noncommunist South under a government headed by a Catholic."[23] Indeed, in many cases entire parishes followed their priests south. In addition to the Catholics, some members of political opposition groups fled south, presumably fearing their chances for survival under a government dominated by the Communist VWP.

As a result of the émigrés' backgrounds and political loyalties, the refugee movement potentially had an important effect on the governments of both North and South Vietnam. For the government of North Vietnam, the refugees' departure could result in a significant drain of professionals and bureaucrats. As Duiker explains: "Although the exodus served to spare the new regime a potential source of opposition, it also deprived the northern provinces of a substantial proportion of their most affluent, creative, and industrious people."[24] American and South Vietnamese policy makers believed that the DRV's loss might be their gain.

On the other hand, many officials within the southern government hoped that the northern émigrés represented a new pool of political support and, in some cases, experienced administrators. American observers anticipated a similar dynamic. Years later, they continued to project onto the situation their expectations that the northerners would bolster Diem's political standing, despite significant evidence to the contrary. For example, in an internal examination of the early years of American involvement in Vietnam conducted in the late 1960s, DOD analysts concluded that the refugees had played an important role in South Vietnamese politics. According to the DOD analysis, the refugees constituted a "politically malleable, culturally distinct group, wholly distrustful of Ho Chi Minh and the Democratic Republic of Vietnam, dependent for subsistence on Diem's government, and attracted to Diem as a co-religionist."[25] Similarly, the journalist Stanley Karnow described the "political importance" of the northerners, who instantly and significantly enhanced Diem's anti-Communist constituency.[26]

These assessments conform to the historian Carl Bon Tempo's argument about the strong connection between refugee assistance and anticommunism in the minds of American policy makers during the Cold War. As Bon Tempo explains: "American leaders believed that refugees—especially those persons fleeing communism, the Soviets, or their allies—were living symbols of Soviet brutality and communism's failure."[27] By assigning high political value and affording special treatment to the northerners, South Vietnamese and American officials contributed to their position as a visible and marginalized minority group. Perhaps because of their faith in such assumptions and their commitment to broader geopolitical goals, most South Vietnamese and American policy makers turned a blind eye to evidence that the northerners' arrival actually exacerbated political tensions and hurt Diem's popularity in the South.

Despite their desire to absorb nearly one million anti-Communists and Catholics, South Vietnamese leaders understood that they lacked the resources necessary for such a major undertaking. At the Geneva Conference, the French had vowed to transport anyone who wanted to rejoin territory controlled by the French Union. However, the US ambassador to Vietnam, Donald Heath, concluded that the French were incapable of delivering on their promise.[28] South Vietnamese officials concurred, and they turned to the US government for assistance. On August 5, 1954, the South Vietnamese Ministry of Foreign Affairs sent a note to the US embassy in Saigon, requesting American assistance in transporting an estimated one million people south of the seventeenth parallel. Four days after receiving the request, the embassy responded. The United States agreed to "extend all reasonable assistance to evacuate all Northern Vietnamese who wished to leave," in an operation that the Americans dubbed "Operation Passage to Freedom."[29]

In the following months, the US government provided enormous amounts of direct assistance to the GVN to help transport the northerners. American policy makers borrowed models and tactics from recent experiences dealing with refugee populations, including their involvement in assisting Europeans displaced during the Second World War. In fact, some of the Americans engaged in refugee work in Europe during the late 1940s went to Vietnam the following decade. For example, the International Rescue Committee sent Joseph Buttinger, its vice chairman, who had been very active in postwar Europe, to direct the organization's refugee operations in southern Vietnam.[30]

Initially, official US agencies took the lead in assisting those Vietnamese who wished to move south. The Military Assistance and Advisory Group (MAAG) shared responsibilities with the newly created Special Technical and Economic Mission (STEM) and the US Information Service (USIS). MAAG helped transport refugees on American and French aircraft and ships and also provided security at reception points in North and South Vietnam. STEM prepared plans for receiving the refugees and for "dispersing refugees from the reception centers and settling them under conditions of security and gainful employment." USIS attempted to help evacuees adjust to their new lives through orientation programs.[31]

The USIS and American intelligence agencies also waged a propaganda campaign to encourage northerners to leave their homes, a subject that has received significant attention from American scholars. These organizations published and distributed leaflets, produced films about the resettlement program, and broadcast recordings over the Voice of America. Edward Lansdale, an intelligence agent at the Saigon Military Mission and one of Diem's closest American advisers, claimed credit for some of the more memorable efforts to promote the mass migration through propaganda and psychological warfare, or "psywar" tactics. The most famous American slogan, "The Virgin Mary is going south," was supposedly created by Lansdale himself.[32] In his memoir, Lansdale described how he "passed along some psywar ideas" to a group of "Vietnamese nationalists" before they left North Vietnam. His unconventional and sometimes sinister tactics included preparing a phony manifesto that called for a mass work stoppage and producing a counterfeit almanac that predicted a dark future for the Communists.[33] According to a handful of observers at the time, some northerners left their homes because they feared a possible US atomic strike on Hanoi.[34] Recent scholarship has fundamentally challenged the conventional wisdom that northern émigrés, especially Catholics, were motivated by (or even aware of) American propaganda efforts. According to a historian who recently interviewed northern Catholics: "Almost none had ever seen a propaganda leaflet, poster, or any other material that advocated departure to the South."[35] Even Lansdale himself later acknowledged the limited effectiveness of US and South Vietnamese propaganda.[36]

Despite their generally heavy-handed behavior, American officials sometimes recognized that their involvement in recruiting new evacuees could be counterproductive and might limit popular support for the Diem regime. Therefore, the US intelligence and information agencies sought to downplay their own role and emphasize that of the government in Saigon. For example, they removed all American labels from supplies in the refugee camps, with the hope of attributing any success in the program to the GVN.[37]

Whatever the direct impact of American recruiting and propaganda efforts, the infusion of foreign assistance for northerners who did seek

The USS *Bayfield* docks at Saigon in September 1954 to offload refugees during Operation Passage to Freedom. Courtesy National Archives, Naval Historical Foundation Photographic Services, Washington, DC.

to leave clearly facilitated their migration. Refugees began streaming out of North Vietnam within weeks of the introduction of US aid. Between August 16 and September 30, 1954, the US Navy transported 106,342 northerners, the vast majority of whom were civilians traveling with their families, villages, or parishes.[38] The British, and especially the French, also actively participated in efforts to help Vietnamese leave the North. According to Louis Wiesner, by May 1955 "allied" ships and planes had carried 768,672 northerners to South Vietnam, and more than 109,000 additional persons had traveled south by their own means.[39]

Whereas the American officials actively promoted migration and physically assisted refugees in leaving northern Vietnam, the Hanoi government launched its own campaign to discourage people from moving south. Rumors circulated that Viet Minh cadres committed widespread atrocities against those who attempted to leave the country. One young naval medical officer, Lieutenant Tom Dooley, attracted great attention with his popular book *Deliver Us from Evil,* which detailed acts of violence supposedly perpetuated against northern refugees.[40] Although it is difficult to determine the accuracy of Dooley's claims or the extent of reprisals directed at would-be émigrés, Dooley's book and other reports did serve an important propaganda function, especially in the United States. They helped galvanize US policy makers and the American public in support of US intervention in the refugee episode. American readers and politicians celebrated Dooley as a model of humanitarian values, and his staunchly anti-Communist account of the refugee crisis lent a moral imperative to US assistance of Diem's regime.

For its part, the North Vietnamese government claimed to adhere to the Geneva Accords by providing transportation to embarkation points for individuals and families wishing to go south. However, according to American reports, the local Viet Minh forces responsible for providing that transportation insisted on segregating men, women, and children. As a result, families feared being separated and not reunited, and many northerners who might otherwise have elected to leave the country dared not take the risk. Photographs of boats filled with bullet holes, which had ostensibly been attacked by hostile forces, circulated in rural areas of the northern provinces and may have further deterred prospective emigrants.[41] Perhaps in response to these fears, Americans aiding the refugees were instructed to pay particular attention to keeping families together and safe as they transported them south. According to an MAAG report: "Extreme care was taken to maintain family groupings." And, during the first six weeks of the refugee crisis, only one family was separated during the move (it was later reunited).[42]

## Resettling the Refugees in South Vietnam

For several years after the beginning of the crisis, officials in both the South Vietnamese and the US governments considered the resettlement of the northern migrants to be a top priority. As late as 1956, in a letter to South Vietnam's interior minister, D. C. Lavergne, the assistant director of the International Cooperation Administration, wrote: "We believe . . . that you will agree that the early resettlement and rehabilitation of refugees is of great political and economic importance to the Republic of

Vietnam. The magnitude and humanitarian aspects of the problem seem to warrant unusual and emergency measures if the problem is to be solved within a reasonable time with the funds available for this purpose."[43]

As Lavergne's letter indicated, the GVN and US government commitment to the refugees derived from both practical considerations about the potentially destabilizing effect of the influx of people and the ideological conviction that through "rehabilitation" the northerners might become strong supporters of Diem's regime. According to this logic, if the regime could effectively incorporate the refugees into South Vietnamese society, the GVN would benefit from having hundreds of thousands of rural Vietnamese who felt indebted to the government for helping them begin new lives in South Vietnam. The refugees, who had actively chosen to leave the North, embodied precisely the type of committed anti-Communists that Diem and his allies in Washington, DC, hoped would inspire loyalty to the GVN among the rest of the South Vietnamese population. In light of Diem's struggle to affirm his legitimacy, the refugees' condemnation of the DRV and of Communist sympathizers in the South might provide a powerful model for other Vietnamese. However, such assumptions suggest more about the significant degree of wishful thinking employed by American and South Vietnamese officials than they do about the realities on the ground.

When the northerners arrived in South Vietnam, they proceeded to reception centers located close to the debarkation points. They were later transferred to resettlement camps built farther inland by Vietnamese and French troops. There they lived in temporary housing, including pup tents provided by the French military. Months after their initial arrival, they finally moved to permanent relocation sites, where they built their own houses and sought long-term employment.[44] In many cases, these sites had been occupied previously but had been abandoned during periods of heavy fighting in the First Indochina War. Strategic considerations often informed GVN and US officials' selection of specific relocation areas. For example, they established many settlements in Communist strongholds, such as the Mekong delta, or in the Central Highlands, which were primarily populated by ethnic minority groups.[45]

Policy makers in Saigon adopted a bold agenda for integrating the new arrivals into South Vietnamese society once they had arrived. Diem and Ngo Dinh Nhu, his brother and closest adviser, considered refugee resettlement to be part of a larger "personalist revolution," which included ambitious resettlement and land-development projects. Concerned with overpopulation in coastal parts of the country, Diem and Nhu believed that "redistributing *people* rather than *land*" might ease population pressure while simultaneously contributing to their goal of economic diversification.[46] They also hoped that resettling Vietnamese loyal to the Saigon government would help address security concerns and advance an ideological agenda centered on community development. The Ngos viewed northern transplants as particularly well suited to spearhead this expansion.[47] The Vietnam expert Bernard Fall explained the Ngo family's vision a few years after the refugee crisis had ended: "Refugees would provide much-needed manpower to put into operation long standing plans for the development of the Southern Mountain Plateau and of more than 200,000 acres of rice land in the Mekong Delta and the Trans-Bassac area that had lain fallow for almost ten years because of the [First Indochina] war."[48]

Diem and Nhu had high hopes for resettling the refugees in the sparsely populated highlands, at the time home primarily to peoples they considered uncivilized savages.[49] According to their vision, settling the northerners in upland areas would not only boost agricultural production there but also serve the strategic objective of creating a human wall between the GVN and its detractors. As the 1950s wore on, South Vietnamese and American officials became increasingly concerned with cutting off supply routes from the North, which passed through Laos and Cambodia into the Central Highlands. But, as Hansen's work suggests, many refugees refused to comply with the GVN's plans and instead decided for themselves where they would settle.[50] The historian Philip Catton's research supports this claim. He explains: "The reluctance of northern refugees to play the role of nation-building pioneers particularly disappointed the palace, which had viewed its coreligionists as perfect settler material."[51]

Like their South Vietnamese counterparts, American officials also placed high value on resolving the refugee crisis quickly and helping the northerners adapt to their new lives. They paved the way for a number of public and private American organizations to provide assistance for refugees once they arrived in South Vietnam. The US government aid agency's in-country team, the US Operations Mission (USOM), worked closely with South Vietnamese officials to coordinate resettlement projects. Beginning in 1955, the MSU public administration team, which was under contract with the US government, also advised the GVN on its refugee policies. Other groups operated at a more grassroots level, frequently interacting with the refugees themselves. Many of these groups were voluntary or religious organizations that distributed food and humanitarian supplies among the refugee communities. They included the International Rescue Committee, the Mennonite Central Committee, the National Catholic Welfare Conference, the World Church Service, and the American Women's Association.[52] After its introduction to Vietnam in 1956, International Voluntary Services (IVS) helped construct permanent villages for the refugees and provided technical assistance in agricultural development. IVS and other nongovernment organizations also functioned as informal mediators by providing a connection between GVN or US officials and the refugees and ensuring that material aid reached the refugee communities that needed help. As one IVS volunteer later recalled: "Every type of work imaginable was done then . . . construction work, establishment of livestock and crop programs, and community development."[53]

Although both contemporary observers and scholars have focused on the positive working relationships between the GVN and Americans during the early years of the alliance, the two sides did not always agree, especially on issues related to financing refugee resettlement. There were significant disputes over how much responsibility each party should have in subsidizing resettlement programs as well as how to distribute and account for specific project funds. With regard to the first issue—funding refugee programs—Vietnamese officials argued that their American counterparts expected the GVN to cover resettlement costs for which they simply lacked adequate money.[54]

Disagreements over distributing and managing funds suggested an even more significant discrepancy in the two governments' nation-building visions. These disagreements illuminated fundamental differences about how to implement the refugee programs. As internal GVN correspondence shows, the Vietnamese generally favored a decentralized model in which locally elected committees would distribute funds and oversee the execution of specific projects.[55] According to Miller, Diem's interest in and self-identification with Confucian teachings influenced his thinking on democracy and administration. Diem insisted on granting the village committees financial responsibility. This position likely stemmed from his assumption that he could exercise more control over local politicians than he could over foreign advisers as well as his hope that committee members would be guided by a sense of their moral duties and obligations.[56]

On the other hand, most Americans argued that the complex and delicate circumstances of administering aid funds called for the expertise of trained accountants and bookkeepers rather than inexperienced committees that might be prone to corruption.[57] The Americans' opposition to village control over financial decision making reflected a bureaucratic sensibility that valued professional expertise over local knowledge and suggested a basic disregard for or lack of trust in local processes as well as a concern over the competence of local people and the potential for fraud.[58] This same attitude surfaced in other areas of nation building, notably among American aid workers focused on agricultural development. In the refugee case, at least, the Vietnamese model won out. GVN officials refused to comply with American recommendations, and USOM put up very little protest in response to the Ngos' decision to shift many of the provincial delegates' duties to the refugee village administrative committees.[59] While some differences of opinion should be expected, these disputes pointed to a basic incompatibility in the different approaches that Vietnamese and American officials took regarding local power and control, and they foreshadowed future ruptures in the partnership.

Resettling the refugees in South Vietnam proved far more challenging than encouraging them to move or physically transporting them south. Most early complications associated with debarkation and resettlement stemmed from the fact that the GVN was ill prepared and lacked the experience to deal with such a large undertaking. The South Vietnamese police personnel stationed at the debarkation points were, according to American observers, relatively unhelpful in assisting with the process of moving people off the boats and into reception centers. Instead, local Vietnamese youth organizations won high praise from American observers for their contributions to the orderly and efficient debarkation of refugees. Similarly, Americans commended Vietnamese Catholic priests, who provided "invaluable service marked by efficient, cooperative and sympathetic relationships with all U.S. agencies involved."[60] These phenomena confirm the low state capacity of the GVN, on which many American aid workers commented at the time. They also suggest a more organized and diverse array of groups functioning in civil society than the conventional scholarship usually acknowledges.

Although some of the northerners had relatives in the South, many refugees arrived in South Vietnam destitute and without any local contacts to help them begin new lives. According to Walter Mode, a member of the MSU group, both Diem and his American advisers considered the refugee movement a "critical situation," with over five thousand new refugees arriving in South Vietnam's ports and cities each day.[61]

To deal with the massive logistic and social problems caused by the barrage of people entering the country, Diem established a new federal agency called the Commissariat General for Refugees, which was widely referred to by its French acronym, COMIGAL. During the first few months of its existence, COMIGAL was plagued with instability and lacked a coherent vision of its mission. As of late September 1954, there had already been four refugee commissioners each of whom offered a different plan for how the agency should deal with the refugee problem.[62] Such problems reflected the general volatility of the new South Vietnamese government as well as Diem's tenuous hold on power at the time. The chaos passed, however, as Diem's administration consolidated its authority, and by mid-1955 COMIGAL had a clear direction and strong leadership. At that time, thirty-seven local units reported directly to Bui Van Luong, a personal friend of Diem's and a Catholic, who remained the director of the agency for the remainder of its existence.[63] Initially, COMIGAL's primary responsibility was to create refugee centers and provide basic building supplies for the new immigrants. The broader aims of the agency focused on a program of assimilation in which the northerners would be integrated into South Vietnamese society.

During its three-year existence, COMIGAL oversaw the establishment of 319 permanent refugee villages in which over 605,000 people settled. The remaining 300,000 refugees resettled themselves without significant assistance from COMIGAL, mostly in Saigon and other southern cities. Some of these refugees may have had preexisting family ties in the South; others likely relied on their own resourcefulness to make a new life. The Mekong delta contained the vast majority of the COMIGAL villages, and most inhabitants were farmers. In addition to 207 villages in the delta, 50 refugee villages were created on the central coast and

62 in the highlands.[64] Although hundreds of thousands of refugees had been settled, nearly all the newcomers still faced significant hardships. According to a report issued by COMIGAL in late 1955, most refugees engaged in farming or fishing, but they lacked field implements, seeds, livestock, and fishing equipment. All the refugee centers needed schools, teachers, and hospitals, and many camps lacked enough water to cultivate the fields.[65]

While some problems, such as inadequate health care and educational opportunities, were commonplace in all the centers, the refugees' experiences varied significantly depending on where they had relocated. According to COMIGAL, the thirty-three thousand refugees who had settled in camps in the Central Highlands enjoyed a relatively high standard of living compared with those living elsewhere. This distinction likely stemmed from the fact that the highlands camps were among the first refugee centers built. Created in late 1954, soon after the refugee crisis began, these camps benefited from more experienced administrators and well-established compounds.[66] Northern transplants who settled along the central coast, particularly those who lived near the city of Nha Trang and the port of Cam Ranh Bay, also enjoyed advantages over newcomers to other areas. In particular, they profited from their proximity to diverse natural resources, rich fishing areas, and surplus farmland.[67] Furthermore, many of the refugees who settled along the central coast were fishermen. As Wiesner explains, refugees who earned a living through fishing tended to fare well because they did not need large tracts of land and required only a small investment in order to become productive citizens.[68]

On the other hand, northerners who settled in the Mekong delta and other areas close to Saigon seemed to suffer greater hardship. An MSU survey conducted in several refugee villages in the delta highlighted some of these obstacles. According to this survey, residents of many villages in Vinh Long Province had no farmland, no sanitation facilities, and no lumber to build houses. Refugee camps in Ben Tre lacked potable water and basic medical supplies. One report from the area illuminated the seemingly insurmountable obstacles facing refugees. These people required such fundamental necessities as "DDT, wells, electricity, homes, and jobs."[69] Ultimately, then, the successes of the refugee episode were accompanied by serious problems.

## Ignoring the Failures of Refugee Resettlement

Driven by confidence in their methods and an eagerness to see the "Diem experiment" succeed, American policy makers failed to appreciate three primary shortcomings of the refugee-resettlement program. First, they overestimated the degree to which northerners were integrated into South Vietnamese society, in part because they lacked an effective means of measuring assimilation. Second, they overlooked how the GVN's refugee policies worsened Diem's political standing in the countryside and exacerbated tensions between local communities and the refugees. Finally, they undervalued the importance of local sentiment and ignored how these tensions sparked increased antigovernment violence, which threatened basic security and the very survival of the state.

Both GVN and American officials believed that the primary goal of resettlement should be for the refugees to become completely self-sufficient and incorporated into local communities, at least in part so that they might enhance the South Vietnamese state's legitimacy. Accordingly, COMIGAL tried to prevent the refugee communities from developing their own administrative units. Instead, existing districts were supposed to absorb these new communities. Furthermore, Diem established COMIGAL as a temporary solution to the refugee problem, with the understanding that the life of the agency would be limited to the immediate crisis period. By mid-1956, the MSU group advised the Vietnamese government that "planning for the orderly dissolution of COMIGAL should begin immediately." COMIGAL anticipated this recommendation and began to transfer some of its functions to permanent government agencies. For example, in mid-1956, it transferred responsibility for providing medical services to refugees to the GVN Ministry of Health.[70]

Other American aid workers concurred with the GVN and MSU group approach to refugee resettlement. As Leland Barrows, the director of USOM, explained to the Vietnamese Committee on Foreign Aid: "This is not a program of public assistance to indigents but a program for aiding the refugees to put themselves through their own efforts in a position to earn a living."[71] One project agreement between the US government and the GVN—dealing with aid to the village of Long Phuoc Thon in Gia Dinh Province—stipulated that US material assistance to the village was "intended to make fully self-supporting 858 refugee families or

4,473 persons within a period of from 6–9 months."[72] A report issued by COMIGAL in October 1955 explained: "The refugees are supposed, within the near future, to identify themselves with the local people."[73] Policy makers in Saigon and Washington valued assimilation not only because it represented a successful resolution to the refugee crisis but also because the refugees' integration into the society meant that presumed government loyalists would be spread throughout the country.

However, the twin goals of self-sufficiency and integration were not necessarily mutually reinforcing. It was entirely possible that a group of northerners might become self-sufficient, especially in cases in which whole villages or parishes moved together. Many such groups seemed to develop a cohesive community, often one based on the strong organization of the Catholic Church, which took care of its own members and did not rely on outside support. However, many groups of northerners exhibited signs of independence without becoming assimilated into the broader society. In fact, by conflating self-sufficiency and integration, GVN and US officials obscured basic shortcomings of the entire resettlement endeavor. They could, and in many cases did, assume that northerners had been accepted into local communities once they no longer relied on or received government assistance.

One of the major difficulties American and Vietnamese observers had when evaluating refugee projects was determining whether and when refugees had been rehabilitated or integrated into the society. For example, the MSU group routinely produced positive assessments of refugee resettlement, particularly in Central Vietnam. However, these reports provided little evidence to support the claims of success. In late 1956, one member of the MSU group visited several camps along the central coast. After conducting interviews and observing four villages in Khanh Hoa Province, he concluded that 80 percent of the 20,000 refugees living in those communities had been "rehabilitated" and integrated into "regular life." Similarly, he found that the 100,000 refugees residing in twenty villages in Binh Thuan Province had been "rehabilitated well" in spite of the fact that they had no access to technical services and that aid money had not been distributed evenly. According to MSU's report, refugees in the relatively wealthy province of Ninh Thuan had fared even better. These 20,000 people were "completely integrated into the communities and are no longer classified as refugees."[74]

The MSU report credited the success of refugees in these provinces to the fact that the area had received extensive US aid and could accommodate more people because of a surplus of previously unused land. Furthermore, the report cited the wealth of natural resources in the region as well as the fact that the central coast saw less insurgent activity and was relatively safer than other areas of South Vietnam. Although the MSU group offered possible explanations for why these refugees had fared so well, their report contained no explanation of the standards used by them or COMIGAL to judge whether refugees had been rehabilitated. The report also failed to mention any other factors that might have accounted for success in this case, such as advantages that this particular group of northerners might have enjoyed as a result of their backgrounds, experiences, or local leadership. Instead of providing concrete examples to demonstrate the effectiveness of US aid, advisers from MSU and other organizations appealed to US and GVN officials' affinity for statistics, however meaningless, and their expectations of a successful outcome to the refugee situation. As this example suggests, American policy makers and aid workers convinced themselves into believing that their efforts played a major role in resettling the refugees.

In fact, the success that northern transplants did achieve often depended far more on their own resourcefulness and the preferential treatment they received from the GVN than on the efforts of US aid workers. As one US official explained, "the remarkable resiliency" of individual refugees proved more instrumental than any support the GVN or the United States could provide them.[75] However, despite positive assessments, such as the MSU report discussed above, over a year after the crisis began the US aid agency found that only "a very small number [of refugees] have been able to create a new independent existence."[76]

## Tensions between Refugees and Locals

Instead of resulting in integration, in many cases the refugees' arrival seemed to generate tensions between the northerners and locals and contribute to Diem's political troubles. Because many of his countrymen saw him not as a patriot but as a repressive leader who favored the Catholic minority and invited foreign intervention, Diem never earned widespread popular support, and he faced a growing antigovernment insurgency. In fact, beginning at the time of the refugee crisis, he brought many of these problems on himself through ill-conceived policies, including the preferential treatment of northern Catholics. As the historian John Prados explains: "Diem naturally gravitated to the northerners, favored them, and expected their loyalty."[77] However, his treatment of the northerners had serious consequences for his political prospects in South Vietnam. According to one scholar: "Diem's favoritism for the northerners was one of the major articles in the later indictment against him."[78] Instead of resulting in the refugees' assimilation and widespread political support, GVN resettlement efforts often bred animosity toward the newcomers and alienated the local population from Diem's government.

Beginning in early 1955, the GVN decided not to permit any more refugees to settle in Ben Tre Province in the Mekong delta because of generally poor security and strained relations between the refugees and the local population. An MSU report described the local people as "antagonistic" toward refugees in many villages. In one area of Ben Tre, the established community refused to allow refugees to use the village well, thus making it quite difficult for refugees to find sources of potable water.[79] In another dramatic and violent episode, some of Diem's political rivals attacked refugees, probably as a form of retribution against palace crackdowns on the group's activities. On July 31, 1955, in the wake of their military defeat in Saigon, members of the Binh Xuyen group burned the village of Phuoc-Ly.[80] Phuoc-Ly was one of the first permanent refugee villages created in South Vietnam and served as a symbol of pro-Catholic government policies. As a result of the Binh Xuyen attack, 190 houses were destroyed, and twenty-four hundred recently resettled northerners were left homeless.[81] These examples reveal the intensity of Diem's political problems. With both opportunistic political rivals and local communities demonstrating their hostility toward the government or the refugees, it would be very difficult for COMIGAL and American aid workers to expect those refugees to be accepted into the community, much less inspire popular support for the GVN.

The practice of providing subsistence payments to refugees also presented numerous problems for the GVN and the refugees themselves. On their arrival, the northern migrants received a small subsistence allowance to help cover their most pressing needs. During the first few months of the resettlement period, this allowance amounted to ten piasters per day for each person. However, officials quickly discovered the complications involved in distributing the stipend, especially once refugees moved throughout the country to permanent relocation areas. Beginning in the fall of 1954, refugees received a lump sum of eight hundred piasters when they arrived in South Vietnam. As further enticement, northerners willing to resettle in the highlands were given an additional two hundred piasters.[82]

According to a USOM report, the subsistence allowances the refugees received while they were in reception camps surpassed the daily income of most Vietnamese peasants. As a result, many refugees resisted moving from reception camps to permanent resettlement areas or villages, where they would no longer be eligible for the allowance. Furthermore, the allowances produced a significant disparity between the refugees, who at least for a time enjoyed cash payments from the government, and the rest of the rural population, who received no handouts and in some cases had very few public services at their disposal.[83] This disparity probably contributed to resentment on the part of the established population toward the northern transplants.

Diem compounded such political dilemmas by adopting policies that openly favored Catholic migrants over non-Catholic refugees and southerners. Catholics generally enjoyed more support than Buddhist refugees, who were often overlooked and received less financial and material assistance from COMIGAL than their Catholic counterparts.[84] According to an MSU report on refugees in the delta's Can Tho Province, Buddhist refugees "[were] left out" of government resettlement programs. The report stated: "Buddhists do not seem to be receiving the same treatment as others."[85] In addition to receiving less money than the Catholics, Buddhist refugees enjoyed far less influence over the implementation of resettlement projects. With the aid of American organizations such as Catholic Relief Services (CRS), Diem's regime attempted to give parish priests more control over administering and financing refugee projects than expert technical advisers from COMIGAL or the MSU group.[86]

Furthermore, Diem's government exhibited preferential treatment toward Catholic refugees at the expense of the established communities. In many cases, the GVN provided the refugees with basic amenities that the local populations lacked. In addition to the subsistence payments, refugees received construction materials to build their houses and equipment such as farming or fishing implements. To make matters worse, Diem also replaced many local leaders who had held prestigious and influential positions within the provincial and the village administrative systems with Catholic northerners. This widely unpopular policy resulted in the creation of what one scholar and participant in the MSU technical assistance group has called a "carpetbag government" in the South.[87] As the historian James Carter writes: "Most governmental positions went, in fact, to either the Catholic minority that now ringed Saigon as recent refugees and/or the Ngo family."[88] These policies likely contributed to tensions between refugees and locals and helped foster the perception that Diem did not have the best interests of the majority in mind.

Many Catholic refugees demonstrated their determination to prevail over the hostility of local communities and the economic hardships they faced by remaining in certain areas of the country. One group of refugees had settled on the property of a Catholic church in Vinh Long Province, in the Mekong delta. Although these refugees had no land on which they could establish farms or raise livestock, they also had "no desire to relocate." Nearby, another group of eight hundred refugees lived on privately owned land. The provincial chief paid their rent out of his own pocket so that they could remain in their new homes. Although these people lacked access to farmland, sanitation facilities, and building materials, they also chose to stay in that village rather than move elsewhere.[89] These anecdotes suggest that many refugees refused to give in to social or economic pressure to leave the areas in which they settled and instead remained despite the hostility of local people, perhaps because they doubted their prospects elsewhere.

Despite their reluctance to succumb to local opposition by moving to a different area, many refugees appear to have retained their northern identity and envisioned themselves as only temporary inhabitants of the South. According to Louis Wiesner, refugees "did not lose their identity in the South." Instead, they arrived in groups, and villages or parishes settled together.[90] As Catton explains, many refugees hoped that partition would be temporary and that they would be able to move back to their original homes at some point.[91] The fact that many refugees anticipated returning to the North, settled as intact groups, and retained many aspects of northern culture suggests that few were fully integrated into local communities.

## Political Instability in Resettlement Areas

In some cases, severe animosity toward the South Vietnamese government threatened to undermine the entire resettlement endeavor. The Cai San development in the Mekong delta provides a particularly striking example of the effects of local opposition, including opposition within refugee communities, to the regime's resettlement policies. In the late 1950s and early 1960s, South Vietnamese and American officials touted Cai San as a success, and the area became an important model for their future land-development projects. But Cai San was also the site of significant antigovernment violence during the first years of Diem's regime, and the northerners' antagonism toward GVN policies previewed future, more serious clashes between rural populations and government authorities.

Despite the challenges facing refugees relocating to the Mekong delta, both American and Vietnamese policy makers encouraged resettlement in the region by funding large-scale projects. The most notable and ambitious of these projects was the Cai San resettlement area, which straddled the provinces of Kien Giang and An Giang in the southwestern corner of the country. Officials intended the settlement to absorb over 10 percent of all the northern refugees and serve as a model for other land-development schemes. On the basis of plans originally conceived by French colonial officials in the 1930s and 1940s, Diem expressed his "unqualified approval" for Cai San.[92] The proposal called for an area consisting of sixteen canals that branched off of larger waterways. Immediately prior to the influx of northerners, the particular location of Cai San village had been largely uninhabited, probably because it had been abandoned during the First Indochina War. According to the MSU group, the Cai San project was designed to "exploit untouched or abandoned tracts" of land in this fertile part of the country.[93]

Vietnamese authorities relied on American funding and equipment and peasant labor to convert the unused land into rice paddies crisscrossed by inland waterways. Around those channels, they then created sprawling villages in which to settle the refugees. The GVN paid refugees to dig the canals and provided each family with a frame for a house and materials to build a thatched roof.[94] Each family also received three hectares (7.5 acres) of land in tenancy. The government envisioned that the newcomers would clear and cultivate the land and that they would later be able to purchase the property in installments.[95]

Initial plans called for 100,000 people to be resettled in Cai San by May 1957. As of August 1956, between 30,000 and 40,000 refugees lived along the canals and used them for transportation, fishing, and irrigation.[96] They grew rice and other crops nearby, on the land they had been loaned by COMIGAL. The vast majority of Cai San's settlers were northern Catholics.[97] The parishes that sprung up along each canal were the central focus of each neighborhood, and the Catholic priests who served each parish became not only religious but also administrative and community leaders.[98]

Initially, at least, GVN and US officials considered the refugee settlement at Cai San a success. The area quickly became an anti-Communist stronghold and seemed to be an island of progovernment sentiment in the middle of a territory where former Viet Minh and Hoa Hao rebels enjoyed significant control and support. As a result, from its inception Cai San served as a showpiece for the entire refugee-resettlement program, and Vietnamese officials as well as foreigners often toured its villages.[99] An article published in July 1955 in the English-language newspaper *Vietnam Press* painted a glowing picture of the progress at Cai San. The article's Vietnamese author reported that, in the two canals that he visited, "houses spring up like mushrooms and the gardens are covered with vegetable beans of a wonderful green."[100]

Vietnamese and American officials also touted Cai San as a model for future strategic development projects. In a presentation delivered in June 1956 before the Vietnamese Committee on Foreign Aid, USOM's director, Leland Barrows, praised the progress that Cai San's settlers had made. He discussed the general achievements of Cai San and recommended that the area be used as an example for other development endeavors. He argued that the positive experience of Cai San encouraged him to think about other instances in which the GVN could institute "rapid redevelopment and re-occupation of idle land." According to Barrows, reclaiming unoccupied land and providing peasants with the opportunity to develop productive farms on that land presented the Vietnamese government with a strategy for improving the political and military situation and simultaneously contributing to the country's economic base.[101] The MSU group also praised the project at Cai San, arguing: "[It] offer[s] the possibility of relocating and rehabilitating thousands of refugees who are now located in unsatisfactory sites. . . . [T]he Commissariat merits high praise for assigning a high priority to these development projects."[102] In the following years, American and Vietnamese policy makers would attempt to replicate the approach they had used with the refugees at Cai San in their other efforts to relocate Vietnamese peasants for tactical and ideological purposes.[103]

But Cai San was not the peaceful and idyllic paradise that policy makers and reporters made it out to be. It had grown from a rural outpost to a bustling village overnight. Gerald Hickey, an anthropologist and member of the MSU group who visited the area soon after it was developed, described it as having a "boom town character." He explained that making the journey there from Saigon felt like traveling to the "frontier."[104] As often occurs in frontier or boomtown areas, however, a significant amount chaos and criminal activity transpired in Cai San. This high level of violence, which was generally directed at GVN officials but sometimes implicated the refugees or American aid workers, challenged the narrative of Cai San as an unqualified success or as evidence of the northern émigrés' support for the Saigon government.

Numerous USOM documents cited high levels of unrest and "hostile activities" in and around Cai San.[105] Some refugees simply refused to move to Cai San, presumably because of the political tensions and violence in the area.[106] In one nearly fatal attack, as mentioned earlier in this book, several South Vietnamese soldiers traveling to Cai San were wounded when their jeep was hit by small arms fire. Apparently, Diem believed that the intended target of the ambush was actually USOM's director, Leland Barrows, whose own jeep reached the site of the attack a mere three minutes after the unfortunate South Vietnamese soldiers.[107] Regardless of whether the real target was the government soldiers or an American aid worker, this incident illustrates the general instability near Cai San and the fact that opposition groups did not shy away from the use of aggressive or intimidating tactics. The historian David Biggs refers to the "frequent episodes of criminal activity on lonely delta highways" near Cai San, and he suggests that neither American nor South Vietnamese policy makers could do much to curb the violence at that point.[108] Although US and GVN officials could not always identify the instigators, much less prevent criminal activity or antigovernment violence, they used such attacks to justify heavy-handed policies designed to locate and eliminate their opponents. This episode previewed the increasing hostility toward government officials—and eventually their American advisers as well—and the Diem regime's responses that developed into a full-blown civil war throughout the rural areas of South Vietnam during the subsequent years.

In August 1956, tensions escalated between GVN officials and settlers in Cai San. That month, Diem announced a number of policy changes that infuriated the settlers. According to Diem's directive, Cai San's priests would be stripped of all administrative authority, and the settlers would immediately be considered "regular citizens," which meant that they would lose the special aid privileges they had previously enjoyed. Most significantly, the GVN required all inhabitants of Cai San to sign tenant contracts.[109] The northerners were enraged to learn that, contrary to what they had previously understood, they would now be responsible for purchasing the land on which they lived and worked.[110] In the aftermath of Diem's announcement, some settlers began rioting, and a number of confrontations broke out between inhabitants of Cai San and GVN officials. As Biggs writes of the episode: "Even in the relatively peaceful days of 1956, deep divisions existed between the mostly Catholic refugees and their priests, on the one hand, and politically connected landowners and government authorities, on the other."[111]

Despite these early examples of unrest, Vietnamese and American aid workers continued to focus on Cai San's potential for resettlement and redevelopment. From the introduction of its mission in Vietnam, IVS was heavily invested in the area. Beginning in late 1956, the IVS agricultural group became particularly involved in efforts to rehabilitate refugees at Cai San. One of the two IVS teams assigned to refugee-resettlement work was stationed at Cai San, and these volunteers lived there for several months at a time. Working alongside local peasants, the American volunteers built demonstration gardens and created communal agricultural areas. They established small orchards and nurseries and then distributed saplings to local refugee families, participated in a GVN-sponsored poultry program, and offered instruction in fishing techniques.[112] IVSers would adopt this same approach to their efforts at economic development elsewhere in South Vietnam during the subsequent decade and a half.

Ultimately, however, IVS efforts at Cai San were cut short because of political problems and instability. On August 31, 1957, IVS closed its Cai San station and moved the volunteers working there to Ban Me Thuot in the Central Highlands. The organization cited "insecurity" in the region as the official rationale for the closure. In addition to general political tensions in the settlement, IVS leaders were responding to the lingering effects of the turmoil that had engulfed Cai San the previous year. IVS apparently had other reasons for withdrawing its volunteers as well. According to the organization's final report for the Vietnam mission, volunteers stationed at Cai San were "unaware of the position of authority exercised by the Roman Catholic priests over the settlers," and the Americans "aroused resentment from a few village leaders."[113]

The unrest at Cai San and IVS's decision to abandon its operation there point to a number of significant problems underlying the entire refugee-resettlement endeavor. Local communities as well as some American aid workers often resented the excessive influence wielded by Catholic priests and their congregations.[114] At the same time, many of the refugees felt that the South Vietnamese government had misled them and that their needs were not being met. Much of the antigovernment sentiment, if not the violence it engendered, resulted directly from these flaws in the implementation of the refugee-resettlement program and GVN policies toward the northern transplants.

## Misplaced Optimism and Lessons (Not) Learned

Despite these shortcomings, American officials celebrated the accomplishments, however limited, of refugee resettlement as representative of a larger success story. Even though some policy makers still harbored concerns about Diem's leadership, many Americans viewed the entire refugee program as an example of Saigon's ability to handle difficult situations and of the role that US aid projects could play in supporting its allies in South Vietnam. Just two years after the refugee crisis began, the US government terminated its support for resettlement programs on the basis of the projection that all refugees would soon be settled and integrated into South Vietnamese society.[115] By 1957, most of the northern transplants had been moved from reception centers and resettled in permanent villages throughout South Vietnam. The following year, COMIGAL, the South Vietnamese bureau that had been created to oversee the resettlement programs, broadened its responsibilities and was renamed the Commissariat General for Land Development. Similarly, the US aid agency's Resettlement Division became the Land Development Division.[116] In 1956, USOM director Leland Barrows concluded that American efforts to help the GVN with refugee resettlement had been effective. He stated: "Undoubtedly, this program compares favorably with any of the several mass refugee movements to which the United States has contributed its assistance."[117]

The perceptions of American policy makers and aid workers about the success of refugee resettlement had significant implications for future American involvement in Vietnam, not least of which was to justify continued intervention. The plight of the northern migrants engaged the sympathies of many Americans, and the experience of helping them establish new lives lent a humanitarian dimension to US nation-building efforts in South Vietnam. Most importantly, the relationship of the GVN and American aid organizations reinforced in the minds of many US policy makers the wisdom and feasibility of supporting Diem and the efficacy of foreign assistance. In a 1956 speech, then senator John F. Kennedy congratulated the Diem government on its accomplishments in dealing with the refugees, whom he described as "courageous people dedicated to the free way of life." In recounting the GVN's achievements during the previous two years, he said: "Most striking of all, perhaps, has been the rehabilitation of more than ¾ of a million refugees from the North."[118] *The Pentagon Papers*, the DOD's definitive internal report on early US involvement in Vietnam, reflected a similar laudatory and positive attitude. The report explained: "U.S. officials defending American aid programs could point with pride to the refugee episode to demonstrate the special eligibility of the Vietnamese for U.S. help, including an early, convincing demonstration that Diem's government could mount an effective program with U.S. aid."[119] And as materials issued by the ICA at the end of 1956 stated: "The groundwork has been laid for long-range progress in economic rehabilitation and development." However, despite (or perhaps because of) their claims of success in the refugee crisis, the aid workers were quick to justify their continued involvement in Vietnam as well as to request ongoing funding from the US government for their activities. Their report acknowledged that South Vietnam's development would require "aid of a considerable magnitude" for years to follow.[120]

As they delivered these self-congratulatory pronouncements, policy makers and aid workers alike overlooked any evidence that conflicted with their narrative of success. They also assumed that their initial positive evaluations of refugee resettlement would hold true in the long term. Not only does this behavior suggest that, from their earliest experiences in South Vietnam, policy makers ignored local concerns; it also reveals a remarkable shortsightedness about the effects of their actions. For those who paid attention, the resettlement episode offered considerable indications, even at the time, of the problematic nature of the US-GVN partnership as well as significant defects in how Diem and others in the South Vietnamese government related to rural inhabitants of the country. Ultimately, American policy makers and aid workers chose to ignore such problems in order to justify continued intervention and ensure political and financial support for their policies in Vietnam.

In the years that followed, the refugee-resettlement period served as a model for Vietnamese and American nation builders pursuing technical assistance and economic-development programs. The policy makers' and aid workers' experiences in refugee resettlement fueled a misplaced sense of optimism that colored how those Americans approached their future efforts in Vietnam. Unfortunately, they drew many of the wrong lessons from the episode and formed flawed assumptions that informed later nation-building policies. Most notably, Americans incorrectly assumed that the conditions that led to the limited successes of the resettlement effort would persist in other contexts. But the attitudes of the mostly Catholic refugees did not mirror the sensibilities of the rest of South Vietnam's population. And, although American and GVN officials shared the same basic goals and approach for resettling the northerners, disagreements in subsequent years over how the partnership should function and how South Vietnam should develop severely hampered their ability to collaborate. For their part, American aid workers would never again enjoy the same degree of support from the US and South Vietnamese governments, the same level of cooperation and acceptance from the local people with whom they worked, or the same feeling of relative political calm throughout the countryside.

Many of the subsequent nation-building failures in South Vietnam might have been avoided had American policy makers and aid workers taken a more objective view of the refugee episode. Instead, they projected onto the crisis their profound desire for a successful outcome to the overall nation-building experiment in Vietnam. Wishing for success, they exaggerated their own role in refugee efforts, ignored the shortcomings of resettlement programs, and missed the warning signs of what those failures would mean for future US involvement in Vietnam.

2

# Civil Servants and Cold Warriors

## Technical Assistance in Public Administration

> The deteriorating security situation in certain provinces was both
> cause and effect of weak and ineffective civil government.
> —Gustav Hertz (1964)

In 1960, Guy Fox, an adviser from Michigan State University (MSU), reflected on the challenges that South Vietnamese and American nation builders had faced as they embarked on their ambitious effort a few years earlier. He described the situation in stark terms, writing: "When southern Vietnam became a fully independent country in 1954, the shortage of trained government personnel threatened the very existence of the new nation." Like Fox, many American policy makers and aid workers believed that South Vietnam's success depended on the creation of modern and American-style public administration in the country. According to members of the MSU group as well as US government officials, two of the most serious problems facing the new state were an absence of law and order and a "vacuum of trained civil servants."[1] Similarly, Leland Barrows, the director of the US Operations Mission (USOM), argued: "The priority accorded the sector of public administration . . . is a recognition not only of the importance of improving the efficiency of public service and the competence of the security services, but also of the priority accorded to this field by the Government of Vietnam itself."[2]

Advisers from USOM and MSU believed that improving public administration and creating a corps of well-trained civil servants would strengthen Diem's tenuous hold on power and reinforce South Vietnam's autonomy and legitimacy. The Americans believed that they could train Vietnamese public bureaucrats to be more efficient in their work, more responsive to the public, and more accountable for their decisions. The MSU group focused primarily on supporting the institutions of the state and working with political elites in Saigon. On the other hand, USOM concentrated on improving public administration in the provinces, thereby representing a more bottom-up approach. However, the American aid workers did not always find a sympathetic or receptive audience and instead frequently met resistance at nearly every level. From basic disagreements over curricular development and teaching styles with their counterparts at the National Institute of Administration (NIA) to more significant disputes with US or Government of Vietnam (GVN) policy makers over the basic contours of democracy and good governance, these Americans were continuously involved in ideological and practical conflicts.

Assistance in public administration would suffer from many of the same deficiencies that plagued other aspects of the US nation-building venture in Vietnam. Members of the MSU group as well as of USOM brought a host of political, ideological, and cultural biases to Vietnam. Most importantly, they assumed that their models and experiences could and should be replicated by the Vietnamese. These advisers also shared the US government's geopolitical agenda, which demanded support for leaders in Saigon regardless of their undemocratic practices or unpopularity. However, their adherence to US policy would prevent the aid workers from being responsive to the diverse interests and vision of the Vietnamese with whom they worked, including political leaders in Saigon.

Although they began as staunch supporters and, especially in the case of MSU personnel, trusted advisers to South Vietnamese officials, many aid workers became outspoken critics of particular GVN policies and of Diem's leadership. Their years of experience and research in South Vietnam resulted in important studies, reports, and information about South Vietnam and its government. In fact, this production of knowledge was perhaps the most important contribution of the MSU and USOM public administration teams. Unfortunately, however, policy makers in Washington and Saigon were loath to accept the aid workers' critiques. Concerned that any criticism or opposition might weaken their already tenuous hold on power or inspire reductions in foreign aid, GVN officials attempted to muzzle any negative reports. Their response led to a battle between South Vietnamese leaders and MSU advisers, in particular, over academic freedom and the proper role of American advisers in Vietnam. For their part, American officials responded negatively to any assessments that challenged US policies. They refused to alter the basic course in Vietnam, even after Diem had been removed from power, and provided only lukewarm support for MSU professors' appeals to free speech. More importantly, both American and South Vietnamese policy makers continued to pursue nation-building projects that alienated large segments of the population and increasingly turned their attention to military concerns rather than political development and good governance.

## The MSU Group and Expertise as Foreign Aid

MSU became deeply involved in the US nation-building effort in South Vietnam as a result of intellectual trends within the academy, broader institutional developments related to the Cold War military-academic complex, and the particular ambitions of a handful of men in East Lansing. In the early 1950s, many American intellectuals championed modernization theory and actively sought opportunities to apply their expertise to public and foreign policies.[3] At the same time, the US government began to look to scholars at the country's leading educational institutions to provide a knowledge base to support and guide policy decisions. For several decades in the mid-twentieth century, many American intellectuals tended to see the world through the same lens as the US government. They shared a mutual understanding about human nature and had a common vision for the US role in leading the international community.[4]

The roots of this partnership between the US government and intellectuals date back to developments in academic life that began decades earlier. During the late nineteenth century, a process of professionalization occurred in colleges and universities across the United States. Scholars in many disciplines moved away from traditional curricula, which emphasized more esoteric studies as well as a divide between the academy and the professions. Influenced by rapid industrialization and social reformers' responses to the transformations that industrialization caused, intellectuals began considering the ways in which their research could be applied to policy. In doing so, they linked their specific work with general social development. As one historian has explained, for the first time in American history universities and academics embraced their "potential for putting knowledge at the service of society."[5]

In the first decades of the twentieth century, the trend of academic research informing social and political policies accelerated. Leading scholars argued that scientific knowledge offered a key to solving the social, economic, and political problems of the day. Although the earliest signs of this intellectual development appeared in "hard science" departments, the movement soon caught on among social scientists as well.[6] These scholars differed from their predecessors as a result of their penchant for using quantitative methods and for conducting model-oriented research. In the twentieth century, social scientists made "a commitment to using rational empirical investigation for the purposes of statecraft and social reform," explains the historian Alice O'Connor.[7] This new type of scholar, with his or her trust in numbers and faith in universal truths, set out to describe human behavior and offer the findings to political and military leaders.[8]

As the historian Ron Robin explains, the American government found behavioral social scientists to be important "interpreters of foreign cultures" and attempted to apply their expertise to foreign policy. Robin argues that scholars "failed to acknowledge that the creation of theoretical knowledge and the formation of practical policy were fundamentally disparate activities" and eagerly accepted their newfound position as advisers to government officials.[9] In fact, this partnership between the producers of knowledge and the power brokers was a central feature of the United States during the Cold War.

US officials sought out partnerships with scholars and institutions, and MSU appeared to be a logical choice. As Ralph Smuckler, one of the chief advisers of the Vietnam Project and dean of MSU's international studies programs, explained years later: "Our government had defined technical assistance to the developing world as an important goal of the U.S., and it became easy to move behind that as a national goal." MSU's history and identity made the school a good candidate for implementing technical assistance programs, he argued.[10] Like other land-grant colleges in the United States, MSU was founded on the principle that certain institutions of higher education should be aimed at educating ordinary people instead of elites and should directly benefit the local population. Although the land-grant colleges were originally designed to help communities within the United States, their approach began to have international implications during the Cold War. Extending their university's services to meet the needs of both the US and the South Vietnamese governments required MSU advisers to adjust the scope of their activities without affecting the fundamental mission of the university.

The MSU public administration team consisted of scholars who strongly believed in the merits of using their knowledge and expertise to serve American interests. Stanley Sheinbaum, one of MSU's participants, claimed that few of the advisers questioned their alliance with the government. He later recalled that, like the others in the MSU group, he took for granted the central role that intellectuals played in promoting the US government's ideology overseas. "It was understood," he explained, "that technical assistance and operational roles were part of the system." He also observed that nearly all his colleagues in the program were "quite convinced of the good motives of the operation."[11]

The public administration team included economists, political scientists, anthropologists, a psychologist, and specialists in taxation and accounting.[12] It favored quantitative methods and empirical research. Throughout their tenure in Vietnam, the professors conducted investigative studies, often using questionnaires and surveys, and then wrote reports based on their findings. As Ralph Smuckler, one of the group's chief advisers and eventual director of all the university's international programs, later explained, for any given project or assignment they would interview many Vietnamese people and then write a report for Diem's government or the US government. "That was just our style," he said.[13] Finally, the members of the MSU group believed that the system of public administration that worked for the United States not only would be appropriate for Vietnam but also would accelerate and ease the nation's transition into modernity.

Members of the MSU group accepted and advanced many of the assumptions underlying modernization theory. They blamed cultural values and traditional practices for what many considered the backwardness of Vietnamese society. However, in doing so, they disregarded Vietnamese history, particularly the profound effects of colonialism. American aid workers also tended to discount the problems caused by the economic disparity and political inequality in the country. As one program plan for Vietnam designed by the US government's international development agency read: "The stagnant economy and inflexible, anachronistic social system breeds discontent and creates fertile soil for Communism."[14] Such thinking exposes one of the primary weaknesses of American aid workers' approach—because they ignored power dynamics and the conditions that led to inequalities, they neither addressed basic political struggles nor offered effective ideas for reform. Instead, they attempted to depoliticize the challenges facing South Vietnam's leadership and relied on cultural explanations for developments in the country.[15]

Ironically, despite the MSU public administration team's aspirations for scientific objectivity, the advisers revealed definite political biases. The close partnership between MSU and the US government defined every aspect of the team's work. As was common to other enterprises involving collaboration between policy makers and scholars, the MSU group produced curricula, textbooks, and research projects that reflected the assumptions, cultural preconceptions, and political concerns of elite government officials. As a result, policy makers in Washington, DC, set the agenda for development programs administered by MSU and other university groups. Those policy makers too often overlooked the expertise of scholars conducting the programs as well as the needs of the people they sought to help.

Like many other intellectuals in this period, the MSU scholars relished their new position as indispensable agents of the American government during the Cold War.[16] Participating in American nation-building efforts in Vietnam raised the profile of MSU, nationally and internationally. John Hannah, the president of the university, and Glen Taggert, the dean of international programs, deliberately pursued any opportunities to enhance the university's status and influence. According to Ralph Smuckler, Hannah and Taggert hoped to compete for funding and prestige with other universities, such as the University of Michigan, the University of Southern California, and the University of California, Los Angeles, that already had government contracts to administer assistance in foreign countries.[17]

Participants in the MSU Vietnam Project believed that they could best serve the Vietnamese people by assisting political elites, developing public administration practices, and promoting good governance. Their vision is best summed up in the group's reflections on what it was trying to accomplish in Vietnam. According to MSU's final report: "Most members believed our activities were valuable not only in increasing administrative efficiency in Vietnam but also in creating among the Vietnamese a critical attitude for seeking truth and knowledge through systematic research, promoting the study of social sciences from the western viewpoint, raising the general level of educational standards, and implanting in the minds of government officials, police officers and teachers the ideas of responsibility and responsiveness to the public, individual dignity and other such concepts, the acceptance of which is a prerequisite for the eventual evolution of free institutions in Vietnam."[18] These objectives amounted to the most ambitious state-building venture undertaken by an institution of higher education in an era when many American universities sponsored development programs throughout the world.

But the project fell short of these lofty goals. The group's members often disregarded the approaches and techniques used by their Vietnamese students and colleagues as well as the cultural values and historical experiences driving those practices. In addition to overconfidence in their own methods and models, the MSU group also brought to Vietnam a set of political and cultural biases and expectations. For example, they believed that academic instruction in administration was critically important to developing a modern government, regardless of the fact that many nations, including the United States, employed a large number of bureaucrats who had no specific administrative training. Moreover, they held narrowly defined ideas about how that knowledge should be transferred and the specific content of courses, with little regard for local practices and limited respect for Vietnamese administrators. Finally, like other American aid workers, they misdiagnosed the basic problem facing the GVN. The GVN lacked popular support, and the country faced significant obstacles related to poverty, corruption, and political instability. But the country did not lack a history of bureaucratic government or eager public servants, as MSU advisers asserted. Vietnamese officials and administrators simply had their own ideas about how best to govern and modernize the country, and those ideas did not always coincide with either Americans' vision or the local population's interests.

## The NIA

The MSU public administration team's primary efforts revolved around training civil servants at the NIA. Their involvement at the NIA reveals how the Americans' approach limited their ability to develop a responsive and responsible government in South Vietnam that could resist the antigovernment insurgency and pressure from Hanoi without alienating its own population. At the most basic level, members of the MSU public administration team demonstrated a tendency to impose their own ideas and methods rather than respond and adjust to the interests and backgrounds of their Vietnamese students and colleagues. As instructors at the NIA, the American professors introduced their students to courses in the social sciences, which previously had been absent from most Vietnamese schools. They encouraged their students to participate in courses that applied classroom skills to practical situations and undertake research that had public policy implications. However, according to Nghiem Dang, a Vietnamese scholar and the assistant director of the NIA during MSU's tenure, this approach to training administrators was foreign to most Vietnamese. Dang argued that public administration in Vietnam historically depended "on the power of persuasion, on setting an example, and particularly on the integrity of the administrators" rather than adherence to normative standards taught in a classroom.[19] His assessment corresponds with the historian Edward Miller's description of the Ngo brothers' views on politics and democracy. According to Miller, Diem and Nhu believed that good governance depended primarily on the morality and model of political leaders as well as the citizens' sense of duty to their community.[20]

Although the MSU advisers emphasized their role in the creation of the institute, the NIA predated the Americans' arrival and had already developed a distinct institutional culture by the time MSU became involved. In fact, it was an outgrowth of a colonial project to improve and develop the public administration system in Vietnam during the waning days of French rule. It was founded by French authorities in 1953 and was originally known as the National School of Administration (NSA). The French conceived of it as a place where aspiring Vietnamese officials could receive career training. Previous efforts by the French to impose their own models for public administration on the Indochinese colonies included the 1914 termination of civil service examinations, which had existed in Vietnam since 1075, and the establishment of the Hanoi École de Droit d'Administration in 1917.[21]

The NSA was originally located in the resort city of Dalat, where the emperor kept a vacation palace on a vast expanse of hunting grounds. During the final years of French rule, the NSA attracted only the highest level of public servants and members of the political elite. Emperor Bao Dai, who ruled Vietnam while it was still part of the French Union, did not consult with the prestigious École Nationale d'Administration in Paris for advice.[22] As a result, though the NSA adopted some French educational models, including an emphasis on the relationship between the law and the state, it developed an institutional identity based on the idea that it was an autonomous establishment, especially after 1954, when Vietnamese officials replaced French educators.[23] It received no technical assistance from France or any other country. This situation further contributed to its image as a distinctly Vietnamese institution. According to a Vietnamese scholar who worked with MSU, the NSA had little success in improving or modernizing Vietnam's corps of civil servants in the few years before Diem came into power.[24]

On their arrival in Vietnam, the MSU advisers immediately recommended moving the school to Saigon, where its instructors could develop closer relationships with government officials and the institute would be more accessible to Vietnamese administrators. On August 8, 1955, Diem accepted the advice and issued a decree, Arrête 483, mandating that the school be moved from Dalat to Saigon.[25] Renamed the NIA, the school greatly expanded its goals and services. During the second half of the decade, the NIA grew significantly in terms of facilities, faculty, and student enrollment. On moving to Saigon in 1955, it consisted of four professors and 147 students. Two years later, it boasted eighteen faculty members and a student enrollment of 217.[26] Admission to the NIA was based on performance in competitive examinations. Those admitted received government scholarships and were obligated to work for the GVN on graduation.[27] The NIA curriculum focused on legalistic approaches rather than practical bureaucratic skills. Advisers from MSU believed this approach to be flawed because, in their view, it failed to prepare students to become

Director Vu Quoc Thong at the National Institute of Administration in Saigon. Courtesy Michigan State University Archives and Historical Collections Vietnam Project, Records (UA 2.9.5.5), Photograph File Drawer.

efficient government employees. The Americans argued that the problem could be remedied by shifting the emphasis of the NIA program of study.

As a result of the MSU group's continual urging, the NIA gradually moved away from a curriculum heavily weighted toward studying the law. American instructors at the institute developed courses in the social sciences, including economics and political science. They also devised a number of practical and managerial courses, and they introduced a program for extended periods of fieldwork. Vietnamese students were now required to take courses oriented toward the practical application of knowledge, such as budgeting, personnel management, accounting, and statistics.[28] In addition, the MSU group recommended that all faculty members replace the traditional annual comprehensive examinations with more frequent tests and term papers.

The MSU advisers added a third year of study to the institute's curriculum, which had originally offered a two-year program consisting mostly of mandatory courses. Intended to provide practical training, the additional year allowed students time to conduct fieldwork and acquire some experience working for the government. Third years spent up to seven months studying outside the classroom. For half that time, they worked in the provinces on local government programs, and they spent the remainder of the time as interns for one of the ministries in Saigon.[29]

Despite the pressure that the MSU group placed on the NIA's leadership, the school adopted the Americans' suggestions for transforming the curriculum reluctantly. In fact, the new curriculum did not go into effect until the MSU advisers had been working at the NIA for nearly five years. In 1955, the NIA offered only three courses in public administration and three in economics. However, by 1959, the school had nineteen courses in administration and seventeen in economics and public finance.[30] In 1960, it offered for the first time two sociology courses, one of which was taught by an MSU instructor. The new curriculum also included classes on research methods and an introduction to the case study method.[31]

The emphasis that the MSU advisers placed on social science courses is hardly surprising, given their backgrounds in related fields. Their belief in the applicability of their respective disciplines constituted a major reason they participated in the Vietnam Project, and they felt most comfortable teaching courses within their areas of expertise.[32] However, by privileging these subjects over others, they created a curriculum that was based not on the particular strengths or educational backgrounds of the Vietnamese faculty but on the types of courses that the Americans deemed important. Furthermore, by forcefully imposing their models on their local colleagues, they contributed to the fear among Vietnamese faculty members that they might lose their autonomy or that the NIA would become an American institution rather than an indigenous one.[33]

Because one of the purposes of the Vietnam Project was to help the NIA establish a program of study that would outlive the Americans' time in Vietnam, it made little sense for the Americans to alter significantly the types of courses that Vietnamese instructors were to teach without also making sure those instructors had access to and a mastery of the new subject material. The Vietnamese faculty taught many of the school's classes, even while the MSU group worked in Vietnam. After the Americans' departure, the Vietnamese faculty was expected to resume all teaching responsibilities while adhering to a curriculum designed largely by foreigners. In effect, the MSU group asked the Vietnamese instructors to begin teaching courses on subjects in which they often had little or no formal training.

## Research at the NIA

In addition to advocating fundamental changes in the curriculum of the NIA, the MSU group strongly encouraged both students and faculty members to undertake research projects, particularly ones with direct policy implications. MSU's public administration advisers generally considered the research division to be among their most important contributions to the NIA. However, their Vietnamese colleagues proved to be far less enthusiastic about doing policy-oriented research. According to Dang, in Vietnam "the traditional conception of public administration seems not to have emphasized [research]," and historically few research volumes were produced.[34] The emphasis on research heightened tensions between the MSU group and the US and Vietnamese governments, and the controversial views the American scholars expressed in some of their studies contributed to the termination of the university's technical assistance program in 1962. MSU's research activities at the NIA reveal many of the underlying assumptions behind the Vietnam Project and the political context that shaped the Americans' associations with their colleagues at the institute. Moreover, the Americans' research agenda illuminates the basic dilemma that resulted from their insistence on exploring and writing about subjects that threatened to undermine either Diem's authority or official US objectives in South Vietnam.

Within the first year of MSU's contract period, the public administration team created an NIA research division and hired two full-time research associates, Gerald Hickey and Alexandra Rolland.[35] As a result of research he conducted while working on MSU's Vietnam Project, Hickey became interested in Vietnam's ethnic minorities. An anthropologist who spoke Vietnamese, Hickey spent a significant amount of time researching in the highlands. He later produced several authoritative studies on ethnic minorities in Vietnam.[36] Many other MSU participants also conducted research or served as advisers for Vietnamese students who performed their own investigations. According to Robert Scigliano, one of the MSU advisers involved in research at the institute, the goals of this program were to "develop the research capabilities and the output of the NIA faculty" and produce studies that would prove useful for future instruction at the NIA and for public policy in South Vietnam.[37]

MSU professors approved and guided student research projects that explicitly sought to generate statistics and analyses that would be useful to government leaders. Not surprisingly, they gravitated toward projects with practical applications for agencies such as the newly created Commission for Civic Action. Because of their close personal contacts with many officials, members of the MSU public administration team were in an excellent position to deliver advice directly to these policy makers.

Under the tutelage of the MSU group, most NIA student research projects attempted to answer pressing questions about the nature of the state in Vietnam and explore the power of and limitations on government authority in the country. While some students focused on national issues and the bureaucracy in Saigon, others turned their attention to local concerns. Several submitted proposals to spend periods of up to six months conducting research in the provinces. The topics of these proposals ranged from a study to determine the impact of rural community development to an examination of the expansion of electric power in outlying areas of the countryside.[38] Others attempted to evaluate various policies of the GVN and offered ideas about the level at which those policy decisions were made and implemented. For example, one NIA student formulated a project to identify the average age of marriage and analyze the reasons couples got married when they did. Conceived in response to the GVN's 1957 "Family Bill," which set twenty-one years as the minimum age for marriage, this project tested the reach of the government by attempting to determine how many people considered this new legislation in deciding when to marry.[39]

In addition to advising student projects, the MSU group encouraged the Vietnamese faculty of the NIA to undertake research of their own or collaborate with the Americans. Diem's government commissioned specific research projects from NIA faculty, with the hope that those projects might guide policy decisions. In fact, Scigliano believed that the MSU group might have its greatest impact by assisting the Vietnamese faculty with projects assigned by the South Vietnamese government.[40] During their seven-year tenure in Vietnam, MSU professors worked in partnership with their NIA colleagues to produce twenty studies on public administration as well as social and economic activities in Vietnam.[41] For example, with the help of their Vietnamese colleagues, the American group produced statistics on the national budget and spending programs for the Budget Office. They provided information on ethnic minority populations to the ministry responsible for government relations with these groups. And they wrote research reports explaining in detail the results of their studies and offering recommendations, including several manuscripts on education that they presented to the Ministry of Education.[42]

Despite the MSU group's eagerness to conduct joint projects with the NIA faculty, the Americans were disappointed to discover that many of their Vietnamese colleagues did not share their desire to collaborate. As Ralph Smuckler conceded: "The one thing we asserted, which was very important to us but not as important to the Vietnamese, was a research focus."[43] According to Scigliano, most "joint research" was actually done by the MSU staff, without significant contributions from NIA faculty members. There were a few exceptions among the NIA scholars, including Vo Hong Phuoc, who worked with Americans on several research reports.[44] However, Scigliano and others in the MSU group believed that generally their Vietnamese colleagues did not value empirical research as much as the American scholars did. Moreover, Scigliano suggested that strained relations between Americans and Vietnamese at the institute prevented effective partnerships. In a letter to the head of MSU's research division, he explained: "I don't believe that our relationship with the NIA faculty, or their motivations and attitudes towards research, and perhaps towards our role, allow for much optimism." Despite this pessimistic outlook, he advised the MSU group to "create an 'environment' for research and stimulate individual persons" at the NIA and "continuously and consciously create the conditions for greater trust and respect, and therefore greater collaboration with the NIA faculty."[45]

## Strained Relations at the NIA

The MSU participants' difficulty working with their Vietnamese counterparts on research projects reflected basic problems in the relationships between American and Vietnamese faculty at the NIA. The Americans and the Vietnamese had conflicting approaches to education and pedagogy, and their divergent backgrounds and values made communication challenging. Perhaps as a result of these differences as well as the power dynamics inherent in their relationships, their professional interactions were often formal and tense. As Dang, the assistant director of the NIA, explained: "In truth, these contacts [with the MSU participants] were rather difficult because of the language and cultural barriers."[46] Perhaps more significantly, the Americans' role as advisers and their condescending manner challenged the Vietnamese professors' authority and knowledge. In many cases, Vietnamese faculty resisted the counsel of the MSU group whenever the Americans' recommendations did not benefit them directly or appeared to insult their status or position.

Soon after their arrival, the Americans learned that Vietnamese instructors and students were accustomed to a formal arrangement in which students did not ask questions and teachers did not encourage debate or dialogue in the classroom. This deeply entrenched system derived from both traditional Vietnamese and French educational styles, which emphasized rote learning. The Americans responded with shock and aversion. Some sharply criticized this teaching style, accusing faculty of "[limiting students'] intellectual expansion to what could be gained from listening to lectures uninterrupted by questions or discussion."[47]

Convinced that NIA students would learn more and become better prepared for their careers if they played an active role in their education, the MSU advisers encouraged their Vietnamese colleagues to make classroom discussion a central feature of their courses. However, the Vietnamese instructors seemed unwilling to change their methods, and they often met suggestions that they do so with apathy. As one of the Vietnamese professors later explained: "The permission granted to students to express

Walter Mode, an adviser in MSU's public administration team, discusses field administration with some Vietnamese students. Courtesy Michigan State University Archives and Historical Collections Vietnam Project, Records (UA 2.9.5.5), Photograph File Drawer.

their own views and raise questions in class constitutes a somewhat radical transformation of pedagogical techniques in a country whose professors are accustomed to speaking from the podium without interruption from a docile audience."[48]

The Americans also invited their colleagues at the NIA to sit in on their classes, with the hope that they would learn from them and apply those lessons to their own courses. But few Vietnamese faculty members showed interest in attending the MSU professors' lectures. These instructors had their own courses for which to prepare, and they resisted being told how to teach subjects within their expertise. Despite the MSU group's suggestion for partnership within the classroom, most Vietnamese faculty also opposed teaching jointly with American professors.[49] Their reluctance to do so likely reinforced tensions between the two groups of scholars. From the students' perspective, it was probably better that the Vietnamese and American instructors did not agree to coteach. Because the MSU advisers taught their courses in either French or English, they needed an in-class interpreter to translate their lectures into Vietnamese or French, depending on the subject material.[50] Students in cotaught courses would then have had one lecturer speaking in Vietnamese, another speaking in English, and sometimes a translator using a third language.

In keeping with their own emphasis on research, the MSU advisers also placed concerted pressure on their Vietnamese colleagues to incorporate more archival research into their own work and teaching. For example, they pressed them to use the new research library at the institute more frequently and assign term papers in an attempt to encourage the students to take advantage of the library's resources as well. Despite these suggestions, most Vietnamese faculty continued to conduct their work without using the library. Nor did they require their students to use the library for their research. MSU professors were disheartened to learn that, with only a few exceptions, the Vietnamese instructors were slow to change either their methods or their views on the applicability and importance of research.[51] By urging Vietnamese faculty members to alter their approach to teaching and scholarship fundamentally, the university group not only offered implicit criticism of their effectiveness but also called into question some core tenets of education in Vietnam.

Formal social relations between the MSU advisers and the Vietnamese faculty further contributed to their difficulties working together. During the first few years of the Vietnam Project, seven of the Americans from MSU shared office space with their Vietnamese colleagues. However, according to the MSU participants, individuals from the two groups rarely formed close bonds either intellectually or socially. As two former participants later wrote: "Contacts were restricted to business matters or superficial conversations."[52] In a monthly report issued soon after the Vietnam Project began, another participant described the rigidity and formality of conferences at the NIA, "with the Vietnamese on one side of the table and the Americans on the other."[53] Some of the Americans attended social gatherings with their Vietnamese counterparts, but the general consensus was that such interactions ultimately did not lead to intimate relationships.

Had the Americans fully considered the scope and significance of what they were asking the Vietnamese scholars to do, they might have been more patient with their colleagues' reluctance to change their ways.

Comfortable in their positions, and used to relating with their students in a particular way, Vietnamese faculty members had little incentive to alter their behavior. More importantly, many of the Americans' recommendations depended on an assumption of superiority. The Americans faced a daunting task in attempting to provide concrete solutions and suggestions for a society about which most of them they knew little, without insulting their Vietnamese colleagues' pride or infringing on their authority.

In dealing with the Vietnamese faculty of the NIA, MSU group members tended to favor their own theories and methods as the appropriate way to improve public administration. There is little evidence that they considered or incorporated ideas and suggestions offered by the Vietnamese. For example, when the NIA director, Vu Quoc Thong, who also served as minister of social action for the GVN, proposed the addition of a graduate program, the Americans immediately objected, arguing that the institute should expand its undergraduate program to four years before adding a graduate division. In this case, Thong demonstrated his willingness to ignore the Americans' counsel when he felt strongly about an issue. Despite MSU's opposition, the NIA introduced a graduate program that admitted its first class of doctoral students in 1958.[54]

Although the Americans attempted to control the direction of the NIA, they quickly learned that they would have to make concessions. At the suggestion of the institute's leadership, the MSU group agreed to abstain from sending representatives to the institute's academic council. As Edward Weidner, the Vietnam Project's first chief adviser, explained, NIA faculty were "very nationalistically inclined and felt that our sitting in on the council meetings would be too much like the French joint university system."[55] This decision likely appeased the Vietnamese, but it also limited MSU's influence over the development of the institute. The arrangement reveals the underlying political tension between the two groups at the NIA and suggests the Vietnamese faculty and leadership's sensitivity with regard to apparent similarities between American involvement in Vietnam and French colonialism. More importantly, it demonstrates that the NIA's Vietnamese leadership attempted to block challenges to the institution's autonomy, even in the face of pressure from MSU advisers.

As a result of the political backdrop and the aggressive ideological framework promoted by both US policy makers and the MSU group, American advisers could never enjoy a truly equal partnership with their colleagues at the NIA. In fact, the fundamentally imbalanced relationships between the Americans and Vietnamese at the institute paralleled the lopsided affiliation between the US and the South Vietnamese governments, in which the Americans attempted to exert their dominance while the Vietnamese worked to assert their own vision and interests. Ultimately, the association between Americans and Vietnamese at the NIA closely mirrored the increasingly strained partnership between the US government and the GVN.

## The Presidential Lecture Series

The MSU group also attempted to extend its reach beyond the NIA by influencing the corps of civil servants who were already working for the GVN. They provided in-service training, launched a professional journal, and offered a series of instructional lectures.[56] The lecture series, in particular, demonstrates how the cultural and ideological biases of the Americans limited the effectiveness of their technical assistance program. In 1956, "following [Diem's] own urging," American professors at the NIA introduced a series of ten lectures that sought to attract mid- and high-level bureaucrats within the Vietnamese government. Designed to provide practical information about public service that could be applied on the job, the Presidential Lecture Series also aimed to stimulate discussion and thought regarding recent and upcoming changes within the GVN. Members of the MSU group delivered lectures at the Saigon City Hall each week of May and June 1956. The lectures covered topics such as "The Role of Management in Government," "How to Develop Executives," "Service to the Public," and "Responsibility and Accountability in Public Service."[57]

Members of the MSU group had a clear vision of what they wanted to accomplish with the lectures, but they walked a thin line between providing useful advice and insulting their audience. They hoped to inspire Vietnamese civil servants to think actively about their duties and responsibilities to the state by encouraging audience participation. According to a proposal for the series, the lectures would "describe rather than prescribe" and should avoid offending the participants by "[making] it clear that the American speaker appreciates what [the Vietnamese] are already doing but at the same time . . . suggest the possibilities of alternative procedures." Discussion was expected to be an essential element of the lectures, and each lecturer devised his own method for encouraging audience participation. Some asked the audience to discuss common administrative problems in small groups, while others fielded questions.[58] The lectures were delivered in English with assistance from a Vietnamese interpreter who translated for the audience.

The lectures emphasized that furthering the public interest and good public relations should be the primary goals of civil servants in a democratic society. They also discussed Vietnam's need for a government that could delegate authority to officials at all levels as well as an administration composed of creative, thoughtful bureaucrats who demonstrated flexibility in their approach to solving problems.[59] The goal of civil servants was presented as humanizing government by identifying with ordinary people and acting as liaisons between elected officials and the population.[60] The final speaker in the series, Ralph Smuckler, commented on the "democratic spirit of youth who are going into administration work" in Vietnam. He explained that his students at the NIA firmly believed that administrators should be responsible "to the people."[61]

Although some of the lecturers focused on particular problems facing administrators in Vietnam, many presented examples that would likely have been unfamiliar to their audience.[62] For example, in his lecture Gene Adrian Gregory referred to an American citizen who asked his congressman for the dome of the US Capitol building, discussed the Teapot Dome scandal, mentioned Abraham Lincoln's trials during the American Civil War, and used an example of a discontented American businessman shopping for a suit in a Manhattan department store. He had no reason to assume that his audience would understand or appreciate any of these examples, and his lecture probably would have been far more effective had he used examples and situations that were familiar to Vietnamese officials.[63]

The use of unfamiliar cases to illustrate arguments was just one of the problems that emerged during the lecture series. Not only did the lecturers believe their audience could relate to foreign examples, but they also presumed that the Vietnamese shared their basic political philosophy and understanding of human nature. One lecturer instructed the audience to appeal to individuals' natural sense of competition.[64] This approach assumed that what stimulated production in the United States would also work in Vietnam, despite that society's distinct history and customs and the ideological underpinnings of its leaders. Such assumptions reveal a fundamental lack of understanding of GVN officials' approach to politics, which was much more oriented around the value of shared sacrifice and the appeal of communal economic and political systems.[65]

The MSU group found it difficult, if not impossible, to judge the effectiveness of the lecture series. As Wickert explained during his presentation: "One cannot change a lifetime of attitudes and behavior in people by having lecturers talk at them."[66] This comment points to one of the primary challenges facing the MSU public administration team: despite their best attempts to measure their success, the American advisers could not determine conclusively the impact of their efforts. The tenuous connection between the intentions of US policy makers and aid workers and the results of specific projects was particularly pronounced in rural areas of South Vietnam, where local figures exercised significant control over decision making on public administration and other matters.

## Disputes with Two Governments

Although the MSU public administration team initially supported the political and ideological aims of the United States and the GVN, it increasingly found itself at odds with both American and South Vietnamese officials. Over time, many of the MSU professors became more openly critical of Diem and American support for his regime. As a result, MSU advisers found themselves alienated from key figures in both governments.

The public administration team's most significant disputes with South Vietnamese and American officials resulted from its various research projects. Not surprisingly, Diem's government strongly objected to any surveys, studies, or reports that criticized GVN policy or portrayed the regime in a negative light. In addition, many of the Americans' research pursuits fueled a growing bureaucratic rivalry between MSU and USOM, the US government's in-country aid mission in Vietnam. USOM worked closely with the MSU group and provided logistic and financial support for it. Many USOM officials objected to MSU research that seemed too esoteric or lacked policy implications. On the other hand, when members of the MSU group offered direct advice to the GVN in areas for which USOM took responsibility, particularly economic policy, the government aid workers protested vociferously and accused MSU of overstepping its bounds.

Despite their personal access to and intimate relationship with Diem, members of the MSU group soon realized that the Vietnamese president intended to keep tight control over all sources of information in the country. As they embarked on research trips in the provinces, they discovered that few local leaders would engage openly because Diem had forbidden them from discussing any official matters with the American scholars. He also required the Americans to clear every investigative trip with him personally and in advance. NIA director Vu Quoc Thong had to submit to Diem's office a written request for each trip that any MSU adviser planned to take. In some cases, he wrote several letters to the president regarding various adjustments to the itinerary or other minor deviations from the American's original research plans.[67]

This requirement meant that the Americans often had to put their research on hold as they awaited approval for their projects. As one MSU professor explained at the time: "Certain aspects of Vietnamese political, social, and economic behavior and organization are foreclosed to research carried out under the clearance procedure."[68] Once the GVN approved a project, American scholars were forced to work under highly controlled conditions, in which candid and frank discussions rarely occurred. Even the director of the NIA refused to tolerate any foreign condemnation of the GVN. For example, Thong expressed anger that the institute's library housed newspapers, such as the *New York Times* and *Figaro,* that contained articles critical of Diem's regime.[69]

In addition to limiting the freedom to conduct research, the GVN also sought to monitor the written products of American scholars' studies and inquiries. In 1957, Diem insisted that all research and publications on Vietnam, whether produced in the country or not, be submitted for GVN approval. Members of the university group reacted strongly against this attempt to curtail their academic freedom. Eventually, the two sides reached a somewhat ambiguous compromise, in which the Americans vowed not to use any notes or records that could negatively affect the security or interests of Vietnam.[70]

About a year later, tension escalated again when the work of one MSU adviser sparked a minor uproar among policy makers in Saigon and Washington. In 1958, John Dorsey wrote an article, "South Vietnam in Perspective," that examined the four-year history of the Republic of Vietnam. He recounted the successes as well as the failures of Diem's regime and American nation-building efforts. Although he was cautiously optimistic in his predictions for South Vietnam, American and Vietnamese officials viewed the article as controversial and possibly subversive. Dorsey discussed the uneven and messy process of democratization in South Vietnam, and he did not shy away from criticism of Diem's leadership or a sober assessment of the limitations of US aid. He argued: "While it would be a gross exaggeration to suggest that disaffection and discontent in South Viet Nam are widespread, it would be equally incorrect to conclude that popular enthusiasm for the regime of President Ngo Dinh Diem is unanimous and that American aid has solved most of the economic problems." He also concluded that the "prerequisite political, economic, and social conditions and experience to sustain a democratic political system have not yet developed" in South Vietnam.[71] However, he conceded that there existed no good alternative to Diem and that the United States had an important and ongoing role to play in the region. In particular, he advocated for increased attention to good public administration, which he viewed as critical to the effective utilization of foreign aid.

Although, on balance, Dorsey's article offered only a mild critique of either the GVN or US policy, American and South Vietnamese officials considered it inflammatory and "dangerous." US policy makers at the International Cooperation Administration (ICA) in Washington objected to its "somewhat critical position of Americans in Vietnam" as well as its references to American military capabilities in Vietnam.[72] In fact, in early 1959 officials at the ICA requested that Dorsey remove any and all specific descriptions of US military force levels and abilities in Vietnam. Dorsey refused to make any changes to the article. Instead, he argued that accepted academic freedom policies governed his work, and he stated that he would perform all necessary editing of the article only after it had been accepted for publication.[73]

For their part, aid workers at USOM in Saigon expressed concern about the potential response to Dorsey's article but resisted openly challenging the MSU group's autonomy or free speech protections. As USOM's director, Leland Barrows, wrote to his superiors in Washington: "While this USOM would not wish to muzzle the opinion of scholars associated with the program in fields of their special competence, articles of political nature, such as this one could cause serious difficulties for our mission here and ICA in Washington."[74] Ultimately, Dorsey removed the figures on American military capacity in Vietnam, and his article failed to incite the severe controversy that US officials had predicted. However, the tension sparked by the article coincided with a general diminishment of MSU's influence in public administration work. This dispute foreshadowed an important factor in the eventual rupture in relations between the GVN and MSU that led to the termination of the group's contract in 1962.

By late 1960, the relationship between the MSU group and Diem's government had turned decidedly sour. For the first few years of their time in Vietnam, members of the group had enjoyed a closer relationship with the Vietnamese president than most other Americans in the country. Wesley Fishel, one of the president's most trusted confidantes, and other leaders of the Vietnam Project participated in frequent "Breakfast Group" meetings with Diem. At those meetings, the Americans commanded his undivided attention and found an avenue for influencing GVN policy. However, as Diem became more embattled, he also became more suspicious of anyone who challenged his authority or decisions. Moreover, during the final years of the 1950s, as security conditions worsened in the countryside, he became increasingly concerned about his ability to retain control over South Vietnam. With tensions mounting, he began to question whether his American allies—even those with whom he had a personal camaraderie—could really be trusted.

At the same time, members of the MSU group, along with other informed Americans in Vietnam and the United States, became more concerned about the stability of the Diem regime and the president's harsh repression of his people. The MSU group's growing disillusionment with Diem paralleled the US government's position. As Miller explains, the relationships between American officials and Diem "reached new lows" in 1960.[75] Ambassador Durbrow and other embassy personnel increasingly pressed Diem to make meaningful political reforms. In addition, some aid workers in Vietnam began to criticize Diem or GVN policies publicly, and concrete conflicts replaced general tensions. For example, one member of the MSU group participated in a candid political discussion with a major in the Vietnamese army, the two sharing their negative views of Diem. Afterward, American advisers discovered that the major was actually a Vietnamese secret service agent working for Diem. As a result of this discovery, the MSU group decided it would be best to avoid the possibility of similar occurrences in the future. MSU removed all its political files from the NIA campus and placed them under lock and key at the MSU headquarters in Saigon.[76]

Diem had good reason to be concerned over his political future. In November 1960, a group of paratroopers from South Vietnam's army attempted to overthrow his government in a coup d'état. Although American officials had no advance knowledge of the coup and remained neutral throughout the affair, they urged Diem to compromise with the rebels in hopes that the GVN would finally implement some of the reforms they had been recommending for years. Diem and his inner circle of advisers considered the American position a betrayal, and they suspected that embassy personnel had encouraged or supported the disgruntled Army officers.[77] Although the coup failed, it heightened tensions between the US government and the GVN even as it exposed the mounting opposition to Diem within the armed forces. And the increase in revolutionary violence throughout 1959 and 1960 suggested not only that the Ngos' internal security efforts were ineffective but also that Saigon faced resistance from a growing segment of the Vietnamese population.

Americans in the MSU group sensed this dissatisfaction and worried that the population would turn against the United States for supporting the regime. One member of the support team in East Lansing wrote a colleague in Saigon: "Please let us know if we are being associated, as Americans, with the 'colonialists'!"[78] Following the upheaval of the coup attempt, the American diplomatic corps encouraged the MSU professors' families, who had been living in Saigon as dependents, to return to the United States. Many families quickly left Vietnam. Some members of the MSU group expressed hope that a reorganization of the GVN would include a change in the leadership of the NIA. The Americans believed that the institute needed new leaders in order to function as an autonomous organization that would remain outside Diem's desperate attempts at control.[79]

At that point, the relationship between Diem and the MSU group had disintegrated beyond repair. As MSU advisers became more openly critical of Diem's regime and the possibilities for democratic institutions to gain hold in South Vietnam, the Vietnamese president increasingly restricted the group's access to him, his advisers, and other officials. Diem particularly resented a number of studies on Vietnam and the GVN that MSU professors published on returning to the United States. Among the studies that most inflamed him were John Donoghue and Vo Hong Phuoc's *My Thuan: The Study of a Delta Village in South Vietnam* and Frank Child's "Essays on Economic Growth, Capital Formation, and Public Policy in Vietnam."[80] Donoghue and Phuoc's examination of My Thuan repeatedly emphasized the lack of security in the countryside and argued that the widespread ineffectiveness of government programs in rural areas resulted from the poor quality of local administrators. As one village information chief told Donoghue and Phuoc: "Generally people are in favor of government policies but do not like the people who carry out those policies." The study also described the continued power and importance in the Mekong delta of the Hoa Hao, one of the politicoreligious groups that had competed with Diem for control of the country in the mid-1950s. Donoghue and Phuoc argued that the GVN must be willing to cooperate with the Hoa Hao in order to win the support of peasants in the delta, a suggestion that Diem was loath to entertain.[81]

When Diem once again demanded that, prior to publication, all MSU participants, including those who had returned to the United States, submit their work to him for approval, the scholars refused to comply. MSU's contract came up for renewal in early 1962, and Diem chose not to extend the agreement for another two-year period. According to the university group's official final report, publications by returning professors and MSU's failure to control open discussion and scholarship triggered the ultimate breakdown in relations between the GVN and MSU.[82] Although the relationship between the MSU group and Diem's government had deteriorated significantly even before 1960, the disagreements over academic freedom dealt a final blow to the partnership.

But Diem was not alone in registering his disapproval of the MSU group's activities and recommendations. Other American aid workers also raised concerns over research projects conducted by the MSU public administration team. During the late 1950s, officials at USOM objected to its village studies, which examined the administrative, social, and economic systems in a number of Vietnamese villages. These officials argued that the studies wasted time and American money and that the findings did not contribute to American policy or offer concrete assistance to the GVN. Instead, they contended that the MSU group should limit its efforts to advising and teaching at the NIA. However, by 1961, aid workers at USOM had changed their tune and begun to support the MSU village studies. By this time, USOM sought to extend American economic aid programs to Vietnamese living in the provinces. USOM officials now found the research done by MSU professors to be useful for their assessments of how to distribute aid and implement assistance projects.[83] In fact, over the next several years, USOM's public administration team relied on the village studies "for orientation and reference material, primarily for counter-insurgency personnel."[84]

While USOM employees sometimes objected to MSU research on the grounds that it distracted the group from its obligations in Vietnam and produced no relevant findings, they also reacted strongly when it appeared that MSU professors might undermine USOM's authority or position in the country. In particular, they expressed anxiety about economic research at the NIA that had policy implications. Concerned that MSU economists who directly advised the GVN would contradict their own recommendations, USOM attempted to limit MSU's influence in matters of economic policy. Fearing that "unapproved economic doctrines might be dispensed at the NIA," USOM requested course outlines from all MSU professors teaching economics classes. When the targeted scholars declined to share their outlines and lecture notes, USOM officials devised a new strategy for challenging MSU's authority. They began to question publicly whether MSU participants had the qualifications and experience necessary to teach courses on subjects such as economic development.

The struggle between the MSU group and USOM for control over the shaping of economic policy reached a tense climax in 1960. A Vietnamese official had cultivated a personal friendship with one of the MSU professors, who also served as his English instructor. When that official showed interest in discussing the merits of devaluation with his American friend, an open conflict ensued between the MSU and the USOM groups. USOM officials threatened to cancel the MSU contract, which was not technically within their power, and expel the American economist who discussed the controversial issue of devaluation with a GVN official. After receiving assurances from the MSU group that the conversation had focused on the abstract economic theory of devaluation rather

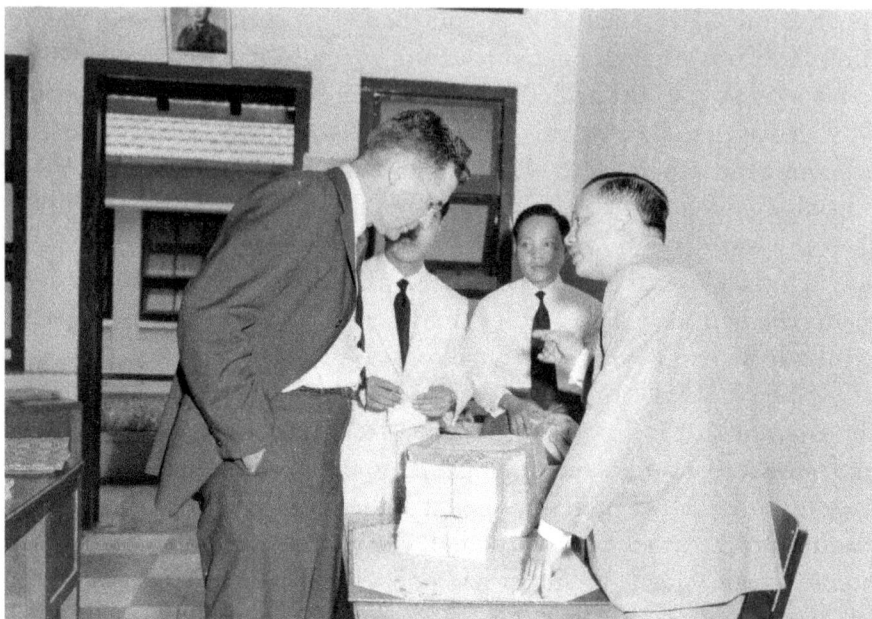

US Operations Mission director Leland Barrows consults with South Vietnamese financial experts. Courtesy Michigan State University Archives and Historical Collections Vietnam Project, Records (UA 2.9.5.5), Photograph File Drawer.

than specific policy recommendations for Vietnam, USOM backed off its threats, and the two American organizations resumed their formal, if troubled, relationship.[85]

This conflict points to an important constraint on the MSU group's effectiveness in Vietnam and also indicates the degree of tension that often defined relationships between the academy and the US government during the Cold War. Although the university group enjoyed somewhat more autonomy than many other American organizations, such as the embassy, military advisers, and intelligence services, MSU did not function with complete independence in Vietnam. Because its representatives relied on the ICA for funding and on the goodwill and support of both the US and the South Vietnamese governments for contract renewals, they had to accept limits placed on them by these forces. These Americans were compelled to work within the parameters of what the US government, and in particular the agencies and individuals responsible for foreign aid, deemed appropriate for nation building in Vietnam.

## USOM's Public Administration Division

Although the MSU group had served as the central advisers on matters of public administration during the early years of Diem's presidency, by the late 1950s USOM had begun replacing it as the most important civilian aid organization in that field. USOM's Public Administration Division (PAD) worked alongside the MSU group until the Vietnam Project ended in 1962. However, the PAD increasingly assumed many of MSU's responsibilities, especially in overseas training programs for government officials and NIA students. For example, in 1959, USOM offered a four-month training course in the United States on customs administration.[86] Two years later, USOM sponsored Nghiem Dang, the vice rector at the NIA, on a three-month study and observation tour in Japan, the United States, and France. During his time overseas, Dang studied topics such as "control of government expenditures and central-local government relations, especially in fiscal affairs." While he was in the United States, he spent time at various administrative agencies, including the Council of State Governments and the federal General Accounting Office. He also met with Vietnamese students who were attending PhD programs in the United States and planning to return as NIA faculty. In France, he spent two weeks observing administrators and faculty at the École Nationale d'Administration.[87]

USOM's PAD also promoted in-service training opportunities and materials that the MSU group and their Vietnamese colleagues at the NIA had produced. In mid-1960, Kalman Dienes, the PAD chief, circulated to his colleagues working in other divisions of USOM information about Vietnamese-language resources available at the NIA. At that time, the NIA's in-service training program had created eighty films and forty-four articles and pamphlets designed to assist Vietnamese administrators working in fields such as education, public health, public safety, and agriculture.[88]

Although the PAD supported and promoted MSU's efforts at the NIA, the two groups served different functions in Vietnam. Most importantly, the work of the PAD was broader in scope than that of the MSU group. In fact, perhaps the most significant distinction between the two groups was that, while MSU focused primarily on providing assistance to elite officials and the NIA in Saigon, the PAD emphasized improving local administration throughout the country. As a result of their attention to local governance and administration at all levels—national, provincial, district, and even village—the PAD played an important role in American efforts to garner support for the GVN in rural areas. Especially as the antigovernment insurgency developed and violence escalated, USOM advisers saw themselves as critical players in South Vietnam's civil war. A USOM quarterly report from 1962 explained the PAD position. It suggested that the PAD had a role to play in the war because the success of counterinsurgency efforts depended on "governmental contacts at the local level with the rural population."[89]

Members of the PAD believed that their work could contribute to improved local governance at the same time that it served counterinsurgency aims. In fact, PAD advisers saw a direct correlation between good governance and security. In more stable areas of the country, where there was less fighting, USOM found local administrators to be more effective and responsive. On the other hand, in areas where the National Liberation Front (NLF) was more active, local government seemed to break down, and officials routinely failed to perform even the most basic services for their constituents. When American aid workers conducted an informal survey to explain why rural populations lacked confidence in the GVN, most people cited the absence of physical security. They also mentioned the "failure of military cadre to perform civil administrative functions."[90]

Unfortunately, many local administrators neglected their administrative responsibilities because they were overwhelmed by security concerns. As one PAD report explained: "The deteriorating security situation in certain provinces was both cause and effect of weak and ineffective civil government."[91] However, PAD advisers also found that, when security concerns diminished, provincial and local officials tended to become more "growth-minded, development-minded."[92] When they were not overwhelmed by military problems, local officials could devote more attention to other pressing social and economic-development needs, such as the introduction of better crops, schools, and medical clinics as well as the construction of houses, roads, and bridges.[93]

An important outgrowth of the burgeoning civil war was the elevated position of the South Vietnamese military within the governing class. By the early 1960s, members of the Army of the Republic of Vietnam (ARVN) had replaced civilian officials in many provinces and districts.

According to USOM reports, these military personnel suffered not only from their preoccupation with defeating the insurgency but also from their lack of training in civilian government. As Gustav Hertz, chief of the PAD team, wrote after visiting several provinces: "One basic conclusion from all field trips thus far is that it will be difficult for local government in the provinces to achieve an acceptable degree of efficiency and service to the people as long as military administrators over-burdened with security duties continue to fill civilian positions or are without adequate civilian assistants." He noted a "particularly critical situation" among district-level officers, who served as a bridge between provincial authorities and village or hamlet leaders. Because many district chiefs were military officers with little knowledge of civilian government, in 1964 USOM and NIA personnel designed a number of training programs aimed at acquainting them with basic administrative responsibilities. Advisers at USOM and the NIA hoped that these training courses would contribute to better working relationships among officials at the province, district, and village levels.[94]

In most cases, officials with military backgrounds had little time or interest in the challenges of civil administration. The higher up the bureaucratic ladder one looked, the more acute this problem seemed to be. According to one PAD report: "Only those officials charged with the responsibilities of local governance . . . appear to be concerned with the need for better informed and more representative governing officials."[95] As a result, the PAD recommended that elected village councils be given greater responsibility and autonomy. However, Bui Van Luong, the GVN's secretary of state for the interior, questioned the wisdom of that proposal, citing political instability and security concerns as impediments for effective elections and civilian administrators.[96]

Despite USOM's emphasis on the importance of village and local officials, most efforts to improve public administration did not reach administrators at those levels. Instead, the GVN's Ministry of the Interior and the NIA designed their outreach and training programs for provincial chiefs and their staffs rather than for lower-level officials. Some members of the PAD team argued that USOM and the GVN could do much more to assist administrators in the villages. For example, in a report he wrote after visiting a number of villages in Binh Duong Province, Henry Bush concluded that most village chiefs and their staff members could read and would benefit from more training materials. He advised his superiors at USOM: "I suspect that we (PAD, RA, USOM as a whole) probably *under*estimate the literacy of provincial *officialdom* at the Province, District, and Village, and Hamlet *Chief* levels, and probably underestimate what we can do with instruction in simple form in print. I suspect we probably *over*estimate the literacy or responsiveness of the *people* (the citizens, the peasantry) at the hamlet level."[97]

USOM advisers found that the quality of local administration varied by province and district. In wealthier, more secure areas, the focus of administrators' authority and energy was at the village level. In more remote, poor, or unstable parts of the country, provincial officials wielded the most authority. There also appeared to be some correlation between local administration and the ethnic makeup of a province. For example, in provinces such as Binh Duong, which were relatively wealthy and predominately ethnic Vietnamese, village leaders enjoyed greater responsibility and control over decision making. On the other hand, in provinces like Phuoc Long, which was one of the poorest in South Vietnam and had a population composed of over 50 percent ethnic minorities, village leaders exercised little power, and provincial authorities issued most administrative decisions and direction.[98] As the PAD adviser Henry Bush explained in a report comparing Binh Duong and Phuoc Long Provinces: "Assuming a spectrum of political and administrative behavior between the above two extremes . . . I infer that, as you get peasant security and prosperity, you get a shift of authority downward toward the people." Bush also argued that the village was the "real future focus of democracy in rural regions."[99]

Although USOM seemed to be making progress in encouraging democratic development in South Vietnam, political chaos in late 1963 limited the effectiveness of the PAD. In the wake of the Buddhist crisis in Hue and increased antigovernment attacks in rural areas, Diem declared martial law in August 1963. The imposition of martial law delayed training programs for local officials and resulted in a temporary closure of the NIA.[100] Even before the NIA had shuttered its doors, it had suspended its in-service training program and the publication of its journal, *Tien-Thu* (Progress). It resumed both the in-service training and publication of the journal at the end of the year, after a nine-month hiatus.[101] However, by the time the NIA returned to its normal operations in December, Diem had been deposed and murdered in a coup. At that point, the GVN faced a more uncertain future than at any time since the first months of South Vietnam's existence.

After the November 1963 coup, Americans providing technical assistance in public administration encountered new challenges. In the immediate aftermath of the coup, there was tremendous upheaval throughout the country, especially among GVN personnel. Leadership in most of South Vietnam's forty-two provinces changed hands. By early January 1964, thirty-four of those provinces had new chiefs at the helm. In addition, USOM advisers estimated that the majority of the country's 235 district chiefs had been replaced in the two months since the coup occurred. As Hertz wrote at the time: "Uncertainty and indecision on both political and administrative matters coupled with changes in personnel continue to handicap the new government."[102] A couple months later, after the leadership of the GVN had changed hands again in late January, Hertz argued that ongoing political instability in South Vietnam "hampered efforts to move ahead with administrative improvements."[103] And a PAD bulletin containing a GVN personnel list and organizational chart warned USOM advisers: "Since these assignments change rather frequently, care should be exercised in checking the continued validity of this transient info."[104]

The turmoil brought on by the 1963 coup also negatively affected the NIA. The institute's operating budget was reduced, and many of its programs were curtailed or postponed. For example, it continued to publish the journal *Administrative Research* but with the time frame for publication delayed by several months. The July–August issue finally appeared in print in December 1963.[105] The faculty of the NIA also suffered from the upheaval in the government. In March 1964, the GVN recruited seven of the institute's sixteen full-time professors to positions within the Saigon government. Although this move suggests the importance of the NIA as a training ground for government officials, it had an adverse effect on its ability to continue producing effective administrators. It did not replace those professors who left to work for the GVN, so the faculty was reduced to nearly half its previous size.[106]

After Diem was deposed, the South Vietnamese military assumed a more central role in the GVN. It now took over many government functions and responsibilities that had previously been carried out by civilians.[107]

Given the prevalence of ARVN personnel in administrative positions, the PAD introduced several training opportunities designed specifically for officials with a military background. For example, in early 1964, USOM provided technical assistance for a joint training course sponsored by the Ministry of the Interior and the NIA. This two-week, intensive training course targeted military officers serving as district chiefs. (At that time, forty ARVN officers held the position of district chief throughout thirty-nine provinces in South Vietnam.) The course covered topics such as the organizational structure and role of local governments, the responsibilities of district chiefs, information on holding elections, and advice for dealing with various political, economic, and social problems.[108]

The growing strength and influence of the NLF also served as an impediment to civilian administration in South Vietnam. Not only did the burgeoning insurgency cause the GVN to respond by enhancing the role of the military in government, but the NLF also established its own parallel administration, especially at the village and district levels. The NLF shadow government collected taxes at a considerably higher rate than did the GVN. According to PAD advisers, most people complied with the NLF's demand for payment in cash or in kind because they felt intimidated by the insurgents. However, the Americans also found that peasants were reluctant to discuss the NLF's tax-collection and other activities or keep NLF-issued receipts of their payments because they feared reprisals from the GVN.[109]

## The Limits of Assistance

The MSU and USOM programs did have some impact on public administration in Vietnam. The MSU group helped develop a nationally recognized institution for training public officials, created a modern research library in Saigon, and exposed thousands of Vietnamese to new approaches to public administration. USOM's primary contributions consisted of outreach and training programs for provincial administrators. Those efforts not only offered a model for local officials to follow but also provided information and knowledge about issues in the provinces to the GVN. However, Diem's intransigence and the political considerations driving US aid ensured that technical assistance programs in public administration existed largely to benefit political elites and support an unpopular government in Saigon. In the end, despite lofty ambitions, both the MSU and the USOM groups fell short of accomplishing their goal of modernizing and improving the public administration system in order to foster a strong, independent nation in southern Vietnam that commanded the allegiance of its citizens. American aid workers' vision of establishing a professional civil service could not resolve the fundamental political and security problems in South Vietnam, especially the Diem regime's legitimacy crisis and the development of a potent antigovernment insurgency.

Both MSU's and USOM's public administration teams found their efforts restricted by the political realities of the escalating war in Vietnam. As antigovernment violence increased during the late 1950s, American and South Vietnamese policy makers came to view the establishment of a skilled public administration system as a secondary concern. By the end of that decade, it became apparent that South Vietnam's future depended on Diem's ability to cultivate support and enhance internal security. The experiences and shortcomings of the public administration advisers ultimately highlight the limited power of academic knowledge to improve a fundamentally flawed government or transform a society in the midst of a war.

# 3

# Sowing the Seeds
# of Discontent

## American Agricultural-Development Programs
## in South Vietnam

The job of the [Government of Vietnam] lies beyond the trial of arms—it is to demonstrate its appreciation of the fundamental aspirations of the farmers. Unless the situation is radically improved it will continue to benefit the anti-Government forces.
—Wolf Ladejinsky (1955)

The fate of South Vietnam, as well as the outcome of American nation-building efforts, hinged on economic and political developments in rural parts of the country. In the 1950s, when the United States became deeply involved in Vietnam, over 80 percent of the population lived in the countryside. As a result, the struggle that ensued there consisted largely of a battle to win the hearts and minds of the peasantry. American policy makers believed that rural development offered an effective way to increase support for the US client state in Saigon and discourage the population from embracing the Communist-led antigovernment insurgency. Beginning in 1955, American agricultural experts from both the US Operations Mission (USOM) and the private International Voluntary Services (IVS) introduced a series of projects designed to transform rural society in South Vietnam. Over the next decade, these aid workers attempted to improve the rural population's standard of living through community development and the introduction of modern farming techniques. Agricultural aid workers believed that the material benefits their programs offered would not only serve as a viable alternative to the land-reform programs promised by Communist leaders but also make the advantages of American-style modernity visible to the entire Vietnamese population.

Despite this ambitious agenda, American agricultural-development programs did not result in either meaningful agrarian reform or lasting socioeconomic change, as the aid workers had hoped. Similarly, agricultural-development initiatives failed to produce widespread loyalty to Ngo Dinh Diem's regime or popular disdain for the antigovernment insurgency, as both South Vietnamese and American officials had anticipated. Although American agricultural advisers may have helped raise the standard of living for some individual Vietnamese farmers and their families, their endeavors neither improved basic economic conditions in rural South Vietnam nor won the battle for hearts and minds. The shortcomings of American rural-development efforts were a central and dominant feature of the overall failure of US involvement in Vietnam. Understanding the limitations of agricultural-development schemes reveals fundamental problems with the approach that the United States took in Vietnam and helps explain why the Government of Vietnam (GVN) could not attract popular support or survive without massive amounts of American assistance.

American agricultural-development programs failed for three primary reasons, all of which derived from the gulf between US and GVN officials' strategic aims and the Vietnamese population's concerns. First, all too often, US aid did not meet the basic needs and interests of Vietnamese farmers. Most Vietnamese peasants were more focused on gaining access to land and basic materials than on sweeping transformations to rural life. However, as a result of confidence in their own expertise and the political priorities driving foreign assistance, American advisers tried to introduce new methods and novel techniques that did not always satisfy local needs. As a result, Vietnamese farmers accepted aid selectively, sometimes embracing specific projects, and other times modifying or even rejecting them. Second, a significant segment of Vietnam's rural society harbored deep suspicions of the Americans' intentions and resented the US government's support of the unpopular Diem regime. With the legacy of colonialism looming large, many people perceived American aid workers as another group of outsiders who did not have the interests of the Vietnamese in mind. Furthermore, increased production or an elevated standard of living for individual families did not outweigh the negative effects of repressive GVN policies in the countryside. As a result, the introduction of industrial agriculture failed to translate into political support for the Saigon government. Finally, the political unrest and escalating violence that emerged as a result of the appeal of revolutionary forces as well as in response to GVN abuses in rural areas overshadowed all the American aid workers' efforts. The civil war placed severe constraints on the Americans' ability to provide assistance to some of the most impoverished and underserved but politically important communities in Vietnam.

## Land, Agriculture, and Communism in Vietnam

During the Cold War, American officials focused on increasing agricultural production in developing countries where a majority of the population lived in rural areas and depended on farming for their survival. Their interest in agricultural development stemmed in large part from their need to offset the appeal of collectivization and communism to the peasantry in such areas. In Vietnam, where peasants constituted an overwhelming majority, Cold War considerations and competition with North Vietnam fueled the US enthusiasm for agricultural progress and for improving rural inhabitants' quality of life. As the historian Nick Cullather explains, by the mid-twentieth century, US policy makers had come to see the American agricultural system, which was diverse, productive, and efficient, as providing national advantages that were "as unique as the atomic bomb."[1]

By the mid-twentieth century, peasants throughout Vietnam demanded meaningful land reform. During the colonial period, the disparity between wealthy landowners, many of whom were French imperialists or absentee landlords, and poor tenant farmers had grown steadily. Such inequalities were particularly acute in the southern provinces, where absentee landlords and plantation owners controlled a disproportionate percentage of agricultural land. According to the historian David Biggs:

"Land reform evolved into perhaps the single most important political issue of the revolution."[2]

After the 1954 partition of Vietnam, a tiny fraction of the population owned the majority of South Vietnam's agricultural land. According to the historian David Anderson, in the southern half of the country 2 percent of owners controlled 45 percent of the land, while 72 percent of owners held 15 percent of the land.[3] A large segment of the Vietnamese population worked as tenant farmers and lived in what one scholar referred to as "economic bondage to their landlord."[4] In the mid-1950s, tenant farmers constituted approximately 40 percent of South Vietnam's population.[5] Even in northern Vietnam, where relatively more people owned some land, most individual plots were so small that the farmers who held them had to work as tenants on larger estates to make ends meet. During the First Indochina War, Viet Minh cadres seized land that belonged to Frenchmen who had retreated to the cities in the wake of the fighting and redistributed it to peasant cultivators. When the war came to a close, the rural population put tremendous pressure on Vietnamese leaders in both the North and the South to rectify the persistent problem of landlessness and assist the millions of tenant farmers who lived on the brink of survival as a result of unfair landownership regulations.[6]

The Vietnamese Workers' Party (VWP) leadership promised a reorganization of existing landholding and farming practices as one of the central components of the party's platform. In the mid-1950s, during its first years in power, the government of the Democratic Republic of Vietnam (DRV) instituted a sweeping land-reform program in the northern part of the country. The program was plagued by corruption and abuses. North Vietnam's land-reform efforts resulted in the murders of thousands of landholders, and the DRV suspended the program within two years of its inception.[7] As the historian Pierre Asselin explains: "[The VWP] had so poorly managed that program that it caused both widespread hardship and resentment throughout the North."[8]

At the time, the South Vietnamese government vociferously criticized the VWP land-reform attempts, claiming that official North Vietnamese policy called for the "liquidation of all landlords."[9] However, Diem's regime also recognized that a large segment of the population insisted on more equitable land distribution and that the South Vietnamese government would have to do something to appease these people. In response to pressure for reform, Diem established special courts to deal with land-lord-tenant disputes and created the Ministry of Agrarian Affairs. GVN reform programs earned little respect from disgruntled peasants, however, because the landowners and officials friendly to them dominated the special courts and the minister of agrarian affairs was one of the largest landowners in South Vietnam.[10] According to Jeffrey Race, an American journalist in Vietnam during the late 1950s who observed land-reform efforts firsthand, the GVN program resulted in no real redistribution of land and proved largely ineffective.[11] Although the South Vietnamese government acquired significant tracts of land from Vietnamese and French landlords, less than half of that land was ever redistributed to peasants, and tenant farmers continued to cultivate the vast majority of land.[12]

## Agricultural Development as a Solution to Rural Problems

US policy makers believed that they could help alleviate rural poverty, introduce the benefits of modernity, and foster political stability through development projects in South Vietnam and elsewhere in the Third World. Ngo Dinh Diem and other South Vietnamese leaders also viewed rural development as a key component of their vision for modernizing Vietnam as well as an antidote to chronic unrest and political opposition. However, while US and GVN officials may have agreed on the broad contours of and basic need for rural development, they often differed on specific projects and the best way to accomplish those shared goals. For example, Diem advocated land resettlement, while many Americans favored land reform as the preferred way to address rural problems.[13]

Despite such differences of opinion, American and South Vietnamese officials were united in their criticism of Hanoi's approach to land reform. Rather than focus on land redistribution, which was popular among the Vietnamese peasantry but smacked of Communist-style, state-oriented development, both US and GVN policy makers emphasized development at the village level and increasing the productivity of land already under cultivation.[14] They believed that improving the rural population's standard of living could placate their demands for collectivization or reallocation of wealth while simultaneously minimizing disorder and advancing national goals. Their distinct approaches to rural problems reflected the deep philosophical and political differences between the North Vietnamese leadership, on the one hand, and the southern government and its American patrons, on the other hand.

Both high-level US policy makers and aid workers in the field presented American-sponsored agricultural projects as a direct alternative to North Vietnamese redistribution initiatives. The official rationale behind the massive US economic and military aid program to Vietnam, which by 1957 was the second largest package offered to any country in the world, reflected the intensity of this competition with the North Vietnamese government.[15] According to a report issued by the International Cooperation Administration (ICA): "Free Vietnam [was] competing with the Communist regime in the north for the political support of the Vietnamese peasants, who comprise 80 percent of the population." In 1958, recognizing the need to improve living conditions in South Vietnam, the US government pledged $18.8 million for "activities which will resettle uprooted people on land now idle" and "defray the administrative costs of land reform."[16] A 1961 US Agency for International Development (USAID) report on American development assistance argued that any assessment of progress "must take into account the competition between North and South Vietnam for the allegiance of the Vietnamese people."[17]

Officials in the Eisenhower and Kennedy administrations believed that the survival of an anti-Communist state in Vietnam—and by extension the existence of capitalism and democracy throughout Southeast Asia—depended on convincing South Vietnam's people that their loyalties should lie with Diem and the United States rather than the Communist revolutionaries. In the minds of many US policy makers, political stability and economic development served as prerequisites for winning the allegiance of formerly colonized people. The ICA, which later became USAID, attached "the greatest importance to helping the free countries of the Far East to develop their economies and improve the lot of their people." A 1958 overview of the agency's Mutual Security Program for Asia stated: "Measures that will further the economic aspirations of the people are as important to the preservation of the freedom of these countries as are military measures undertaken to counter internal and external threats to their security."[18]

As a result of policy makers' misplaced faith in economic progress trumping political self-determination, agricultural-development programs figured prominently among US foreign aid packages during the mid-twentieth century, especially in developing countries such as Vietnam. To a large degree, overseas agricultural programs were an outgrowth of recent trends in farming and rural development within the United States. In the early twentieth century, improved technology, newly trained agricultural experts, and students of the Industrial Revolution radically transformed the practice of agriculture in America. According to the historian Deborah Fitzgerald, during the twentieth century an "industrial logic or ideal in agriculture" emerged as the fundamental feature of rural development and socioeconomic change on America's farms. Fitzgerald argues that, in the first decades of the twentieth century, a new generation of specialists who had studied at agricultural colleges introduced the "principles of efficiency" and "rational management techniques" of industrial factories to American farms. Relying on scientific and technological innovations, such as tractors, combines, and chemical pesticides, these "agents of industrialism" enthusiastically applied the techniques of mechanization, cost accounting, and specialization to farming.[19]

While efforts to make farming modern altered the rural landscape and practices of farmers in the United States during the early twentieth century, Americans also began exporting this new agricultural philosophy overseas. For example, in the late 1920s the US government sent between one and two thousand technical experts to the Soviet Union as agricultural advisers. According to Fitzgerald, those advisers enjoyed the "opportunity to both offer assistance to those in need and to try new agricultural ideas that may not be easy to do in America."[20] Although most participants in the Soviet advisory program considered the project unsuccessful, US foreign aid officials were not deterred by this experience and continued to promote similar agricultural-development schemes in other parts of the world.[21] In the 1940s, the Rockefeller Foundation initiated the Mexican Agricultural Program, which was designed to address the supposed gap between Mexico's food supply and its population. American policy makers looked to the effort to transform Mexico's agricultural system as an important model for other parts of the postcolonial world, particularly Asia. As Cullather explains, Mexico became "a staging area for the conquest of hunger in Asia."[22]

Policy makers' optimism about the universal and international applicability of American farming methods suggests that they often assigned greater value to the perceived expertise of agricultural advisers than to historical experience or local conditions. Moreover, government support for land-grant colleges and the ongoing trend of professionalization within the fields of agricultural science ensured training opportunities and the production of expertise in these areas.[23]

Despite vast differences in time, geography, and political context, American agricultural-development efforts in Vietnam borrowed heavily from and proved strikingly similar to the 1927 Soviet advisory enterprise in particular. Fitzgerald explains that the agricultural technicians who went to the Soviet Union approached their work with "faith . . . in the power and persuasion of rational, demonstrable scientific fact."[24] American aid workers in Vietnam shared this conviction. They also faced similar challenges in implementing their programs, challenges that stemmed from their identification with the US government.

Many agricultural advisers embraced the official American view regarding the role of foreign aid in fighting the Cold War, and, as such, they played a central role in executing modernization policies. Although much of the aid workers' daily work occurred at the local level and affected only the people with whom the Americans came into direct contact, many saw themselves and their labor as part of a larger effort. Some even espoused ideological arguments identical to those of the US government, particularly at the beginning of their time in Vietnam. In one of his letters to family and friends, the agricultural adviser Don Schmidt explained that the overall goal of foreign aid was to "defeat communism by developing people."[25] Another aid worker, Leslie Small, wrote about the links between war and underdevelopment, stressing the idea that "guerilla tactics thrive on needy and dependent populations." Small argued that, if Vietnamese people could see positive results from US and GVN assistance, it would be easier for them to resist the Vietnamese Communists' attempts at political control.[26]

## Agents of Agricultural Change

Two organizations—a government agency and a private group of volunteers—spearheaded American agricultural-development programs in South Vietnam. Aid workers from USOM and IVS partnered to introduce new technologies, products, and techniques to Vietnam's farmers.

These men hailed primarily from rural areas of the United States and had studied modern farming practices at some of the top American agricultural colleges. They worked directly with the Vietnamese Ministry of Rural Affairs in promoting GVN-sponsored development initiatives, and they also provided technical assistance at the grassroots level.[27] Unlike many other American advisers in Vietnam at the time, agricultural aid workers often lived in the Vietnamese countryside and had daily contact with Vietnamese peasants, some of whom worked with the Americans.

Advisers from USOM engaged in a huge number and wide range of agricultural activities in Vietnam. Their Farm Improvement Division included projects to increase rice production and encourage the development of tropical plants, including sugar, for export. They introduced fertilizers, new types of field crops and seeds, and livestock programs. Their agricultural extension program aimed to address problems faced by farmers in outlying areas. As Lawrence Doran, a USOM extension adviser, described his activities, extension work sought "to encourage [farmers] to adopt new practices to improve agricultural production and farm family living conditions."[28] Some aid workers advised the Ministry of Rural Affairs on agricultural-economics or land-settlement programs. Others helped establish rural credit agencies and cooperatives, set up fishing facilities, or designed irrigation systems. Still others staffed the Agricultural Information Service, which produced and distributed leaflets and photographs, coordinated radio programming, and operated a mobile audiovisual unit to promote new agricultural techniques and practices.[29]

USOM also assisted the GVN in its efforts to promote agricultural education, introduce home improvement programs, and work with rural youths. It funded and administered training programs for Vietnamese staff members. Usually, Vietnamese farm agents were invited to participate in short-term training sessions, either in Vietnam or elsewhere in the region. In some cases, Vietnamese staff members received longer-term training and college degrees at American universities.[30] Relying on the model of the American system, aid workers also helped establish an agricultural college at Blao (Bao Loc), in the Central Highlands. The Blao Agricultural College was created to remedy the problems associated with the shortage of local people who had background and experience in agricultural studies or a "strong desire to serve rural people."[31]

USOM's Home Improvement Division worked closely with rural

women in Vietnam. Its goals were to help them make a "vital contribution to the development of their families, their communities, and their nation." USOM's stated goals suggest a certain distrust of local practices and an assumption that Vietnamese women had much to learn from American advisers. Home improvement agents were supposed to teach Vietnamese women skills needed for "caring for children, providing good food for families, growing fruits and vegetables, improving their homes, caring for the sick, and working with their neighbors," as if they did not have any prior experience performing such tasks.[32] USOM's Rural Youth Division worked with the GVN to establish "4-T" clubs, modeled after American 4-H clubs. These clubs invited girls and boys between the ages of twelve and twenty to participate in agricultural activities and learn how to be more productive farmers.[33] The efforts of American aid workers and their Vietnamese counterparts produced measurable results. By early 1964, there were 447 women's clubs with over fourteen thousand members and 1,100 4-T clubs with over forty-four thousand members in South Vietnam.[34]

Because of the ambitious nature of its efforts and the scope of its activities, USOM's Agricultural Development Division required a large number of American advisers and technicians. However, the mission lacked enough manpower to realize all its goals. USOM turned to private aid workers to fill in the gaps, entering into a contractual relationship with IVS, a nongovernment organization, to help implement agricultural-development programs in Vietnam. IVS volunteers generally had less contact with GVN officials and provided more grassroots-level assistance than their colleagues at USOM.[35]

Inspired by a sense of duty to their country and the commitment to helping less fortunate populations, many IVS volunteers arrived in Vietnam brimming with idealism and optimism. Most had grown up on or near farms and brought to Vietnam prior experience and training in agriculture. In conducting searches for possible agricultural volunteers to work in Vietnam, IVS specified the following qualifications for employment: prior experience working on a farm, a degree from a recognized agricultural college, and "a spirit of dedication and [ability] to work on a people to people basis."[36] With only a few exceptions, these young men had just graduated from college and were seeing another part of the world for the first time. Some volunteers had never left their home states, straying from family farms just long enough to complete their degrees. Richard Peters, who grew up on a farm in California's San Joaquin valley and attended the University of California, Los Angeles, later recalled that his background and prior experience mirrored that of most of his colleagues in the IVS mission.[37] Perhaps as a result of their youth and idealism, the volunteers sometimes demonstrated a tendency to romanticize Vietnam and its people. As one man wrote home, describing his impressions of how Vietnamese celebrated Christmas: "It seems sometimes that the Vietnamese appreciate their simple life more than we do our rich one."[38]

Unlike IVS missions in other developing countries, the one in Vietnam received its funding entirely from the US government and operated under the authority of USOM.[39] According to this arrangement, USOM provided IVS with funding to support the volunteers, technical advice, and materials such as seeds, livestock, construction materials, medications, textbooks, and other educational tools. In exchange, the volunteers, who referred to themselves as *IVSers*, lived and worked in rural areas of the country, implementing American aid programs, and often serving as intermediaries between higher-level aid workers and local officials.[40] Although the relationship between USOM and IVS offered tangible benefits to both parties, IVSers in Vietnam operated with considerably less autonomy than did their counterparts elsewhere as a result of their financial dependence on the government.

During the early years of IVS involvement in Vietnam, both the organization's leadership and the volunteers embraced their relationship with the US government.[41] The IVSers firmly believed in their mission, and many saw themselves as the only Americans capable of executing grassroots development programs. As the organization's final report stated: "During the first five or more years of IVS/VN, the volunteers were the sole representatives of the U.S. foreign aid effort out among the people." As a result, IVSers generally concluded that their commitment to Vietnam's people outweighed their desire or demands for greater autonomy. The young volunteers saw themselves as "agents of agricultural change," and they believed that technological advances and increased productivity signified positive developments for farmers.[42]

In many instances, the roles and responsibilities of IVS and USOM overlapped. The main IVS office in Saigon was located within USOM's headquarters. IVS agricultural volunteers often outnumbered USOM employees and doubled as provincial representatives for the agency in the field. USOM reports always included details on the activities of the IVS-ers who worked on agricultural projects.[43] In addition, USOM sometimes recruited IVSers to take on special projects in rural areas, for which they were better suited than government aid workers, who had less experience working with villagers and, in many cases, could not speak Vietnamese. According to IVS's terminal report, the close association between IVS and USOM "created a relationship which had political significance."[44]

Relations between the IVS volunteers and USOM employees were generally good on both the personal and the professional levels. One volunteer, Mike Chilton, described the close association between the two organizations, writing that the volunteers served a vital role as intermediaries between USOM representatives and Vietnamese farmers.[45] Aid workers at USOM's Rural Affairs Division showed their appreciation for the IVSers, and the two groups seldom encountered conflicts in their working relationships. In a recent interview, Rufus Philips, a close colleague of the counterinsurgency expert Edward Lansdale and the head of USOM's Rural Affairs Division in Vietnam during the 1960s, conveyed his respect for IVS volunteers and spoke about their commitment to providing assistance to the Vietnamese. He described how, unlike many other American organizations, both USOM aid workers and IVS volunteers attempted to solicit ideas from the Vietnamese rather than simply imposing their programs on the people.[46] Philips's recollection suggests that some low-level aid workers may have been more attentive to the needs of the Vietnamese than high-ranking officials or government bureaucrats were. However, such responsiveness was certainly not the norm among American nation builders in general, and many IVS agricultural volunteers' actions and writings indicate a lack of consideration for local economic and political interests.

Despite the ambitious vision and good intentions of American aid workers, US agricultural-development programs failed to transform the lives of South Vietnam's rural population fundamentally or win hearts and minds to the anti-Communist cause. The main reasons for these shortcomings were that US aid simply did not meet the most basic material needs of Vietnamese peasants—in fact, it often conflicted with their cultural practices and political interests—and it was inextricably linked with US support for the authoritarian government in Saigon.

# Failing to Address Peasants' Basic Material Interests

USOM and IVS focused on introducing new methods, technologies, and products that were designed to alter the ways that farmers behaved. The approach of these aid workers derived from their faith in industrial agriculture, their ideas about development and progress, and their assumptions about the backwardness of Vietnamese peasants. However, farmers in Vietnam tended to prioritize access to land and basic materials, and they did not uniformly embrace aid workers' suggestions. Instead, they adapted new technologies and methods to suit their own needs. Although some individual farmers enjoyed increased production or saw some improvement in their economic position, GVN and American aid programs never addressed larger structural issues rooted in socioeconomic disparity, and, as a result, they proved largely ineffective.

Some American advisers recognized the fact that Vietnam's peasants had very basic and immediate needs and interests. In July 1955, Wolf Ladejinsky, one of the foremost American experts on agriculture and land reform in Asia, submitted a report to the ICA that outlined his recommendations for development assistance to Vietnam.[47] His report, based on research trips to rural Tay Ninh, Soc Trang, Bac Lieu, and Can Tho Provinces, suggested that Vietnamese farmers' immediate needs outweighed their political and ideological concerns. According to Ladejinsky, Vietnamese peasants desperately required access to credit, assistance with irrigation and drainage systems, buffaloes and other draft animals, and fertilizer. He argued that, although farmers sought to end feudal patterns of landownership, their desire for basic materials took precedence over their interest in rent reduction. As a result, he concluded that the establishment of cooperatives and farm extension services would have only "peripheral" success in Vietnam.[48] Years later, other American advisers echoed this advice. For example, in his end-of-tour report, the USOM agricultural economics adviser Richard Pringle recommended that both the United States and the GVN needed to focus on "reduced urban/rural disparity" through "more productive farm credit."[49]

Ladejinsky and other advisers placed the burden of agricultural and economic development on the South Vietnamese government. Ladejinsky wrote that the GVN must play the central role in helping peasants, suggesting that US aid could be only marginal to that endeavor. Specifically, he argued that the GVN needed to "demonstrate its appreciation and understanding of the fundamental aspirations of the farmers." He insisted that the long-term key to the success of the Republic of Vietnam (RVN) lay in the provision of material aid to Vietnam's farmers rather than events in Saigon. However, American advisers often found that South Vietnamese policy makers were reluctant to take the lead in financing or implementing agricultural programs. Ladejinsky was highly critical of Vietnamese officials' "lack of zeal and zest" and the fact that they seemed "disturbingly unconcerned" about the rural population.[50] GVN officials claimed that they simply lacked the funds to provide material support for farmers. Furthermore, they demonstrated a preoccupation with industrial development and forced rural-resettlement schemes while trying to garner political support among the urban middle class.[51]

Although many US advisers advocated straightforward material assistance, American aid workers on the ground repeatedly resorted to a more sweeping vision of fundamentally altering the way Vietnamese farmers went about their business and modernizing rural society through the application of an industrial agricultural logic. Despite his emphasis on the importance of supplying credit and farm equipment, even Ladejinsky argued that the United States should focus on placing more American technicians in the field to transfer knowledge and demonstrate the advantages of new ways of doing things.[52] However, aid workers found that people throughout the country often lacked enthusiasm for foreign interference and guidance and were reluctant to adopt new methods.

USOM advisers and IVSers discovered that most people they encountered focused their time and energy on ensuring their families' survival and basic comfort rather than on increasing their profit margins. Individuals with this outlook on life were seldom prepared to assume the risks that accompanied changing established agricultural practices, on which their livelihood and survival depended.[53] In many cases, Vietnamese farmers had strong economic motivations as well as cultural reasons for maintaining their accustomed methods and avoiding financial risks. Consequently, community leaders accepted aid money, and peasants adopted seeds, animals, and tools, even as they resisted altering their habits. Aid workers found it far more difficult to convince Vietnamese of the merits of new techniques or methods than it was to distribute cash or materials. This pattern confirms the accuracy of Ladejinsky's and other advisers' recommendations for how best to assist rural populations.

According to Alan Berlet, an IVS volunteer stationed in the Mekong delta town of Can Tho, most Vietnamese were unwilling to incorporate new agricultural practices. However, the farmers of Can Tho accepted money and other forms of material aid with "outstretched hands." When Berlet provided instruction on how to use new tools and machines, the Vietnamese responded with a "token display" of interest and continued practicing their old ways of farming. As Berlet wrote in a letter home, people refused to shift their thinking and consider novel ways of using new materials, especially ones that did not meet their immediate needs.[54] Similarly, the IVSer Bob McNeff described the challenges he faced when encouraging Vietnamese to overcome their reluctance to try something new. McNeff worked in Phan Rang, an area conducive to breeding livestock. There he attempted to develop a local industry to produce grain for animal feed. After discovering that farmers frequently ignored his advice, he concluded that local inhabitants were hesitant to accept his suggestions because they had no previous experience growing grain for this purpose. He struggled to convey to these farmers the profitability of cultivating livestock feed, and he acknowledged that his efforts were met by slow progress at best.[55]

## Challenges to Cultural Practices and Political Interests

In addition to their reliance on proven techniques, Vietnamese peasants sometimes had significant social or cultural reasons for maintaining certain ways of planting, harvesting, and raising livestock. Religious beliefs, family customs, and time-tested processes directed the daily routines of Vietnamese and ethnic minority farmers alike. When the Americans' development schemes interfered with any of these deeply rooted beliefs or practices, peasants in Vietnam simply refused to participate in the programs.

Most Americans involved in agricultural development believed that rural people were essentially conservative and would refuse to accept new approaches or technologies unless they were convinced of the overwhelming benefits of adopting them.[56] In this sense, Vietnam's rural population seemed remarkably similar to farmers in the United States. As the historian Deborah Fitzgerald explains, in the early twentieth century many American farmers initially exhibited reluctance to use certain equipment, especially tractors and other large machines, that was inappropriate for the size of the farm or the type of crop being raised.[57] According to American aid workers, Vietnamese farmers demonstrated a comparable lack of enthusiasm for new machinery and techniques. As a result, both USOM and IVS placed great emphasis on demonstration and informal teaching to convince local farmers of the wisdom of novel methods as well as the usefulness of unfamiliar crops or tools.[58]

Because of their close contact with rural populations, the IVS volunteers were especially attuned to Vietnamese peasants' general unwillingness to alter existing farming patterns. In their letters to family and friends, many commented on the complicated nature of attempting to influence others to change their behavior. Their anecdotes illustrate this point and suggest several explanations for the reluctance to accept new techniques. When coupled with their suspicion about the volunteers' intentions and loyalties, many peasants' aversion to taking unnecessary risks or their cultural predilections outweighed other incentives to alter their practices.

Many aid workers recognized the significance of local customs and argued that traditional farming methods were often more appropriate, given the realities of rural inhabitants' existence. For example, in Nha Ho, where the IVSer Everett La Rue was stationed, most families owned small plots of land that ranged from a quarter of an acre to ten acres. Cultivating these small plots did not require large, modern farm equipment, and the farmers rarely benefited economically by introducing new equipment or novel techniques. They had reasons for using certain methods, and, in La Rue's words, "quite often the validity [of these methods] outweighs an entirely new concept."[59]

An anecdote related by another volunteer illustrates La Rue's point. Don Schmidt, who was also stationed in Nha Ho, participated in a crop experimentation project. Schmidt believed that he could find and introduce a new type of bean that would be more productive in Vietnam's conditions. In his "rather ambitious program of evaluation," he tested two hundred varieties of beans from thirty-six countries. He assumed that many of them would prove superior to the kind grown by Nha Ho's farmers. To his surprise, he discovered that the local strain, a small black bean

International Voluntary Services volunteers John Sommer, Peter Hunting, Gene Stoltzfus, and Willie Meyers (*left to right*) in Phuoc Tuy Province, November 1964. Courtesy Gene Stoltzfus Papers, 1940–2012, HM1–101, Photographs: Vietnam, International Voluntary Service, 1963–1967, box 4, folder 2, Mennonite Church USA Archives—Goshen, Goshen, IN.

that farmers in the area had cultivated for years, was the only variety that was resistant to the region's heavy infestation of insects and other pests. According to Schmidt, the "valuable lesson" of this experience taught him to "appreciate the merits of what the illiterate but intelligent Vietnamese farmers themselves have developed and learned."[60]

In both their writings at the time and in later recollections, many volunteers pointed to individual cases in which a farmer, family, or community accepted American assistance and modified their behavior. At the same time, nearly all the volunteers observed a more general phenomenon: rural inhabitants demonstrating a fundamental resistance to change, especially when pressured to do so by outsiders. One volunteer, Larry Laverentz, wrote: "Change must be slow and must conform to many of the present ways of doing things." Laverentz continued: "This is only natural since their customs have been handed down from generation to generation for centuries with possibly only slight alteration in many cases."[61]

Another volunteer reached similar conclusions. Harvey Neese explained to his family and friends that most of the Vietnamese with whom he worked were reluctant to try unfamiliar methods. According to Neese, the laborers at the experimental station in Ban Me Thuot "keep a very close watch on Americans and any mistake registers in their brains and stays there." When he learned that the local farmers always shelled peanuts before planting them, he encouraged them to save themselves some work and plant the nuts in their shells. Believing that peanuts planted in the shells would not grow, the farmers advised him against wasting his time by trying to plant them. However, he ignored the advice and planted some peanuts with shells "as an experiment." Neese reported that the Vietnamese were surprised to find that the nuts grew well. He concluded: "It is hard to break the Vietnamese away from age-old customs which might just be the hardest way to do a certain thing. This is what I'm here for   to show them easier ways to farm." Despite professing such confidence in his methods, Neese admitted that he was sometimes wrong. Moreover, he confessed that, although he had been hired as an adviser, during his time in Vietnam he had learned to accept advice, too.[62]

To the surprise of some volunteers, the IVS agricultural team discovered that Vietnamese rarely accepted American advice indiscriminately. For this reason, the final results of many agricultural-development projects looked quite different from the original conception or design of those endeavors. Local farmers chose to adopt some aspects of the American aid programs and reject others, depending on what they believed would benefit them and their families.

The IVSer David DePuy found that, even though people might request assistance, the ways in which they implemented the aid often differed significantly from the volunteers' original intentions. With the support of the GVN and USOM, IVS initiated a "pig program," in which volunteers offered local farmers advice on how to raise pigs. Hoping to promote better nutrition among rural inhabitants and develop an export market for pork products, USOM provided farmers with pigs and materials to build concrete pigsties. After arriving in the coastal city of Phan Thiet, DePuy began working on this program. When he visited a nearby village, he was happy to learn that some farmers in the hamlet had benefited from the program. More importantly, he discovered that, on learning of their neighbors' success in raising pigs, many other farmers requested assistance in building their own pigpens. As DePuy optimistically noted to his family and friends: "This is the type of reaction that we want from these programs, because the few stys we can build will do little to help the economy of Viet Nam; but if neighbors will copy neighbors, a multiplied effect will result."[63]

Despite his enthusiasm about the Vietnamese farmers' request to expand the pig program, DePuy quickly realized that local interest in a project did not guarantee its success. More importantly, he learned that the results rarely conformed to the Americans' intentions. Apparently, the farmers accepted the money and cement provided by the program but refused to participate further. Instead of building pigpens, the farmers used the cement and money for other purposes, such as improving their own houses.[64] Similarly, Bob McNeff, who also worked on the pig program, reported that farmers in Phan Rang learned to raise pigs quite successfully but did not want to part with the animals once the time came to sell them. In both cases, the peasants' behavior defeated the purpose of a program intended to help them enter the pork business and increase their profits. Arguing that the farmers involved had been selected from "insecure hamlets," DePuy reasoned that political insurgents had botched the program in an effort to see the GVN- and US-sponsored endeavor fail. He concluded that limiting the program to farmers from "pacified areas" would enhance its chances for success in the future.[65]

DePuy's analysis of why the pig program did not work as planned reveals a flawed assumption common among Americans working in Vietnam at the time. Many Americans could not believe that Vietnamese people might use materials for their own purposes or decline to accept aid workers' advice without also supporting the Communist insurgency. According to this simplistic worldview, which was reinforced by the rhetoric of the Cold War, Vietnamese villages were either insecure or pacified, and all inhabitants acted accordingly by either participating in or subverting US aid projects.[66] In fact, peasants in Vietnam exhibited complex motivations and loyalties that were driven by political and economic concerns as well as social norms and cultural traditions. Even though he initially failed to grasp this dynamic, DePuy eventually took the view that most Vietnamese farmers acted in what they perceived to be the interests of themselves and their families. In the months following his disappointing discovery of the farmers who refused to construct pigsties with the materials they had been given, he visited fifty other hamlets to observe the results of the initiative. He found that most farmers deviated from the official plan in order to build other structures that better met their needs. He also noted that most of these farmers expressed no sympathy for the insurgency. Instead, they showed their appreciation for American assistance in allowing them to improve their lives in ways in which they saw fit.[67]

In some extreme cases, however, Vietnamese peasants simply refused to comply with the aid workers' suggestion. One IVSer referred to the "trying moments" of his job. This volunteer described his frustration over learning that some Vietnamese farmers working at the IVS experimental stations quit early, failed to water certain vegetable plots, and dumped seed lots "ignorantly," thereby ruining that particular batch.[68] Another volunteer confided in his family and friends that most of his efforts had been met with direct opposition from local inhabitants. He explained his belief that such resistance stemmed from the fact that IVS was a "pioneer organization" and that the Vietnamese exhibited a "general mistrust of complicated mechanical devices."[69]

Everett La Rue, who was working on irrigation projects in the drought-prone region of Nha Ho, described how the villagers of one hamlet had been given three water pumps five years earlier. Although inhabitants of this town would have benefited from the pumps, no one had installed them. La Rue gave a nod to practical limitations, conceding that the villagers owned few of the tools and little of the machinery necessary to install the pumps. But he also echoed other volunteers' culturally deterministic explanations by describing peasants' behavior as rooted in tradition and opposed to American-style modernity. He wrote: "In general, the farmers reject improvement because they are used to doing something in a certain manner handed down to them for centuries."[70]

A USOM report from 1960 suggests similar patterns in other parts of the country. According to this report, farmers living in the outskirts of Hue, in Central Vietnam, also resisted innovation and maintained local traditions. For example, peasants in neighboring villages employed vastly different methods for pumping water to irrigate their fields. In one area, farmers relied on foot-operated treadle machines. A few miles away, they used buckets to lift the water by hand. And, several miles farther on, they depended on natural forces—powered by the river, large bamboo water wheels known as *noria* moved water to the fields. Although these farmers were almost certainly aware of their neighbors' irrigation techniques, none of them seemed interested in changing their practices. And, when American aid workers tried to encourage them to adopt more efficient methods for pumping water, they simply refused.[71]

## Agricultural Aid to Ethnic Minorities

In addition to their work with Vietnamese farmers, IVS volunteers attempted to bring agricultural improvements to ethnic minority groups. Working with these communities presented additional challenges. Some minorities had misgivings about the GVN, not only as a result of their historical antagonisms with Vietnamese leaders, but also as a result of Diem's policy of forcefully assimilating minority groups into the central state.[72] Like their Vietnamese neighbors, many ethnic minorities viewed American aid workers with suspicion and hesitated to adopt their advice. In several cases, minority leaders refused to accept IVS assistance or materials because they believed that doing so would cause harm to their communities.

Anthropologists have identified fifty-four distinct minority groups living in Vietnam, and members of these diverse societies speak different languages and have distinct cultural traditions.[73] Many of Vietnam's ethnic minority communities, including the Rhade, Jarai, and Maa groups, live in the Central Highlands.[74] Despite their linguistic and cultural differences, many minority groups display basic similarities in their political organization, religious ceremonial practices, housing construction, and agricultural practices. Historically, these communities engaged in swidden agriculture, also known as slash-and-burn or dry-rice farming, and they supplemented their diets by hunting and gathering as well as by cultivating secondary crops in small kitchen gardens.[75] As a result of their small populations and relative geographic isolation, Vietnam's ethnic minorities enjoyed a great degree of autonomy until the beginning of the twentieth century, though they had been subject to periodic raids by lowland Vietnamese populations in previous centuries. During the twentieth century, French and Japanese administrators attempted to build an anti-Vietnamese coalition with these groups, and later US officials enlisted them in the fight against the Communist insurgency.[76]

In the years following World War II, the South Vietnamese government attempted to incorporate the minorities into the body politic by eliminating many of their traditional practices. With the help of IVS and other American aid organizations, the Vietnamese pursued policies meant to modernize agriculture and animal husbandry in the highlands and settle the minorities into permanent villages.[77] These objectives were based on often-inaccurate assumptions about the minorities' lifeways. Vietnamese officials believed, for example, that they used only dry-rice farming techniques and that all highland groups were nomadic. In fact, many tribes practiced swidden agriculture along the steep mountain slopes as well as wet cultivation in valley areas, and some groups lived in established and permanent villages.[78] The stated objectives of the Social and Economic Council for Southern Highlander Country, established by Emperor Bao Dai in 1952, reveal the biases of Vietnamese officials. Members of this council blamed the widespread conditions of famine and ill health among minorities on "agricultural methods dating from the early history of man."[79]

American policy makers shared, or at least did not question, many of these Vietnamese prejudices. As a result, US agencies assisted the GVN with efforts to modernize minority communities by expanding plantation crops, such as coffee, tea, rubber, rice, and sugar cane, introducing irrigation and electricity, building roads and bridges, and using "scientific therapy" to replace the minorities' reliance on shamans for health matters.[80] However, this state-sponsored crusade proved difficult to accomplish and alienated many ethnic minorities. As a result, American aid workers participating in agricultural-development projects for these communities encountered numerous challenges.

Ted Lingren, an IVS volunteer stationed in the highlands at Bao Loc, attempted to help the neighboring Maa community by introducing vegetable gardens into the area. In mid-1961, several foreign missionaries living near Maa villages asked Lingren and other IVSers to assist the Maa people in creating the vegetable gardens. Lingren agreed, and he prepared to distribute seeds and cuttings, help people start vegetable plots, and build fences to protect domesticated animals. According to Lingren, when local chiefs learned of his plan, they voiced their strong objections. Lingren wrote that these village leaders claimed that introducing new crops would invite "evil spirits" to enter the villages. Despite the chiefs' grave warnings, two villagers decided to plant some sweet potato seeds they had obtained from Lingren. Soon other villagers followed their example. Lingren wrote that, when other villagers saw the success of these new crops, and when it became apparent that introducing sweet potatoes did not provoke retaliation from the spirit world, inhabitants of the Maa villages as well as other minority groups requested comparable assistance for themselves.[81] Lingren never questioned his assumption that Maa leaders were primarily motivated by superstitions. He failed to consider, at least in his letters, whether the local leaders might actually be voicing concrete political concerns, such as apprehension about retaliation from antigovernment insurgents or fear of losing their authority, when they referred to "evil spirits."

Bob Knoerschild, another IVSer doing agricultural extension work with non-Vietnamese groups living in the Central Highlands, also encountered some resistance from the people he intended to help. Knoerschild focused on assisting people who had been recently resettled in permanent villages. In an effort to secure political control over the upland areas of the country, the South Vietnamese government forcibly removed many ethnic minorities from the lands they had traditionally managed and resettled them in newly constructed villages. As a result, they could no longer practice traditional agricultural methods. Knoerschild sought to help people in resettlement villages adjust to their new surroundings by planting family gardens and teaching permanent farming techniques. Stripped of their conventional means of survival, many resettled people willingly accepted IVS assistance and advice, Knoerschild reported. He noted, however, that at least one village chief expressed his reservations owing to fears that "malignant spirits" would accompany new crops and agricultural systems.[82] As in the letter written by Lingren, Knoerschild's report lacks any discussion of the possibility that the local leaders might have used the term *malignant spirits* as a euphemism. In fact, the chief's reference to spirits may have been a veiled attempt to voice concerns about violent retribution against those who cooperated with the GVN and Americans or a general uneasiness about being caught in the middle of Vietnam's civil war.

US technical assistance did not succeed in fundamentally transforming agriculture or improving the basic economic position of most peasants in Vietnam. American agricultural efforts also failed to accomplish a second goal—they did not produce widespread support for the Saigon government. Two key conditions help explain this shortcoming. First, the legacy of colonialism and foreign interference left many Vietnamese suspicious of the intentions of outsiders. Their society's long experience of foreign invasion and occupation shaped their perceptions of the motivations of outsiders and made some wary of accepting assistance from foreigners, even those who claimed to have the best interests of the people in mind. Second, US support for the Diem regime, which implemented numerous unpopular and repressive policies, and their own associations with both governments further limited the aid workers' ability to win the confidence of Vietnamese peasants. Not only did many rural residents question whether the GVN held the interests and well-being of the people in high regard, but many Vietnamese also worried that Diem's administration might quickly be replaced by another.[83] Because of the Saigon government's partnership with the United States, Americans became tainted in the eyes of those Vietnamese who were concerned by either Diem's authoritarian tactics or the GVN's chances of survival.

## The Legacy of Colonialism

As reports from IVSers reveal, Vietnamese farmers responded to many of the American aid workers' suggestions with suspicion and caution. Given their recent experience with colonialism, many people were reluctant or slow to adopt radical changes to their daily lives, especially at the suggestion of a foreigner. The observations of Vietnamese who worked with IVS suggest some of the reasons for the peasants' general lack of enthusiasm in response to the Americans' efforts. In addition, articles written by local journalists and scholars who were concerned with foreign aid to South Vietnam illuminate Vietnamese perceptions regarding the US government and American organizations. Understanding how some Vietnamese people viewed IVS in particular and development assistance more generally provides important insight into ways in which Vietnamese history affected the outcome of US aid.

A letter written in mid-1961 by one of IVS's Vietnamese employees highlights some of the reasons why Vietnamese and ethnic minorities harbored deep suspicions about the intentions of American aid workers. Bui Duong Chi, a twenty-two-year-old student at the time, worked as an interpreter for IVS. In a letter to Don Schmidt, a friend and IVS volunteer stationed in Thap Cham, Chi provided some thoughtful explanations as to why many Vietnamese had developed negative impressions of Americans, even those who worked to improve the lives of rural inhabitants. He began his letter with a highly critical generalization about Vietnamese perceptions of Americans: "To most Vietnamese, who live in towns and big cities, the word 'American' symbolizes a rich man with a head full of race prejudice who locks himself so carefully in his own way of living that it is impossible for other people to approach him or vice versa."[84] Although he admitted that his personal experience of living and working with IVS-ers convinced him that not all Americans were guilty of such a charge, he insisted that there were concrete reasons for many of his neighbors' negative view of American aid workers. According to him, these reasons stemmed both from the population's historical experiences with colonialism and from mistakes made by Americans as well as Vietnamese.

Chi cited Vietnam's recent status as a French colony as the primary obstacle to better relations between IVS volunteers and the local population. The overwhelming "cost" of France's civilizing mission had made it difficult for many Vietnamese families to trust any outsiders, he claimed. With US involvement in the form of "huge aid programs" coming on the heels of the crumbling French Empire, Vietnamese had trouble distinguishing the motivations of the Americans from those of their European predecessors. Chi explained: "People in a deplorable situation unhesitatingly received the help, but bitter experiences the French left behind still keep them suspecting the good will of another 'civilized' country from the West."[85] Most American officials and aid workers never fully grappled with the legacy of French colonialism in Vietnam. Moreover, very few of them seem to have recognized any parallels between their own efforts and the earlier French colonial project.

In addition to the lasting effects of colonialism, Chi highlighted some of the other obstacles that prevented Vietnamese from being completely open to American assistance. He referred to the "striking difference" in the standard of living of most Vietnamese and the Americans who lived in the country, arguing that such a disparity made mutual understanding or cooperation nearly impossible. To make matters worse, a small group of Vietnamese benefited disproportionately from US economic aid, thus exacerbating inequalities within Vietnamese society. Chi believed that this socioeconomic divide must be bridged, writing: "Something must be done or it will be an unbearable thing to be poor with some rich around [*sic*] and a sin to be rich amidst poverty." According to him, the way in which US aid programs were implemented and the timing of their introduction to South Vietnam created the impression among many that Americans were more concerned with the security of the United States than with helping underdeveloped regions of the world. As a result, many Vietnamese questioned the motivations and loyalties of aid workers and accepted their advice with caution, often for practical or political reasons. This interpretation of the situation was an astute and accurate assessment of the US government's inclination to provide far greater amounts of military than economic aid to Vietnam, even in the years before the war. Finally, Chi argued that both Americans and Vietnamese were guilty of casting each other's societies in a negative light that was informed by gossip and racial prejudices.[86]

Despite the pessimistic tone of his letter to Schmidt, Chi included a more hopeful postscript in which he referred to his "deep sympathy toward American people" and his "fierce national pride." He shared his wish that Americans and Vietnamese might arrive at a cultural understanding. In his own reflections on the letter, Schmidt concluded that Chi touched on some "vital points . . . as to why the U.S. is not making more rapid progress in its struggle against Communism despite our expenditures of millions of dollars in foreign aid."[87]

Bui Duong Chi's explanations for Vietnamese attitudes regarding US economic aid dovetail with the arguments of some prominent intellectuals and journalists who were writing at the time. Contributors to Vietnamese magazines and journals frequently discussed the dilemma posed by South Vietnam's willingness to accept foreign aid and its simultaneous struggle to preserve its independence. Vietnamese economists and other scholars published articles brimming with nationalistic rhetoric. They argued that the survival of their nation depended on South Vietnam's ability to develop economically and raise the standard of living of the country's inhabitants. However, they also maintained that progress should never be considered a higher priority than economic and political independence from foreign governments as well as the Communist Party.

A number of articles appearing between 1957 and 1959 in *Phong Thuong Mai,* a journal concerned with economics and business that was published in Saigon, highlighted Vietnamese apprehensions regarding the problems associated with receiving foreign assistance.[88] For example, in an article titled "The Problem of Foreign Aid with Respect to Economic Independence," the journalist Ky Tam argued that the recent history of European colonization had dampened the national spirit, damaged the population's dignity, and led to "extreme backwardness" in Vietnam's economic and political systems. Writing at the height of the Cold War and in the midst of an international process of decolonization, Tam referred to a new world order in which all previous relations between East and West had been replaced. In this evolving climate, Asian nations that had defeated the "yoke of slavery" aspired to greater international cooperation, while more powerful and wealthy countries looked for ways to attend to the needs of the world's poorest people and to bolster the "psychology of a new Asia."[89]

In addition to overcoming these obstacles, Tam argued, the South Vietnamese government also faced another challenge—preventing its own collapse in the face of national reunification under a Communist flag. Tam's anti-Communist critique warned that South Vietnamese leaders needed to act quickly to establish the conditions for a vibrant economy and a democratic government in order to avoid becoming a casualty of the "dictatorial designs" of the revolution. In his estimation, the GVN required a strong leader at its helm to "defend peace without sacrificing independence and implement progress in economics without sacrificing the essential freedoms of our children." Tam believed that South Vietnam had no choice but to accept foreign aid. According to him, the basic objective of foreign assistance should be to promote self-reliance and independence in countries that had recently been decolonized. He also linked foreign aid with the fundamental competition between North and South Vietnam. Because the regime in Hanoi received money and materials from a number of Communist countries, the GVN also needed external assistance in order to raise living standards and participate in the capitalist market system. Tam explained that only with these economic developments in place could South Vietnam resist the type of political chaos that would threaten its sovereignty.[90]

Another article that appeared in *Phong Thuong Mai* several months later also predicted dire consequences if South Vietnam did not develop economically. However, in this article, titled "Change Will Come to Our

Economy," Nhut Moc argued that relying on foreign assistance would not help the country. Instead, he suggested that financial and material aid from outside governments had the overall effect of swamping South Vietnam's markets with products that few people could afford. He claimed that, as long as Vietnam's economy remained weak and there were not enough consumers for all the goods imported into the country, aid programs that focused on stimulating growth by increasing imports would prove unsuccessful.[91] Many prominent non-Vietnamese journalists and scholars echoed Moc's critique at the time and in subsequent years.[92]

Moc's basic argument was that Vietnam must reverse its trade imbalance in order to achieve a healthy economy. Rather than concentrate on acquiring new products through a commercial system heavily weighted toward imports, Moc suggested that the GVN promote an economic program based on augmenting South Vietnam's exports. He argued that the country had many potential but previously untapped export commodities. For example, it produced duck eggs, coconut oil, cinnamon, scrap iron, and rice in excess and could export these goods. If the basis for economic growth shifted to exports, people would earn more money and would not be dependent on the government to provide as many goods and services. In Moc's estimation, foreign aid passed through the hands of the South Vietnamese leadership but rarely reached those in need. As a result, aid programs strengthened and enriched the central government but did little to improve the standard of living or increase the purchasing power of the majority of South Vietnam's citizens.[93]

Although Nhut Moc's critique of foreign aid specifically attacked the American Commercial Import Program (CIP), many of his arguments help explain Vietnamese attitudes about other programs and foreign assistance more generally.[94] His argument that foreign assistance seldom benefited the general population, usually contributing only to the wealth and power of the government, reflected the observations of Vietnamese as well as American aid workers. According to the scholar George Kahin, between 1955 and 1958 at least 80 percent of US economic aid to South Vietnam was channeled through the CIP, which provided luxury consumer goods for a small but growing middle class.[95] Several IVSers recognized the problem inherent to the import program and voiced their frustration that economic aid did not always reach the most distressed areas of the country or the most vulnerable populations.[96]

More importantly, in his call for economic independence and self-reliance, Moc offered an explanation for the actions and behavior of many Vietnamese families and communities that viewed American assistance with suspicion. Many people in rural Vietnam viewed outside intervention, whether it came from the GVN or a foreign government, as an encroachment on their autonomy and an impediment to their economic survival. As one IVSer concluded, most Vietnamese communities closely guarded their independence, and peasants exhibited "little or no feeling of debt or loyalty to the Republic government."[97] Even those individuals or villages that benefited from development assistance were hesitant to credit the government for their improved standard of living. As long as the majority of Vietnamese remained fiercely committed to self-reliance, local autonomy, and economic self-sufficiency, it would prove difficult for any group perceived as representing outside interests to convince the people that they owed their allegiance to the nation of South Vietnam or a foreign power.

## "The Political Burden of Being American"

American aid workers' relationship with the unpopular Saigon government likely proved even more damaging than did their status as foreigners. Many Vietnamese harbored a profound distrust of the GVN, at least partially as a result of its heavy-handed methods for eliminating political opposition and dealing with insecurity in rural areas. Some Americans understood this dynamic. As a State Department memo from 1960 explained, Vietnamese peasants held a "traditional view of the government as something to be feared and avoided." Theodore Heavner, the American consul at Hue and the author of this report, based his account on his experience traveling throughout the countryside of Central Vietnam and having conversations with individuals "at all levels of CVN [Central Vietnamese] society" during the previous two years. According to Heavner, the "communist style control and indoctrination techniques" utilized by the GVN alienated the rural population and overshadowed any projects designed to address the peasants' economic problems.[98] Another State Department report from 1960 suggests that GVN policies negatively affected agricultural production. American observers blamed a sharp decline in farm productivity and income in some areas on the "harsh, if not brutal, tactics of security personnel in ferreting out Communists" as well as the policy of forcing peasants to construct *agrovilles*.[99]

Many American aid workers had difficulty maintaining a balance between their obligations to the GVN and those to the Vietnamese population. USOM and IVS advisers were supposed to cooperate with officials at South Vietnam's Ministry of Rural Affairs and implement GVN-sponsored programs. However, they often found Vietnamese officials at the national and local levels to be intransigent and trying partners, and they disagreed with some projects favored by the palace. For example, many American aid workers objected to Diem's emphasis on resettlement and the development of unused lands as opposed to land-reform measures. As a result of such disagreements, in late 1957 USOM temporarily suspended aid to the Land Development Division, which was one of Diem's pet projects. The following year, it permanently cut off assistance to the program.[100] USOM's decision reflected fundamental differences in the American and GVN views on land, labor, and social organization.

As a result of these ideological differences as well as the perceived superiority of their approach, American aid workers were quick to criticize South Vietnamese officials. In his end-of-tour report, the USOM adviser Richard Pringle complained about the ways in which the "reactionary attitudes" of GVN officials had handicapped agricultural-development work. In particular, Pringle criticized the "prevalent industrial/urban preference in general [GVN] policies" and argued that rural-development projects might serve as an important counterweight to the Saigon regime's favoritism toward urban dwellers.[101]

Similarly, the IVSer Ray Borton recalled that many local Vietnamese administrators demonstrated an unwillingness to assume responsibility for development projects. According to Borton, American aid workers frequently had trouble obtaining money, equipment, and machinery promised to them by the GVN because Vietnamese officials believed that, if they held on to their own resources, the US government would eventually provide whatever the aid workers needed. Through his interactions with provincial-level representatives of the Ministry of Rural Affairs, Borton realized that few Vietnamese wanted to become too closely associated with the South Vietnamese government. Apparently, even public officials working at the provincial and village levels understood the GVN's unpopularity and sensed that the regime in Saigon had a tenuous hold on power.

As a result, they sought to remain flexible and keep their options open in case another government replaced the current one. Following their lead, Borton tried to distinguish himself from the US government and military forces. He argued that, even in rural areas, Vietnamese people were "always suspicious" of Americans because of the perception that the US government supported the unpopular administration in Saigon.[102]

The dilemma of the aid workers' association with government policies was compounded for the IVS volunteers, who tried to distinguish themselves not only from the GVN but also from the US government. As Borton later explained, IVSers engaged in a "constant discussion of the philosophical problem of their dependence on the U.S. government." According to Borton, no volunteer wanted to be associated with American government programs or be seen by the Vietnamese population as an employee of the US government. He claimed that many volunteers understood that Vietnamese harbored feelings of mistrust and resentment toward the South Vietnamese regime and that the IVSers' connection with either the GVN or the government's American supporters would adversely affect their relationships with the people they were trying to help.[103]

Many volunteers recognized the importance of demonstrating to their Vietnamese neighbors that IVS was different from the US government and other American organizations. The IVSers argued that it would be easier to earn the population's trust if they resided in Vietnamese communities and maintained modest lifestyles. Most volunteers considered securing the confidence of local people to be a prerequisite for implementing aid projects. Reflecting on this assumption soon after his arrival, one volunteer wrote: "Our associations with the Vietnamese people, other than those with whom we work, will have in some way not clear to me, an important effect on the way I do my job and how successful I am at it."[104] Some volunteers claimed to see tangible results from their decision to distance themselves from other American agencies. According to Harvey Neese, the Vietnamese tended to regard IVS more favorably than they did USOM or other American organizations because its volunteers had strong personal relations with the local communities.[105]

When offered the opportunity to live in a residence owned by the US government or share a house with non-IVS Americans, many volunteers declined. For example, one small group of IVSers chose to move out of the more comfortable USOM housing and settle in a local house because they felt that doing so would improve their relations with the community. Another volunteer, Charles Frances Lay, complained to his family and friends when American officials advised that, owing to deteriorating security conditions, his IVS team should move into the regional US military compound. Lay, who was stationed in the Central Highlands town of Ban Me Thuot, conceded that the Military Assistance and Advisory Group (MAAG) house was more comfortable than were his previous arrangements. However, he understood that living there prevented him from having daily contact with the Vietnamese community. Shortly after moving in, he decided to leave the compound and find his own house where his Vietnamese friends and neighbors could visit him in the evenings and on weekends.[106]

In retrospect, many volunteers saw their organization's complicated and dependent relationship with both the American and the South Vietnamese governments as a central cause of the failure of their programs. After completing their service in Vietnam, a few former volunteers documented their experiences in articles and books describing the fundamental problems that arose from IVS's association with the US government. In their personal account, *Vietnam: The Unheard Voices,* Don Luce and John Sommer argued that the volunteers found themselves "caught in the middle" between their desire to help the people of Vietnam and their connections with the US government. Acutely aware of the "political burden of being American," IVSers tried to "preserve a separate identity" in the eyes of many Vietnamese but found this challenge nearly impossible. According to Luce and Sommer: "Even those Vietnamese who did appreciate the essentially neutral role of the IVS volunteer were afraid that close association would compromise them in their relations with other Vietnamese."[107] Such observations suggest that many rural inhabitants feared the possibility of retribution by antigovernment insurgents if they appeared to support the GVN or American involvement in their country. Ultimately, the volunteers' inability to escape their connection with the US government and the Diem regime hampered their ability to help Vietnam's rural communities.

## Political Instability and Violence

Although other significant problems limited the effectiveness of American agricultural efforts, political unrest and violence throughout the countryside gradually came to overshadow all other challenges to development assistance in rural areas of Vietnam. As the antigovernment insurgency coalesced and incidents of violence increased during the final years of the 1950s and at the beginning of the following decade, it became nearly impossible for agricultural advisers to perform their work. The civil war between the GVN and antigovernment forces, which by late 1960 had coalesced under the leadership of the National Liberation Front (NLF), had a dramatic impact on the lives of Vietnamese peasants as well as American aid workers.[108] Throughout his tenure, President Diem maintained a relatively secure hold on South Vietnam's major cities. However, as it became apparent that the reunification of Vietnam would not be achieved through political means, the NLF launched an intensified campaign in the smaller towns and rural areas of the country. This campaign included political assassinations, the intimidation of rural inhabitants, and skirmishes between the South Vietnamese armed forces and the NLF.[109] Diem's policies only reinforced the instability. As his regime instituted more repressive measures for controlling the rural population, Vietnamese peasants increasingly lent their support to antigovernment forces.[110]

By the early 1960s, the period of relative calm that most Americans had described in the first few years of American involvement in Vietnam had evaporated.[111] In 1959, to deal with the growing insurgency, Diem's regime introduced two particularly repressive and unpopular policies: the agroville program, which forcibly relocated rural Vietnamese into "pacified" villages, and Law 10/59, which required anyone accused of crimes against the state to be tried by a military tribunal without the right of appeal.[112] Shortly after those policies took effect, the North Vietnamese government officially recognized and pledged to support an armed insurgency in the South. Finally, in December 1960, the antigovernment insurgents announced the creation of the NLF, which represented the first organized resistance to the GVN, and vowed to topple Diem's regime.[113]

The political unrest in rural areas had a profound effect on agricultural production. As early as 1957, a USOM adviser reported that insecurity in the countryside was alienating the peasantry and contributing to poor rice production. USOM's Milton Esman placed much of the blame on the GVN-sponsored Self Defense Corps, which was charged with keeping the peace in rural areas. He described the Self Defense Corps as "undisciplined rabble, which uses its weapons to terrorize and highjack the peasantry, creating in effect the very insecurity which it is designed to combat."[114] Another American report issued in 1960 linked a decline in farm productivity with insurgent activity as well as GVN policies for combating the insurgency.[115] And a USOM report from 1963 painted a similar picture. According to the report's author, who had visited the Mekong delta province of Ba Xuyen: "A rice co-op . . . was obviously suffering in its activities from the ramifications of VC [NLF] activities. Interestingly a Chinese-owned mill and rice wine distillery next door to the co-op was less so. His greater flexibility, political as well as financial, allowed him to still carry on a substantial though greatly reduced business."[116]

Because they lived and worked predominantly in rural areas, agricultural aid workers had firsthand knowledge of the effects of the burgeoning civil war. The explosive nature of the security situation in rural parts of Vietnam restricted their access to certain areas of the country and limited their ability to implement new projects. They could not extend their programs to villages or areas that were deemed unsafe or unstable. Some IVS-ers had to move to different stations and abandon their projects altogether because of the escalating conflict. Still others continued their work at IVS agricultural stations but had to make some lifestyle changes in order to better protect themselves from the violence plaguing the region.

In 1960, IVS transferred Verle Lanier and Floyd Burrill out of My Tho, one of the largest towns in the Mekong delta, because of concern for their safety. Lanier and Burrill worked at the My Tho rice experimentation station, where they tried to develop new strains of rice and increase the production of delta area rice farms. Prior to his transfer in late 1960, Lanier had been stationed in My Tho for over a year and wrote to his family and friends on several occasions about the success of aid programs in the region and the progress being made by many local rice farmers. However, when suspected NLF sympathizers burned down a warehouse at the My Tho station, the IVS leadership reassigned him to the IVS team in Saigon and transferred Burrill to the Hung Loc crops station. As Lanier wrote on January 17, 1961, several weeks after his transfer: "The peaceful serenity of the rice paddy and the quiet dignity of the tropical jungle of South Vietnam has [sic] been encroached upon by gunfire in recent months."[117]

Although the Mekong delta was a particular hotbed of antigovernment activity, political violence erupted in other areas of South Vietnam as well. In the weeks leading up to the April 9, 1961, presidential election, American and Vietnamese officials advised tighter security in several of the areas where IVSers worked. Anticipating general unrest and the possibility of NLF attacks, the provincial chief of Hung Loc recommended that volunteers in the region travel to the experimental station only two or three times per week and refrain from staying overnight, as they had done in the past. However, IVS did not want to take any chances. The organization temporarily moved its volunteers from the Hung Loc station to Saigon or Ban Me Thuot, where the men assisted with other projects during their monthlong stay.[118]

Even though Ban Me Thuot appeared safer for Americans, that outpost in the Central Highlands had been threatened by guerilla activity six months earlier. As a result of a steady increase in attacks and raids in the area, in October 1960 the IVS team moved off its farm and into the MAAG residence. Although the volunteers initially thought that the arrangements would be temporary and they would soon be able to return to the farm, it became apparent that hostilities would continue and they would be more secure living closer to the military unit. They enjoyed the more luxurious conditions at the MAAG house, but they eventually decided that, in the words of one volunteer, they "couldn't do an effective job if the local people thought [they] were connected with the military."[119] The group settled for a compromise, moving out of the MAAG residence and into a house closer to the center of town that was more easily secured than the farm.

Violence in the countryside not only forced some volunteers to relocate but also limited their ability to reach people living in outlying villages. As political instability intensified, Bob Knoerschild found it nearly impossible to continue providing assistance to ethnic minority groups that had previously shown interest in IVS projects. Beginning in late 1961, Knoerschild and other volunteers working in Bao Loc established an agricultural extension program that allowed them to work with various Maa communities. Knoerschild traveled to some Maa villages that were located in remote areas of the Central Highlands to help the villagers with their cultivation of cacao. However, he lamented that after his initial trips he could not return because, in his words, "the area is infested with Communist guerillas" and the Maa people had fled to resettlement areas.

According to him, the Communist insurgency and civil war prevented ethnic minority groups from practicing traditional forms of agriculture, notably swidden farming, thereby making it much more difficult for them to survive and remain on their ancestral lands.[120] Another volunteer, who had been in Vietnam for only a few weeks at the time, observed: "We are held back in our effectiveness by two apparent factors: our range of travel which is limited by uncertain security and our numbers which are at present twenty one."[121]

As the war escalated, there was a fundamental shift in the objectives of American nation building in general and agricultural-development programs in particular. While these programs had always revolved around winning hearts and minds and cultivating support for Diem, early efforts focused on increasing agricultural production and improving the lives of Vietnamese farmers. By the early 1960s, however, the explicit objective of all technical assistance had become defeating the insurgency. In a reflection of the priority that US policy makers placed on winning the military struggle, in 1962 all American agricultural-development activities had been reorganized and classified under the broader category of counterinsurgency programs. As a result, the focus of American aid workers explicitly shifted from providing technical assistance in agriculture to supporting the political and military campaign of the US and South Vietnamese governments. USOM officials considered agricultural-development work valuable in that it involved "activities which can contribute to the counterinsurgency military operations and psychological warfare."[122] As a report from 1964 explained: "The emphasis of [agricultural] project assistance programs is on counterinsurgency and the principal objective is to aid the GVN in its effort to gain the support of the rural people of Vietnam."[123] In the end, the civil war in South Vietnam not only altered the work of American advisers but also rendered irrelevant any of the progress they had made in modernizing agriculture in Vietnam. As a 1963 USOM report concluded: "The lack of security continues to be the number one deterrent to a more effective agriculture program for Vietnam."[124]

## Conclusions

When considered separately, any of the factors limiting agricultural-development efforts in South Vietnam appear daunting. In many cases, the American aid workers' insistence on introducing new and sometimes inappropriate methods, technologies, and products did not satisfy the material needs or cultural and political interests of the Vietnamese population. Overcoming peasants' distrust and their fear that Americans had imperial designs for their country would have been difficult, if not impossible, for any group of foreigners, particularly coming on the heels of French colonial exploitation. However, the close relationship between the US government and the GVN ensured that the Vietnamese would have trouble distinguishing the aid workers' goals from broader, often unpopular policies. Finally, as the military conflict escalated, not only did it become more difficult for agricultural advisers to travel throughout the country and work with local people; it also became more dangerous for farmers in Vietnam to trust the Americans and embrace their programs openly.

Agricultural aid workers, and especially the IVS volunteers, saw firsthand the destructive effects of GVN and US government policies. They witnessed the groundswell of public opinion turning against the South Vietnamese state and its American sponsors. Perhaps more than any other Americans in Vietnam at the time, they were in a position to appreciate the challenges to South Vietnam's survival and suggest alternative strategies for helping rural populations and winning the battle for hearts and minds. Unfortunately, too many aid workers were blinded by a sense of righteousness with respect to their cause and approach, and US policy makers never sought to learn from the experiences of these young men. Instead, American officials continued to ignore the needs and demands of the population, support unpopular and repressive regimes in Saigon, and accelerate the path to war by relying on military solutions to economic problems and political unrest.

# 4

# Policing the Insurgency

## Police Administration and Internal Security in South Vietnam

> History teaches us that soldiers make poor police officers. As a rule, civilians dislike being controlled by the military.
>
> —Jack Ryan (1957)

When a small group of police experts from Michigan State University (MSU) arrived in Saigon in late 1955, they found general instability throughout the country, a new government that enjoyed only a tenuous hold on power, and Vietnamese security forces in poor condition. In December 1955, Ton That Trach, the director general of South Vietnam's civil guard, informed the head of Ngo Dinh Diem's cabinet that the country's security was completely lacking in all areas. Trach argued that, in order to maintain control over the civilian population, the country's police forces desperately needed weapons, equipment, communications materials, and assistance in dealing with traffic problems in the overcrowded cities. Although Trach had originally solicited support from the US military advisory group, Vietnam's officials turned instead to the civilian MSU team for assistance in these four key areas.[1] This decision reflected the early confidence South Vietnamese and American policy makers had in nonmilitary modernization efforts, and it reveals the high value they placed on maintaining stability and defending the new state.

In the following years, American and Vietnamese nation builders devoted tremendous resources and energy to strengthening South Vietnam's military and police forces. Between 1955 and the early 1960s, 80 percent of US aid money financed security projects in South Vietnam, and a significant portion of the remaining funds subsidized communications, transportation, and infrastructure programs that indirectly contributed to military or police efforts.[2] This commitment underscores the US government's focus on shielding Diem's regime from political or military threats from the earliest years of American intervention. During the first few years of South Vietnam's existence, MSU played the largest role of any American group in aiding civilian law enforcement.[3] The university's efforts to professionalize and modernize the country's police forces met with disappointment and constituted a major failure in US nation-building policy.

Members of the MSU police administration team believed that they could help Diem consolidate his control over South Vietnam by improving security and introducing Western-style, democratic law enforcement organizations to the country. Like their colleagues in public administration, however, participants in MSU's police team demonstrated unwavering confidence in their expertise and a willful blindness to the political conditions in Vietnam. Civilian police advisers were unrealistic about Diem's weaknesses, which derived from his autocratic and often brutal ruling style and his inability to overcome the general perception that his regime lacked legitimacy. Police team members also underestimated the strength and nature of the antigovernment insurgency. Finally, they disregarded the fact that many of their suggestions bore little relevance to the actual political and military problems facing the Government of Vietnam (GVN). The case of technical assistance in police administration presents one of the most striking examples of how US modernization efforts were divorced from reality and how the overtly political nature of the aid programs limited their effectiveness. As a result of their fundamental misunderstanding of the core problem facing Diem—the fact that most people did not support the basic aims of his government—the police team recommended reforms that proved inappropriate and insufficient in light of the vehement opposition to the GVN. By the early 1960s, South Vietnamese officials had largely abandoned modernization efforts in the field of law enforcement in favor of a more confrontational, military response to the widespread insurrection.

## MSU's Diagnosis

The MSU group and other American advisers identified a number of key problems that they believed limited the effectiveness of South Vietnamese law enforcement and contributed to poor internal security. First, they noted the basic dearth of supplies and infrastructure, including an underdeveloped and decentralized police communications system. Second, they believed that the lack of coordination or clear distinction between the country's various law enforcement organizations caused confusion and inefficiency while heightening bureaucratic rivalries. Finally, they considered the strained relations between police and the general population not only detrimental to law enforcement but also a contributing factor in the rise of the insurgency. However, their diagnosis of the shortcomings failed to address the simple yet obvious problem facing police in South Vietnam—they functioned in service of a state that not only lacked popular support but also relied on law enforcement organizations to implement repressive policies.

In order to remedy the problems they identified, American police advisers called for significant aid in the form of weapons and communications equipment as well as funding for infrastructure projects throughout the country. They also provided training opportunities for policemen, both in Vietnam and in the United States. American aid workers firmly argued that enhanced training presented one of the best opportunities for improving poor police-community relations. Finally, the MSU team, in particular, emphasized the need for a new organizational structure to eliminate overlapping responsibilities and reduce rivalries among the various law enforcement organizations in South Vietnam.

But advisers from MSU and their allies in other aid groups faced staunch opposition. Not only did officials in the GVN reject many of their ideas, but US military personnel also disagreed with their prescription for improving South Vietnam's internal security. In fact, American efforts to aid South Vietnam's police forces exposed two distinct, and not necessarily compatible, approaches to nation building that the United States undertook simultaneously. The first of these relied on short-term funding packages and emphasized military solutions to internal security problems. The second took a broader view of the role of American intervention and focused on long-term economic, political, and social development under the guise of modernization. The story of American technical assistance to South Vietnam's police forces, and especially the crisis over the civil guard, reveals the tension between those two approaches and helps explain how proponents of the military course eventually won.

The MSU group's seven-year tenure in South Vietnam would result in few measurable achievements and little lasting influence on Vietnamese civil defense forces. The police team's shortcomings derived primarily from its members' failure to understand that better police training, institutional reorganization, and the creation of technologically advanced crime laboratories would not address South Vietnam's fundamental political and military problems. The conflicting visions offered by the MSU advisers and South Vietnamese officials regarding the role that police should play in modern nation-states, as well as disagreements between the MSU group and American military leaders, served to weaken further the university team's efforts. These disputes alienated MSU from the central authorities in Vietnam. Ultimately, the MSU police advisers would find themselves marginalized by the more powerful forces in the South Vietnamese and American governments and unable to reverse the rising tide of political violence in the country.

## Instability in South Vietnam and the MSU Police Team

Throughout his eight-year tenure as South Vietnam's leader, Diem placed a high priority on expunging all political opposition and maintaining absolute control over law enforcement organizations. This was partly a response to the fact that his government had been under siege from its earliest days. He initially focused on destroying a number of politicoreligious organizations and other opposition groups that were jockeying for control over the new nation. These groups included the Binh Xuyen, a crime syndicate that had dominated the Saigon police for years. During his first year in power, Diem crushed the sects by waging a full-blown military campaign against them in the streets of Saigon. He relied on American weapons and assistance from US counterinsurgency specialists. Although he and his American supporters proclaimed the rival groups to have been defeated, members of these organizations continued to challenge his government throughout the second half of the 1950s. In the wake of these battles, as the GVN struggled to solidify its authority over its political opponents and local law enforcement, Diem and his brothers focused on developing the capabilities of the police. In doing so, they hoped not only to improve internal security but also to balance the power of the army with strong civilian law enforcement organizations.[4]

Although an organized antigovernment insurgency did not coalesce until roughly five years after he came to power, Diem treated internal security as a grave and pressing issue from the beginning of his tenure.[5] His brothers, Ngo Dinh Nhu and Ngo Dinh Can, created and managed the Can Lao Nhan Vi Cach Mang Dang (Personalist Labor Revolutionary Party), which served as a central, if somewhat shadowy, institution in the South Vietnamese government. Described by one historian as a "state within a state," operating behind the guise of the GVN, the Can Lao depended on an intricate web of informants throughout the country to identify and apprehend suspected Communist guerillas as well as any individuals associated with political opposition to the central government.[6] In addition, Diem focused on converting the security forces organized by the French colonial administration into law enforcement organizations that he could control. He also sought to rebuild Vietnam's infrastructure, which had been badly damaged during the years of war against the French. Doing so would allow for the transport of security forces and government access to remote areas of the country.[7]

Although American policy makers did not always approve of Diem's authoritarian tactics, the US government proved a willing accomplice to his efforts to consolidate his control over both South Vietnam's police forces and its population. On the basis of the assumption that military aid and technical assistance in civil law enforcement could bolster his regime long enough for the GVN to cultivate popular support and ensure the survival of South Vietnam, American officials assigned an array of organizations to help Diem strengthen the country's defense and police forces. In addition to the MSU group, these organizations included the US Military Advisory Assistance Group (MAAG) and the US Operations Mission (USOM).

Although the US government directed the bulk of its aid to financing, training, and advising South Vietnam's military, American and GVN officials concluded that the country's police forces also required assistance. Diem, his brothers, and the GVN's interior minister believed that Vietnam's police lacked sufficient training and that the MSU group should direct its energies toward practical instruction for all the Republic of Vietnam's law enforcement agencies.[8] Representatives from several American agencies, including the US State Department, MAAG, and USOM, initially agreed with the Vietnamese leadership that civilian organizations also needed support and that "civil internal security" should be a top priority in the country.[9] The MSU group was a logical choice to aid South Vietnam's police, given the strength of the university's own Police Administration Department in East Lansing, its commitment to providing the GVN with technical assistance in public administration, and the friendship and political connections between Diem and Wesley Fishel, a young but influential professor in the university's Political Science Department.

The majority of participants in MSU's police team came to the program from various American law enforcement agencies rather than from MSU or other universities. Arthur Brandstatter, the chairman of MSU's on campus Police Administration Department, worked from East Lansing as the campus consultant for the police section of the Vietnam Project and spent little time in Vietnam during the tenure of the program.[10] Jack Ryan, a former FBI agent who served as deputy and later chief of the Vietnam Project's police team, also hailed from MSU's campus, where he taught police administration. Otherwise, most police advisers for the Vietnam Project came from law enforcement organizations in Michigan and other parts of the United States. For example, Howard Hoyt, the first leader of the team, was the former police chief of Kalamazoo, Michigan. Richard Rogers had been chief of the Midland, Michigan, police department, Gilbert Shelby had served as a Detroit police officer, and Corey Diamond had worked as a fingerprint expert for Michigan's state police force. Other participants came from the New York State Department of Civil Service, the Federal Civil Defense Administration, and the CIA.[11]

Throughout its time in Vietnam, the MSU police team contained a small group of CIA agents embedded within its ranks. These agents were assigned to advise and train Vietnamese police in counterespionage tactics, an area in which the MSU group had little experience or expertise. In theory, the CIA unit was forbidden from conducting its own intelligence; however, it is highly unlikely that the agents actually abided by this restriction.[12] This type of arrangement, in which the CIA used nongovernment organizations to obscure the activities of its agents, occurred frequently during the Cold War. According to the scholar Michael McClintock:

"The CIA retained its normal use of police programs as cover for its own advisory personnel and skewed the overall impact of Public Safety by far toward the political police side of law enforcement [in South Vietnam]."[13] The presence of the CIA contingent within MSU ranks, which caused concern among university advisers and their Vietnamese contacts, became an increasingly contentious issue as time passed. The link between the CIA and MSU not only fueled tensions within the university group but also appeared hypocritical, given the Americans' appeals for an open, democratic system of law enforcement in Vietnam. In addition, MSU's connection with the CIA revealed the minimal amount of autonomy that MSU advisers actually enjoyed.

During the first few years of Diem's rule, American advisers were divided over whether Vietnam's police should fall under the jurisdiction of civilian administrators or military authorities. These competing visions derived from their proponents' divergent assumptions about the nature and root causes of the problems facing Diem's regime as well as opposing views about the most effective method for handling political opposition. Completely overlooking the political roots of Diem's difficulties, members of the MSU team believed that the GVN's primary challenge consisted of a widespread lack of confidence in civilian police forces and the government. They also concluded that outdated, inefficient systems limited the effectiveness of South Vietnam's police. As a result of these assumptions, they thought that they could help Diem garner popular support and consolidate his control over the country by improving basic security and introducing law enforcement organizations that were based on American models and techniques.[14] They advocated reforming South Vietnam's police through increased training, a structural reorganization of security forces, and the introduction of modern scientific identification methods. They argued that a modern state needed police who were subject to and charged with upholding a system of laws. They insisted above all that South Vietnam's police operate with transparency as civilian law enforcement organizations.

Civilian aid workers at USOM generally agreed with the MSU advisers' view on the role of police in a democratic society and their prescription for dealing with internal security issues in South Vietnam. Internal USOM documents from the late 1950s suggest that employees of the aid agency harbored significant concerns regarding Washington's overemphasis on military assistance to the GVN. USOM called for increased nonmilitary funding to support long-term economic development and promote financial stability in Vietnam. As a memo detailing funding priorities for the 1957 fiscal year explained, the US government's policy of favoring military and security aid could have disastrous effects on important, nonmilitary projects designed to strengthen the South Vietnamese state: "The result would be an adequate security force but a strained economic situation, without any near-term prospect of substantial increase in Vietnam's capacity for self-support."[15]

Even as late as 1964, after USOM's Public Safety Division (PSD) had shifted away from many of the recommendations that the MSU group championed in earlier years, the aid agency continued to argue for a clear distinction between civilian law enforcement organizations and the military. In USOM's "National Police Plan for Vietnam, March 1964," Frank Walton, the PSD chief, explained the agency's view of the proper role of police in society. He described the basic goal of police as "attack[ing] conditions which tend to cause [the population] not to support the constituted government": "*Foremost among the measures which must be taken is the provision of security and protection to the citizen.*" Walton was critical of the fact that "police operations today, particularly in emerging countries, bear considerable resemblance to military operations" in their tactics, logistics, intelligence gathering, and communications systems. He emphasized the differences between civilian law enforcement and military action, noting that police work is ongoing while military engagements are temporary and occur during a period of warfare or crisis. He also argued that police officers should be local figures who were intimately familiar with the population, politics, and terrain. He concluded that the police should be representatives "*of* the people; responsive *to* the people."[16]

South Vietnamese leaders offered a radically different prescription for how the police should operate. Diem's cohort saw its authority threatened by both internal and external forces. They also worried about the prospect that American policy makers might suddenly decide to withdraw US support, on which the regime depended for its survival. At the same time, Diem understood the negative political and psychological implications of his dependence on American aid. He did not want to leave himself open to accusations that he had simply replaced French colonialism with American imperialism. As a staunch nationalist who was aware of the general anti-imperial sentiment in Vietnam, he was loath to appear beholden to the United States.

Because of their insecure position in this precarious situation, GVN officials attempted to steer a course in which they established and maintained absolute control. They promoted a vision of the police as a paramilitary organization, charged with eliminating all opposition to the central state as well as serving as a counterweight to the army.[17] Diem was determined to remain in power, and he often relied on force to demonstrate the legitimacy of his regime. Although he sometimes compromised when it appeared that the United States might reduce funding for the aid package to South Vietnam, he frequently insisted on charting his own path, and he demonstrated little patience for procedures that might limit his authority. He demanded that law enforcement officers comply with his orders rather than with legal codes outside his control. Finally, he and his brothers contended that Vietnam needed a tough military approach to maintain security and defeat what they simplistically described as a Communist insurgency that was directed and controlled solely by officials in Hanoi.[18]

American aid workers in South Vietnam frequently registered their frustration with and disapproval of the GVN's approach to internal security and policing. In an August 1960 report for USOM, William Ellis argued that Diem's authoritarian tactics were counterproductive in dealing with the threat of insurgency, writing: "Diem's suppression of legitimate political opposition is only indicative of his general reaction to the current security crisis." Ellis also explained the direct connections between popular dissatisfaction with the GVN and the growing insurgency: "[Diem] has not adequately appreciated that the security problem breeds on discontent and that the communists are as much a resultant as a prime cause."[19]

Unlike most aid workers from USOM and MSU, the American military establishment generally supported Diem's approach for dealing with internal security in South Vietnam. American military leaders and many CIA operatives argued that South Vietnam's police and military forces should overlap. Edward Lansdale, a CIA agent who had assisted right-wing leaders in defeating the antigovernment Huk insurgency in the Philippines a few years earlier, tried to persuade his close friend Diem of the wisdom of this position. According to his memoir, Lansdale advised the

GVN president to establish at least one branch of the police as a "military reserve organization."[20] Diem sided with Lansdale and the US military advisers over MSU. He advocated close ties between civilian and military forces, particularly with regard to relations between the civil guard and the South Vietnamese army. In fact, the subsequent dispute over the civil guard became a major point of contention among the MSU group, Diem's government, and US military leaders in Vietnam.

American civilian aid workers were critical of the US military's appraisal of the situation and its recommendations for improving internal security in Vietnam. For example, in his report from 1960, Ellis described the Military Assistance Advisory Group (MAAG) as "a disciplined monolithic organization tolerating little difference of opinion," and he argued that MAAG's approach "tends to limit constructive, imaginative thought." More importantly, he charged American military advisers with misunderstanding and underestimating the southern insurgency and the threat it posed to the GVN. He wrote: "The MAAG holds the rather anomalous view that the Viet Cong security problem is an annoying diversion, rather like a buzzing mosquito, that prevents the armed forces from concentrating fully on the real threat from the north." He continued to explain that, notwithstanding the MAAG and GVN view, nearly half of South Vietnam's military and paramilitary forces were preoccupied with trying to vanquish the much smaller group of insurgents. He concluded: "It is easy to envisage a situation requiring all the GVN forces merely to maintain internal security."[21]

As a result of the fundamental discrepancy in their views of the problems facing South Vietnam as well as the most effective methods for dealing with them, American civilian aid workers found that the GVN rarely embraced their suggestions for improving law enforcement. Members of the MSU police team in particular also failed to convince more powerful elements within the US government of the wisdom and applicability of their approach. Most American military leaders and CIA officials agreed with Diem's diagnosis, asserting that South Vietnam's political problems could be solved only once the military threat posed by the armed insurgency had been extinguished. Military advisers argued that the need to professionalize or "Americanize" South Vietnam's police forces paled in comparison with the more fundamental necessity of defeating armed opposition and defending the state. However, both the MSU and the

US military viewpoints ignored the basic political problems facing the GVN. Most significantly, they failed to consider the widespread demand for Vietnam's reunification and independence among the government's detractors as a legitimate position.

## Material Aid and Training Programs

Although they held fundamentally different views regarding the nature and the role of the police, the MSU police advisers and GVN policy makers agreed that South Vietnam's law enforcement organizations could protect the population and uphold laws effectively only if they secured access to weapons, equipment, and vehicles. In the mid-1950s, the South Vietnamese police were severely lacking in basic supplies and communications networks. According to a survey conducted by Charles Sloane, a member of the MSU group, police in the eleven provinces of Central Vietnam operated without the aid of radios or telephones. Instead, all communication, even contact with central headquarters, depended on runners, bicycles, or, in rare cases, jeeps. In addition, law enforcement agents in these provinces had few weapons and little ammunition. With an average of twenty-five rifles within each province, "many men working [did] not have any type of firearms and some that [did] have firearms [had] no ammunition."[22] Police officers in the relatively large city of Phan Thiet, which consisted of about sixty thousand residents, had no vehicles, radios, or transmitters. They patrolled the city and outlying districts on foot and by bicycle, and their only contact with the Saigon police headquarters was by telegraph.[23] One of the major features of the MSU group's program involved supplying South Vietnam's police forces with hundreds of thousands of dollars worth of equipment and weapons.[24]

Not only did South Vietnam's police forces lack an infrastructure for communications and transportation as well as basic weapons, vehicles, and other supplies, they also had little access to training. According to American aid workers, this lack of training manifested itself in general feelings of ill will and resentment between the police and the population throughout the country. The MSU advisers recommended better training for police officers as a remedy for strained police-community relations. GVN officials agreed with the Americans' emphasis on training and instruction. For example, when a riot nearly erupted in Nha Trang as a result of popular dissatisfaction with the police of that coastal city, the Interior Ministry transferred a police chief there from Saigon and issued him explicit instructions to improve public relations between officers and the community. Chief Bang, the newly appointed head of police, reported to his superiors and the MSU team that the introduction of more well-trained officers could help ease tensions between residents and local law enforcement.[25]

The training programs that did exist in South Vietnam were haphazard and not standardized. Prior to American involvement, most young men who had been recruited by Vietnamese police agencies had little practical experience. In some cases, such as the municipal police force in Central Vietnam, police officers were required to pass an examination that tested their basic knowledge of the legal system as well as their ability to write reports. Other police organizations selected personnel without administering any exams or enforcing any minimum requirements.[26] Furthermore, few of the police recruits received any organized training on their selection for employment. Instead, new officers were assigned to work with older, more experienced men and were expected to learn on the job. Only a small number of officers took part in training courses held at South Vietnam's two police schools. A modest police school in Hue, established in 1954, offered three-month periods of instruction to classes of sixty men.[27] Others attended the national police academy in Saigon. When they returned to the field, graduates of the two academies were usually expected to hold in-service training sessions for those of their colleagues who did not have access to formal instruction.[28]

Within the first two years of their contract period, the MSU police team provided training programs for thousands of Vietnamese law enforcement agents. Many of these programs focused on weapons instruction and especially on how to operate American-made firearms, which flooded the country as a result of US material aid to Vietnam. As the influx of new weapons accelerated, so too did the demand for Vietnamese security forces that could properly and safely use them. The Americans trained officers of the Saigon municipal police, members of the Vietnamese Bureau of Investigation (VBI), and guardsmen from Diem's presidential security force to use .38-caliber revolvers and other firearms. In several large cities, they provided demonstrations of the effective operation of tear gas and Remington riot shotguns.[29]

In addition to firearms instruction, American advisers launched training programs in other subjects, including communications, fingerprinting techniques, and the English language. In one exemplary case, American aid workers cooperated with Tran Chanh Thanh, the minister of information, to establish a school that would teach police officers how to repair and maintain radios. Students at the school attended a lecture on radio communication each morning and then spent the rest of the day working with a technician to perform repairs on radio systems. These men were expected to maintain and improve radio communications throughout the country on completion of the program.[30]

At the request of Vietnamese officials, the MSU police team delivered thousands of hours of lectures to high-ranking security officers and future instructors within the various police agencies. These lectures covered fifty-one subject areas and were translated into Vietnamese and published as manuals for general use among law enforcement organizations. Many of the lectures covered technical or practical issues, including "Court Procedure in Viet Nam," "Care and Preservation of Evidence," "Highway Patrol," and "Traffic Accident Investigation." Others addressed more esoteric and nontechnical aspects of police work. The MSU team's introduction of topics such as "Police Public Relations," "Police Responsibilities," and "The Position of Police in Society" reveals its concerns about training law enforcement officers who would not only know how to use their equipment and file reports but also exhibit good interpersonal skills.[31] The MSU police team hoped to produce officers who understood their role in society, were responsive and respectful in their relations with the community, and adhered to the rule of law. In the university advisers' minds, well-behaved police forces played a central role in good governance.

The MSU team also sent a number of Vietnamese police personnel to the United States for further training. In anticipation of the officers' study tours, the American advisers encouraged a handful of police officers to enroll in English-language training. In late 1955, Nguyen Ngo Le, the director general of the national police services, selected nineteen police officers representing each of Vietnam's three major law enforcement agencies to participate in English classes. Le and his colleagues had high expectations for these men and anticipated that they would introduce American methods and sensibilities to their fellow police officers. However, the students did not perform as well as either their superiors or the MSU advisers had hoped. Less than two months after the inception of the program, one student had withdrawn from the program to enter a military school. The English instructors expressed concern over the ability of half the remaining students to complete the course successfully. According to the instructors, the nine students in danger of failing did not work hard enough, were inattentive in class, and lacked discipline. Howard Hoyt, the head of MSU's police team, explained that the students' failure was the result of unrealistic expectations from their supervisors, who required the students to perform a full day's work in addition to their intensive study program.[32]

Despite a large investment of money—upward of $350,000 for the English-language program alone—and Vietnamese leaders' participation, the English-language program for police could hardly be considered a success. Poor morale and low motivation on the part of the police students, who hailed from all the major security forces, hindered their ability to learn English.[33] The police supervisors aggravated the situation by not fully supporting the students and refusing to permit them a respite from their regular duties. The behavior of both students and supervisors reflects their ambivalence about the value of learning English. The Americans' emphasis on English-language training might have seemed like a secondary concern to Vietnamese law enforcement officers who faced more immediate and concrete security problems.

The police team's insistence on including English-language courses illuminates one of the basic problems associated with MSU's training programs—in many cases, the instruction provided to South Vietnamese law enforcement officials had little or no connection to the realities of the security situation in the country. The university group emphasized English-language acquisition so that Vietnamese police officers could participate in training programs in the United States or the Philippines that would provide significant exposure to American-style law enforcement methods. However, studying English did not prepare Vietnamese policemen to deal with the most pressing security issue facing the GVN—the political insurgency. Similarly, instruction in proper reporting techniques did not necessarily ensure that Vietnamese security forces could effectively identify and apprehend antigovernment guerillas or defuse the explosive situation caused by violence perpetuated by the GVN and insurgents alike. Ultimately, the training opportunities offered by the MSU police team were too detached from the problems facing Vietnamese police on the ground to result in widespread changes, either in police-community relations or in the effectiveness of law enforcement.

## Reorganizing South Vietnamese Law Enforcement Organizations

The MSU police team did not focus solely on material aid or training. In fact, its central recommendation for improving internal security called for a basic reorganization of law enforcement bodies. In the mid-1950s, a handful of different groups—mostly holdovers from the French colonial period—were charged with law enforcement and the maintenance of internal security. But those groups had only a minimal presence in rural areas of the country. As the historian William Rosenau explains: "Police serve as visible signs of a state's power and authority." But law enforcement organizations were basically nonexistent outside large cities in South Vietnam.[34] In addition to the municipal police force in Saigon, the national Sûreté (established by the French and eventually replaced by the VBI) took responsibility for criminal activity, such as river and highway banditry. The small but well-trained imperial gendarmerie, Vietnam's rural police force, operated as an elite rural police force, while the civil guard managed security in the provinces. Finally, in many villages, various local organizations known as self-defense corps—including some opposed to Diem's rule—functioned as paramilitary units to protect inhabitants of the villages and outlying areas.[35] The university advisers considered this "excessive number of law enforcement organizations" a significant obstacle to the GVN's ability to control South Vietnam. In their estimation, Diem had not adequately defined the legal responsibilities of those agencies.[36]

In theory, these security forces each had distinct responsibilities that did not overlap with the duties of the other groups. However, in practice they often enforced different standards, investigated the same cases without cooperating, and sometimes even contradicted each others' findings. According to the Americans' observations, the lack of clear jurisdiction among the security forces resulted in considerable confusion as well as inefficiency and increased costs. In the words of one MSU adviser: "One of the greatest boons to law enforcement in Viet Nam would be the enactment of legislation which would clearly define the laws which each police organization would be responsible for."[37]

In an attempt to correct the problems associated with having too many law enforcement organizations with ill-defined duties and authority, the MSU police team proposed that the GVN consolidate all the forces into three agencies. Its plan centralized law enforcement authority by recommending that all internal civil security matters be handled by the Saigon municipal police, the civil guard, or the VBI.[38] The university advisers called for the elimination of all other police forces, which they considered extraneous and wasteful.[39] They recommended that all three agencies report directly to the Ministry of the Interior and be wholly separate from South Vietnam's military.

According to the MSU plan, the three major organizations would have distinct duties and responsibilities, but each organization would work in concert with the other two. The municipal police force would have jurisdiction over the capital city of Saigon as well as the surrounding urban areas, particularly the neighboring city of Cholon. It would consist of between five and six thousand uniformed and armed officers divided into several large departments, and its primary functions would resemble those of a large American city's police department. The civil guard would serve as a rural security agency and handle all police matters outside Saigon and Cholon. With a force of forty-five to fifty thousand men, it would maintain law and order in villages, small cities, and rural areas. The VBI would handle police matters that fell outside the realm of either the municipal police or the civil guard. As a smaller force of approximately four thousand men, it would be primarily responsible for criminal investigations in the country. Its agents would be "specialists in plain clothes," charged with maintaining central criminal files and records as well as operating national, "scientific" criminal detection laboratories. Using the FBI as a model (even for the agency's name), the MSU group planned to train VBI agents to analyze intelligence and coordinate action against criminal offenders. In addition to these responsibilities, the VBI would handle all matters concerning immigration and customs, narcotics, postal inspection, and tax evasion.[40]

Initially, an American committee for police and civil security that included members of the US embassy, USOM, and even some military advisers supported the MSU reorganization plan.[41] Unfortunately for the university team, however, consensus among the American players would prove fleeting. Within a couple of years, MAAG had abandoned MSU's plan, primarily because of differences in opinion over the role and nature of the civil guard. By 1959, even USOM, which had for years staunchly supported MSU's position on civilian law enforcement, bowed to pressure from US military advisers and GVN officials. This rejection of the university group reflected a broader shift within US policy toward military escalation in Vietnam.

## The VBI and Modern Intelligence Systems

The MSU group's efforts to assist the VBI revolved around the police team's belief that Diem's government needed good intelligence and accurate information about as many citizens as possible. Criminal offenders could be apprehended only if police knew who was responsible for the infraction. Similarly, GVN officials could eliminate political subversion only if they knew who was loyal to the regime. In order to deal with the problem of recognizing common criminals as well as antigovernment insurgents, the police team recommended that the VBI establish an identification bureau. This department would be responsible for issuing ID cards as well as making, classifying, and storing fingerprints.

The MSU advisers saw the introduction of these identification techniques as an important component of their assistance to the Vietnamese security forces. Consequently, they began encouraging the GVN to establish national fingerprinting and ID card programs immediately on their arrival in the country. As Jack Ryan explained: "The creation of a modern Identification Division is absolutely vital to the operation of any police organization." However, creating such a bureau amounted to no small task, especially in a country such as Vietnam that historically lacked any comprehensive system for keeping track of and identifying the population. In order to launch a fingerprinting department within the VBI, American advisers would first have to supply the agency with the necessary equipment, such as fingerprint cardholders, plate glass, rollers, and ink. Next, they must train Vietnamese technicians to take, read, and use fingerprints. Finally, the Vietnamese government would need to pass and enforce laws authorizing the police to obtain fingerprints of arrested or suspected criminals.[42] Similarly, to implement a countrywide ID card program, the Vietnamese would need cameras, photographic paper, laminating machines, and other materials. They would then require training to use this equipment and issue the cards.

When the MSU police advisers began advocating for an identification department, they quickly encountered a basic problem. In the past, Vietnam's security forces had used two different fingerprint classification systems and had not integrated the prints into one collection. Both these systems, the Parisian and the Pottecher, had been abandoned by most Western and Southeast Asian law enforcement agencies as outdated and inefficient. The relatively small police departments at Hue and Dalat used the Parisian technique, which could not accommodate a large number of prints, while one of the Saigon departments used the Pottecher system, and the other Saigon agency used a makeshift combination of both. Neither of the two methods could meet the demand for identifying Vietnam's large population. Perhaps more importantly, neither procedure allowed the police to exchange information with other Southeast Asian law enforcement agencies, which all used the more modern Henry classification system.[43] The American advisers introduced the Henry system to the VBI, and they also attempted to streamline existing records by consolidating old fingerprint cards from the Parisian and Pottecher systems with the new Henry procedure.[44] However, their efforts to create a comprehensive fingerprinting program were cut short and never achieved the widespread results for which they had hoped.

The fingerprinting and national ID card programs constituted a deliberate attempt to make Vietnamese society more legible and thus more easily controlled by outsiders as well as domestic political forces.[45] Because of his tenuous hold on power, Diem supported both programs. After all, he had at least as much interest as the Americans in developing reliable identification methods for his intelligence agency. In fact, according to one former MSU police team participant, the ID card program was one of the few projects that the Americans did not have to "ram down the throats of the Vietnamese."[46] Despite backing both projects in their early stages, however, Diem eventually refused to continue assisting the MSU group in implementing either. In their efforts to administer the programs, the MSU advisers made a number of recommendations that undermined GVN central authority. Diem responded to these challenges by resisting the group's suggestions.

During the first three years of MSU's contract period, the university group trained 340 police officers as fingerprinting technicians. Yet the American advisers and the GVN officials could not agree on how to deal with fingerprints once they had been taken.[47] Policy makers at the Ministry of the Interior argued that a distinct identification bureau should be established in each province for the storage and classification of local fingerprints. The MSU team rejected this proposal, citing inefficiency, extra costs, and the "probability of error in searching fingerprints" housed at provincial facilities. Instead, the MSU advisers advocated collecting all fingerprints at one central location. In fact, they adamantly argued that American material assistance for the program should be restricted to the Central Identification Division at the VBI in Saigon.[48] This dispute slowed the work of taking and classifying fingerprints and contributed negatively to the already strained relations between Interior Ministry officials and the MSU group.[49] Despite the large amount of money spent and the hundreds of fingerprint technicians trained, five years after the introduction of the program the VBI still faced a tremendous backlog of unclassified prints. As late as June 1960, the American advisers concluded that the VBI had not adequately incorporated the Henry fingerprint system and still required additional supervision and guidance.[50]

The MSU group also encountered problems implementing the national ID card program. Conceived in 1957, this program was designed as a way for the Vietnamese police to identify individuals quickly and keep closer tabs on the population. In 1959, four mobile teams, each consisting of one fingerprint technician, two photographers, and eight clerks, began traveling to the provinces around Saigon to issue cards. However, the program produced limited results. The ID card teams issued only 225,838 plastic laminated ID cards linked to a national register before deteriorating security forced an abrupt suspension of the program in February 1960. According to an MSU report, "the steady increase in acts of terrorism, raids and assassinations" targeting GVN officials and their supporters made it unsafe for the mobile police teams to travel outside the cities or for rural inhabitants to participate in government-sponsored programs. Although the VBI resumed the program under MSU supervision a few months later, the GVN restricted operations to the immediate urban area of Saigon-Cholon.[51]

In fact, by the time MSU and the VBI introduced the ID card program, violence in the rural areas had become endemic. Although previously assailants had usually targeted GVN officials, now their attacks increasingly involved civilians. For example, during a five-month period in 1957, a mass murder in Chau Doc claimed the lives of seventeen people, guerilla fighters gunned down the district chief of My Tho and his family in broad daylight, and the bombing of a café in Cholon injured thirteen people. Americans were not immune from the violence. On October 22, 1957, three separate bombing incidents in Saigon left thirteen Americans wounded. Conservative GVN estimates from 1958 cited 193 civilian murders and 236 abductions that year. The French journalist Bernard Fall concluded that the South Vietnamese government had lost nearly 20 percent of its village chiefs by the end of 1958. According to the CIA agent George Carver: "A pattern of politically motivated terror began to emerge. . . . [B]y the end of 1958 participants in this incipient insurgency . . . constituted a serious threat to South Vietnam and its political stability."[52]

Each year, as the number of politically motivated attacks swelled, Diem's regime responded with increasingly repressive tactics. The success of the insurgency prevented the Vietnamese forces and MSU advisers from fully executing the ID card program, which had been designed to defeat that very insurgency by making it easier for the Vietnamese police to conduct surveillance. It was becoming clear that efforts such as the ID card and fingerprinting programs could not adequately protect the people of South Vietnam. Diem and many US officials began looking for more aggressive ways to curtail the opposition. They saw a well-trained and heavily armed civil guard as a promising method for doing so.

## The Civil Guard Dispute

Perhaps the MSU police advisers' most significant failure derived from their inability to convince Vietnamese officials to embrace their recommendations for the civil guard. Their protracted conflict with the GVN and the US government over the future of the civil guard reflected a shift in official American policy in South Vietnam toward increased militarization. This conflict also contributed significantly to MSU's gradual loss of authority over police operations in the country and foreshadowed the American involvement in the ground war.

According to the MSU group's vision, the civil guard would be a professional law enforcement agency with guardsmen outfitted with and trained to use "modern mobile communications and firearm equipment." The police team modeled its recommendations on state police forces in the United States. It expected the organization to operate locally and with some autonomy while adhering to national laws and regulations. The American advisers hoped that members of the civil guard would "become a part of the community in which they live" rather than a force sent from Saigon to the provinces during difficult periods.[53]

However, the university advisers were not naive about the rapidly increasing level of violence in the Vietnamese countryside. They anticipated situations in which a regular civil police organization might be unable to preserve peace and order. Therefore, they advised that the civil guard train some elite companies that would be more mobile and have the ability to strike harder than regular guardsmen. The government could dispatch these companies to respond to trouble spots or particularly grave threats to internal security. Because they must remain available to be sent anywhere in the country, these units would not likely become integrated into the community. However, like all units of the guard, they were to consist entirely of civilians and would be forbidden from using military tactics. According to the MSU police team, if internal security reached the point of emergency, the president could then call in the military at his own discretion.[54]

The clear distinction between the civil guard and the Vietnamese military, as well as the separation of the duties and powers of these two groups, lay at the heart of the MSU group's diagnosis of how to improve law enforcement in South Vietnam. The police team insisted that civilian police organizations, rather than the military, handle all matters of internal security. On this point it held firm, even when Diem and other American advisory groups advocated militarizing the police forces. During their time in Vietnam, the MSU police advisers came under pressure from Diem and MAAG to convert the civil guard into a national paramilitary group.

The different visions for the civil guard offered by the MSU group and USOM, on the one hand, and the GVN and American military leaders, on the other, stemmed from the two sides' divergent diagnoses of Vietnam's security problems as well as their conflicting political ideologies. In particular, the MSU team expressed ideas about the relationship between the police and state building that differed radically from those of the GVN and MAAG. The university advisers believed that the greatest threats to internal security in Vietnam emerged from inefficient or old-fashioned systems and routine criminal activity. They argued that South Vietnam needed police officers who effectively enforced the law and served the communities in which they worked. In their minds, civilian police played an important role in supporting the state by upholding its legal systems and protecting its citizens.

By contrast, Diem and most of his American military advisers saw Vietnam's security problems as the result of a powerful political insurgency composed of internal enemies of the state as well as aggression from the Democratic Republic of Vietnam (DRV), a foreign power. Accordingly, they promoted taking a hard line and using quick military strikes to wipe out any opposition. From Diem's point of view, paramilitary organizations offered many advantages over civilian law enforcement agencies. They would be accountable to the president and his demands. As a result, Diem would enjoy significant control over their behavior. Ultimately, he and US military leaders believed that security forces should defend the interests of the central state, which in this case were tantamount to Diem's personal political interests.

The MSU group demonstrated unwavering faith in the notion that only civil law enforcement agencies could effectively solve the problem of Vietnam's internal security. As Howard Hoyt explained to Arthur Gardiner, the head of USOM in Vietnam: "The solution to problems of an internal security nature stemming from the activities of subversive elements or criminals lies in the establishment of close cooperation between the population and existing civilian police organizations." The police depended on information from the population to combat subversive infiltration, terrorism, and criminal activity. As a result, Hoyt argued, a deep mutual respect must exist between the police and the people. When the local population did not respect or lacked confidence in police agencies, they could not be expected to share information with the authorities. More importantly, if their fear of criminals and insurgents outweighed their trust in the police, citizens would likely remain silent or even assist those criminals and insurgents.[55]

Following this logic, American aid workers argued that the Vietnamese government should refrain from using the military to solve internal security problems. In a memo to Wesley Fishel, the chief adviser of the MSU group at the time, one police team member wrote: "History teaches us that soldiers make poor police officers. As a rule, civilians dislike being

Howard Hoyt, deputy adviser for Michigan State University's police team, and Bui Van Tinh, the minister of the interior of the Government of Vietnam, examine a map of Saigon-Cholon in 1955. Courtesy Michigan State University Archives and Historical Collections Vietnam Project, Records (UA 2.9.5.5), Photograph File Drawer.

controlled by the military."[56] Echoing and expanding on these sentiments, Hoyt argued: "History is replete with instances where military forces have been utilized by a government to police the population. With certain exceptions, all of these attempts have failed by virtue of the fact that military orientation and training are directed toward military operations, not police work." Furthermore, Hoyt contended that military units not only were ill equipped for daily police responsibilities but also tended to rely too heavily on demonstrations of force without regard for civilians' safety and well-being.[57]

Under the leadership of Hoyt and his successor, Jack Ryan, the MSU police team repeatedly shared its views about the importance of establishing civilian law enforcement organizations with policy makers in the US and Vietnamese governments.[58] Officials at the International Cooperation

Administration (ICA) in Washington subscribed to MSU's view that the civil guard should function as a "pure police" force rather than a paramilitary organization.[59] But they also worried that Diem would not accept the "civilian concept" for the civil guard.[60] The officials at ICA correctly anticipated the GVN position. Throughout the late 1950s, Diem ignored the university team's advice and failed to implement its specific recommendations. Instead, he supported the activities of paramilitary organizations and pressured his American patrons to provide military-style weapons and increase funding to the civil guard. As Hoyt explained in 1959, Diem was "adamant in his favoring the use of the military approach to the internal security problem."[61]

Diem wanted the civil guard to be a "second-line army," trained, disciplined, and supplied by the Ministry of Defense. As American officials and scholars have noted, his interest in the guard as a paramilitary organization did not stem solely from his concerns over internal security. Analysts at the US Defense Department later observed: "Diem wanted the Civil Guard equipped very much like his regular army—possibly with a view to assuring himself a check on army power."[62] The historian William Rosenau describes this approach to the civil guard as a delicate balancing act. Diem hoped to use the guard both as a check on the Army of the Republic of Vietnam (ARVN) as well as a means of augmenting the size of the military and ensuring his own political survival.[63] Similarly, the historian Ronald Spector argues that Diem saw the civil guard as a potential counterweight to the influence of the South Vietnamese army. According to Spector, the guard was to be staffed largely by Catholics, many of whom were former militiamen from North Vietnam and might serve as a loyal counterforce in the event the army turned against the president.[64] But, as Edward Miller has suggested, these arguments do not tell the full story. In fact, as Miller shows, less than one-third of the guardsmen hailed from Vietnam's northern provinces.[65]

Contrary to the idea that Diem viewed the civil guard primarily as a counterbalance to the ARVN, the two groups overlapped in many aspects, including their roles, their organizational structure, and especially their personnel. The leadership of the civil guard consisted of many high-ranking ARVN officials. The military background of the guard's leadership reflected Diem's emphasis on creating a force that functioned like another branch of the armed services. Between April 1955 and April 1959, three of the five directors general of the civil guard came from the ranks of the ARVN, while the top echelon of the force consisted entirely of ARVN officers. Furthermore, regional military commanders controlled all provincial-level police activities, whether they were carried out by the army or conducted by civilian agencies.[66] One member of the MSU police team observed in 1956 that throughout Central Vietnam the civil guard operated solely as a "relieving military force" to assist the army in pacifying rural areas and did not actually handle any police matters.[67]

GVN officials and American aid workers also disagreed over the organizational structure of the civil guard. In addition to establishing the guard as a paramilitary force, Diem promoted a decentralized model for its organization. In contrast, advisers from MSU and USOM advocated for a more centralized organizational structure. In their written reports and informal conversations with the president and his ministers, they recommended that the leadership of the guard be centralized under a director general and that the guard adopt certain national standards. Rather than accept these recommendations, Diem called for the civil guard to be controlled by provincial chiefs. Under this plan, all rural security forces, including the civil guard, would be responsible only to the provincial chief and not to a director in Saigon. The provincial chiefs would deal with internal security problems and criminal activity on an ad hoc basis, sometimes relying on multiple police organizations to identify, apprehend, and punish perpetrators.[68] Furthermore, Diem vowed to deal personally with any provincial chiefs found to be uncooperative or unable to handle local security concerns. His promise to manage problem cases demonstrated his desire to maintain full control over all security forces in South Vietnam, even if that meant pitting various agencies against each other.

His approach also highlights the high priority Diem placed on having loyal provincial and village-level administrators. By retaining control over local leaders, he hoped to prevent the creation of a unified organization that could challenge his authority. He knew that it would be easier to replace one ineffective or disloyal provincial chief than to dismantle a bureaucracy that might not always serve his own political interests. Although his vision for the civil guard may have been appropriate, given his own ambitions and the realities of Vietnam, where much daily decision making occurred at the local level, his civilian American advisers considered his strategy to be inefficient and unproductive. At a more fundamental level, they regarded his methods as incompatible with their views on how the police should function within a modern state.

Diem lobbied his American supporters in Saigon and Washington for increased material aid for the civil guard. He was primarily interested in acquiring military weapons for the guardsmen. His demands intensified after 1957, when he proposed transferring the civil guard from the Office of the Presidency to the Ministry of Defense.[69] He explained to officers in MAAG that he wanted American weaponry for the civil guard in order to "bolster their morale."[70] He also used incidents of violence in the countryside as evidence of the guard's need for more arms. For example, after insurgents attacked a French rubber plantation north of Tay Ninh in January 1958, he appealed to Ambassador Durbrow for greater levels of material support to the guard. The attackers had burned buildings and stolen money from the plantation's offices, and they had been able to escape with almost no challenge from local law authorities. According to Diem, the guardsmen in the area could not respond effectively because they lacked adequate weaponry.[71] High-level American military officers such as General Samuel Williams agreed with Diem that providing the civil guard with more advanced weapons could tip the scales in favor of government forces in the countryside. In secret correspondence with his superiors at Pearl Harbor, Williams wrote: "I greatly sympathize with Diem on the matter of equipment for the guard."[72] Although he and other American military personnel supported GVN demands for heavy weapons and other material aid, civilian policy makers were less inclined to concur with Diem's wishes.

Diem was likely emboldened by the US military and CIA support for his vision. Although in 1955 the leadership of MAAG and the CIA claimed to support MSU's recommendations, American military and counterinsurgency advisers soon broke with the university group. For these Americans, Cold War concerns and a predilection for using military force trumped any genuine commitment to democratic nation building in South Vietnam. Lansdale, one of Diem's closest American advisers, believed that the civil guard was "badly outmatched in trying to cope with guerillas." He urged Diem and American officials to establish the guard as a military force and was unhappy to learn that USOM refused to back that proposal. His memoirs reveal his disapproval of the USOM and MSU model for the civil guard: "The result was a police force sketchily trained and armed along the lines needed for keeping order in an American city and pathetically unready for the realities of the Vietnamese countryside." Expressing particular contempt for USOM, he quipped: "American bureaucrats are a stubborn breed."[73]

American military advisers expressed similar sentiments. Officials at the US Department of Defense were "extremely interested" in efforts to bolster the civil guard if it could serve as "an effective internal security force" and provide relief for the army. However, one Colonel Evans told a civilian aid worker that he was "opposed to Guard Civile being what he called a 'village policeman type,' making friends with the people, etc."[74] Admiral Felix Stump, the commander in chief of US forces in the Pacific at the time, strongly criticized the MSU team's position on the civil guard. Stump argued that the university group did not understand that Vietnam's internal security situation called for fundamentally different approaches to law enforcement than those that worked in Michigan.[75] General Samuel Williams, chief of MAAG from 1955 to 1960, also disagreed with MSU and USOM plans for the guard. He advised Diem that transferring oversight of the organization to the Ministry of Defense made perfect sense.[76] According to Lansdale, he "[begged] the U.S. Mission to change its policy of assisting the Vietnamese police, but to no avail." Despite opposition from USOM and MSU, Williams managed to supply the civil guard with American military weapons and ammunition, at least for a brief period.[77]

Debates over the civil guard, which pitted MSU and USOM against the GVN and MAAG, plagued relations among those groups through 1957. In the middle of that year, when it became apparent that neither side would budge on the issue, the US government suspended its material and technical support for the guard.[78] In July 1957, USOM's director, Leland Barrows, temporarily shelved all commodity orders for the guard as well as police and security services in Vietnam. According to members of the MSU police team, Barrows decided to suspend material aid to South Vietnamese law enforcement until the GVN "clarified its position as to whether the civil guard was to be a civilian police agency or a military one." In January 1958, the ICA resumed financial support for public safety projects but continued to block funding for the civil guard.[79] During this time, the MSU police team continued to provide limited amounts of instruction to guard officers at a training school in Cap St.

Jacques while urging Diem to convert the guard into a civilian force.[80] However, by the time the US government resumed large-scale assistance to the guard at the end of the decade, policy makers' support for aid to purely civilian law enforcement was waning, and the MSU advisers no longer exercised much power in the field of technical assistance to police organizations.

In early 1959, USOM's newly formed PSD officially replaced MSU as the primary American civilian group advising the civil guard.[81] At that time, the PSD had ten regular employees, with five vacancies.[82] However, given the magnitude of the security crisis, the USOM leadership argued that the PSD needed to grow quickly. A USOM report from July 1959 advocated for an expansion of the PSD to twenty-one American advisers, many of whom should be proficient in Vietnamese.[83] Although USOM occasionally consulted the MSU team for assistance in "special fields," after 1959 the university advisers found themselves excluded from serious decision making with respect to the future of the civil guard.[84] The final defeat of the MSU model came in December 1960, when Diem transferred responsibility for the guard to the Ministry of Defense.[85] Because Diem served as his own defense minister, this move indicated his desire to assert direct control over the guard. He clearly hoped to enhance the strength of both the guard and the army while allowing neither to become dominant or solely responsible for internal security. With the successful implementation of Diem's vision of a militarized civil guard that would both complement and compete with the ARVN, American aid workers all but abandoned the idea of having a large, civilian rural police force.

Although the debate over the nature of the civil guard was resolved by the beginning of the 1960s, the force continued to disappoint Diem's American advisers. Even with access to military weapons and training, the guard repeatedly turned in poor performances when tested in the field. For example, in November 1962, insurgents mined and destroyed a vehicle and railroad bridge over the Truoi River about twenty-five kilometers south of Hue. A unit of guardsmen stationed at the bridge had been unable to prevent the attack or detain those responsible. However, perhaps the most damning aspect of this incident is the fact that members of that same guard unit had been reprimanded by the provincial chief the previous year after they had been caught fast asleep while on the job.[86]

Although the incident at the Truoi bridge is a particularly egregious example of the ineffectiveness of the civil guard, many PSD advisers criticized their poor performance. A USOM report from July 1959 detailed the shortcomings of the guard and advised against expecting "any immediate spectacular results." According to the chief of USOM's PSD, the guard "has some capability as a fixed guard force at important installations, but with the present state of training, lack of material support, lack of flexibility due to organization, and general lack of overall direction, [it] cannot be considered an effective security force."[87] Later reports and correspondence from USOM police advisers corroborate this negative assessment. In particular, these documents cite intransigence on the part of both GVN officials and members of the guard.[88] Brooks Anderson, a PSD adviser from 1962 to 1964, described the "constant lack of responsive cooperation from members of the National police." Although Anderson conceded that there had been some improvement in rural law enforcement after the November 1963 coup, he argued that "much work still needs to be done to create a better public servant image" of the civil guard and other police forces. He also recommended that the guard be brought back under the Ministry of the Interior.[89]

Ultimately, the civil guard remained more a paramilitary organization than a civilian police force. The MSU police team's inability to influence Diem and MAAG on this issue constituted one of its greatest defeats in Vietnam. More broadly, GVN and American policy makers' decision to abandon the rural police model for the civil guard paralleled their rejection of long-term political- and economic-development efforts in favor of short-term military solutions in South Vietnam.

## The Legacy of MSU's Involvement in Police Administration

The MSU team's participation in police administration raised many questions about the appropriateness of a university group implementing US foreign policy. Members of MSU's police team worried about their role in advancing Diem's autocratic aspirations even as they contributed to the police state in South Vietnam. Throughout their time in Vietnam, many expressed serious reservations about how the GVN and American political and military leaders used police forces to secure and bolster South Vietnam.

As the university group became more involved in aiding Diem's security forces, members questioned how their work corresponded with broader US goals, which claimed to support democracy in South Vietnam. One of the police advisers, Victor Strecher, suggested that the group conduct a research project to study the "political-philosophical aspects of providing technical assistance to law enforcement organizations which may employ improved techniques of operation in a less than democratic manner." In early 1960, Strecher, who was also a professor of police administration at MSU, submitted a research proposal to Lloyd Musolf, the chief adviser of the Vietnam Project at the time. This proposal enumerated Strecher's concerns regarding the moral and legal responsibilities of American police advisers. His recommendations for the study reveal a certain anxiety on the part of some MSU participants over how to balance their assignment to develop "technically competent instruments of law enforcement" with their desire to promote democratic institutions and protect the people of Vietnam.[90]

The proposal highlighted the tension that resulted from MSU's involvement in South Vietnam's internal affairs and civil security. Strecher posed important questions about whether the United States should aid police agencies that "function within a framework of almost unlimited authority." He urged fellow aid workers to consider whether they should concern themselves only with the end results of their work or whether they should take into account the means used to achieve those results. Finally, he argued that the university team would have to decide which GVN policies should be deemed internal matters and therefore lay outside the MSU group's purview.[91]

Other members of the group exhibited similar misgivings about the police advisory program. According to Ralph Smuckler, the leaders of the MSU group devoted significant time and attention to their concerns regarding the police program and its impact on the university, the GVN, and the people of Vietnam. Smuckler and his colleagues such as Art Brandstatter, the head of MSU's Police Administration School, and Glen Taggert, the director of the university's international programs, deliberated over whether a university group was the "appropriate vehicle" for helping Vietnamese security forces. Furthermore, they worried that the issues involved in providing technical assistance in this area might be "too sensitive, too close to the heart of power and control in a society such as Vietnam, for university people to manage."[92]

Although the philosophical and political ramifications of their program concerned many members of the MSU police team, most participants justified their work as primarily focused on assisting the people of South Vietnam. They also cited their commitments to the US government and MSU.[93] However, one participant in the MSU group took a more openly critical view of MSU's police team and the repercussions of the university's involvement in such work. Stanley Sheinbaum, the campus coordinator of the Vietnam Project, resigned from his position and later left academic life entirely, at least in part because of his disgust over the MSU police program. Sheinbaum was the only person to leave the MSU group because of his objections to the university's police work, and his case is atypical. Nevertheless, his story provides an interesting glimpse into the internal dynamics of the group and also illuminates the highly controversial nature of the most basic assumptions driving American nation-building projects.

Hired in 1955 as the MSU Vietnam Project's campus coordinator, Sheinbaum was based in East Lansing and visited Vietnam only twice during the university group's tenure there. His primary responsibilities included selecting participants for the Vietnam Project and acting as a liaison between the university group in Vietnam and its government sponsors in Washington, DC. Perhaps most importantly, he coordinated the programs of study and activities for the Vietnamese civil servants and police officers who came to the United States for training.[94] In 1956, during his first trip to Saigon, Sheinbaum visited the university advisers and reported back to MSU on the project's progress. According to his account of his visit, he learned soon after arriving in Vietnam that one floor of the university group's five-story headquarters building was off-limits, even to program administrators like himself. When he inquired as to why he was not permitted to enter the restricted area, his American colleagues refused to explain. A Vietnamese employee of the university group eventually told him that the floor in question housed the MSU police team and a unit from the CIA.[95] Sheinbaum claimed that he knew nothing about the cooperation between the MSU group and the CIA before visiting Saigon and speaking with this Vietnamese employee.[96]

After spending three months in Vietnam, Sheinbaum returned to East Lansing. He was outraged and had decided to confront MSU's administration over his findings. Not only did he feel betrayed by the university;

he also began to question seriously the fundamental objectives driving the Vietnam Project. He was deeply worried about MSU's involvement in South Vietnam and what it meant for the university's reputation as well as the future of Vietnam. As he later explained: "I was sort of horrified by [MSU's connection with the CIA]. What's a university doing being a cover for a CIA operation? In fact, what's the U.S. doing? We're supposed to teach them democracy and what not!"[97] On his return to campus, he argued with university administrators, and, as he later recalled, he lost many friends as a result of his objections to the Vietnam Project.

Sheinbaum's vehement opposition to MSU's cooperation with the CIA and his disagreements with the university's leadership ultimately had little impact on the program. Most of his colleagues did not share his strong opposition to the CIA arrangement. As Sheinbaum later conceded, other members of the Vietnam Project were "quite convinced of the good motives of the operation," but he himself "got caught up in this purism" and did not think the university should act as a "Cold Warrior." According to him, only one other member expressed similar anger over the link between MSU and the CIA. However, this man had a practical streak, and, as Sheinbaum put it, he decided that "these things have to be done to win the Cold War."[98] Although Sheinbaum continued working on the Vietnam Project for a few more years, eventually his strained relations with the university's administration and others in the technical assistance group became overwhelming. In 1959, after years of frustration with the Vietnam Project and having been passed over for a promotion and pay raise, he finally resigned from MSU and academe altogether. As he told one historian, the university technically did not fire him but "left [him] no alternative but to get the hell out."[99]

Sheinbaum was the only member of the MSU group to denounce the connection between the CIA and MSU publicly. Most other participants in the Vietnam Project described the CIA's involvement as unproblematic and a matter of common knowledge. Smuckler later claimed: "While we did not publicly announce it, the presence of the intelligence personnel had been an acknowledged relationship, known well to the Vietnamese government and to anyone else in Saigon with an interest."[100] In their 1965 "official history" of the Vietnam Project, two MSU group members, Robert Scigliano and Guy Fox, dealt with the CIA collaboration as a matter of fact and without apology.[101] Between five and eight CIA agents worked with the MSU police team and shared office space in the university group's Saigon headquarters.[102] Although the MSU police team documents contain few references to the CIA link, it is clear that some, if not all, of the advisers knew about the presence of a CIA unit.[103]

Despite the MSU group members' claims that the university's link with the CIA was insignificant, the arrangement posed many problems. Between 1954 and 1975, the CIA occupied a central position in US efforts to prop up the GVN and fight the antigovernment insurgency. In the estimation of one scholar, the CIA played a "decisive" role in Vietnam. As John F. Kennedy's undersecretary of defense explained in a 1970 interview, Vietnam became a "proving ground" for the CIA's new tactics and equipment as well as its new ideas about how to wage counterinsurgency warfare.[104]

MSU's cooperation with the CIA compromised the group's independence and autonomy. According to the scholar Michael McClintock, the CIA "carried more clout than anybody else did, certainly through the end of '61."[105] The MSU group claimed that its chief adviser would supervise the CIA unit's behavior and ensure that the agents would, in the words of one MSU participant, "not be running around as agents working for the CIA."[106] Given the position and influence of the intelligence agency in Vietnam, however, it is highly unlikely that the CIA unit embedded in MSU's police team would have complied with the university group's request that the agents not conduct their own intelligence or engage in spying. With a CIA unit entrenched in their ranks, MSU advisers had little power to deviate from agency directives. More importantly, accommodating the CIA weakened the MSU group's argument that it was interested only in promoting police forces that were subject to the rule of law and public scrutiny. MSU's link with the CIA undermined the university group's claim to its Vietnamese counterparts that it was truly committed to transparency and democratic law enforcement in South Vietnam's police organizations.

The ramifications of MSU's cooperation with the CIA continued to haunt the university group for years after its contract expired. In 1966, with the help of Sheinbaum, the journalist Robert Scheer published a scathing article about MSU's technical assistance program and CIA involvement in *Ramparts* magazine. This article, along with other negative press about the Vietnam Project, provoked a congressional investigation of MSU and served as a rallying point for antiwar activists.[107] Following the publication of the *Ramparts* article, thousands of students and faculty members protested MSU's involvement in Vietnam on the university's campus in East Lansing as well as at other colleges and universities throughout the United States.

## Tensions with Local Police

Disagreements over the organization of law enforcement bodies and especially over the nature of the civil guard reflected broader discord among the various individuals and groups working with South Vietnam's police. Not only did American aid workers disagree with many GVN officials; they also had problems working with Vietnamese police officers. MSU police advisers discovered that Vietnam's law enforcement authorities— even those working at the local level— were often slow to adopt their suggestions, if they did so at all. Many members of the university team failed to recognize how the Vietnamese might perceive them as self-interested, powerful outsiders trying to impose their views on others. The psychological and political effects of colonialism, as well as Diem's oppressive methods for dealing with opposition, likely informed how Vietnamese police officers responded to the MSU team and its programs.[108]

Many participants in the MSU group worried that negative interactions with Vietnamese officials and counterparts would restrict the effectiveness of their programs. By mid-1957, relations between the university group and the Vietnamese had reached such a low point that the leaders of the Vietnam Project felt it necessary to address such concerns. In July 1957, Fishel held a meeting to discuss the image of the university group in the eyes of the Vietnamese government and the "community." American participants and Vietnamese employees of MSU attended the informal meeting. Fishel opened the gathering by summarizing the view of many in the group, stating: "In our daily contacts, we have the impression that there is an increasing anti-American feeling among the Vietnamese officials." He then asked his colleagues to propose suggestions for how the university advisers might minimize such sentiments and improve relations between the two groups. In the conversation that ensued, some of the Vietnamese employees offered ideas and opinions that revealed the depth of misunderstanding on both sides. Their contributions also illustrate

Bui Van Long (*fourth from left*), the commissioner general for land development of the Government of Vietnam, thanks Wesley Fishel (*second from right*) for a donation from the Michigan State University group to rebuild a school that was destroyed by fire. Courtesy Michigan State University Archives and Historical Collections Vietnam Project, Records (UA 2.9.5.5), Photograph File Drawer.

many of the problems stemming from the power differential between the American aid workers and their Vietnamese partners.[109]

The Vietnamese participants at the meeting admitted that many officials held unfriendly or reluctant attitudes toward the university group. One participant, a Mr. Quan, explained that the Americans might have been "indiscreet" and given the impression of supervising or investigating rather than cooperating and advising. He urged the Americans to consider how their behavior might appear to insult the pride of Vietnamese officials. He suggested that protecting their reputations or "saving face" was a priority for most Vietnamese. He argued: "In any case, always bear in mind the importance of the face question in Oriental countries." A Mr. Chuong, another employee of the MSU program, expanded on Quan's assessment, claiming: "In general the Vietnamese in their relations with the Americans have an 'inferiority complex' whereas the Americans often have a 'superiority complex.'"[110]

In response to their Vietnamese colleagues' comments and suggestions, the Americans at the meeting vowed to approach their work with greater cultural sensitivity. Despite a general consensus that every effort should be made to improve relations with the Vietnamese, members of the public administration and police teams differed over how to achieve this goal. Representatives from the public administration team spoke about offering their services only when the GVN specifically requested them, rather than imposing methods or advice on officials. They also argued that the university group must develop good social contacts with the Vietnamese. One aid worker even suggested that MSU's Vietnamese employees design a guide for social behavior. Fishel charged the five Vietnamese in attendance with creating a handbook titled "Social Codes for the Americans in Vietnam."[111] On the other hand, Jack Ryan, the only member of the police team present at the meeting, took a more pragmatic view of the conflicts and hostilities between the Americans and the Vietnamese. Arguing that "different culture, traditions, customs and mentality" resulted in daily frictions and "deeply rooted misunderstanding," he lamented that there could be no easy solution to such problems. He proposed that members of the university group focus on their work and not force social relations with Vietnamese officials. He implored the group to "remember our goal and aims here and carry it [*sic*] out without paying attention to the rest."[112]

A week after the meeting, Phon Anh, one of MSU's Vietnamese employees who had participated in the discussion, wrote a private letter to Fishel in which he expressed his views about the problems between the university group and Vietnamese officials. Although he recognized that some tension did exist between the groups, Anh suggested that the situation was not so critical as to warrant meetings such as the one Fishel had organized. In fact, he argued that future discussions about MSU-GVN relations might provoke "a still more reticent attitude toward MSUG and other American agencies" on the part of government officials if they learned of them. Anh reminded Fishel that the MSU group "should not be lulled into the common fallacy that if one is extending assistance one can always expect downright co-operation or good will from the people assisted." He cited several political factors informing Vietnamese attitudes about Americans, notably the negative effects of Vietnam's recent experience of French colonialism and the fact that many Vietnamese questioned American intentions for their country. He explained that many American aid programs appeared "too aggressive" to Vietnamese officials, who were concerned with maintaining their own authority while also currying favor among the population. As he put it: "Too many offers and acts aimed with good faith at assisting Government agencies are misunderstood and misinterpreted as attempts to meddle in their operations." Vietnamese officials therefore found themselves in the difficult position of balancing their need for assistance with their strong desire to prevent creating the impression that they were "under the American spell."[113]

In his letter to Fishel, Anh urged the American advisers to proceed with their aid projects while exercising flexibility and tolerance. He described the attitudes and behavior of Vietnamese officials as the result of "sincere but somewhat exaggerated self-confidence." Finally, echoing Ryan's comments, he recommended that the MSU group worry less about social interactions and more about their professional duties. He argued that Americans should adopt rules of conduct only if they allowed for flexibility and adaptation in the face of diverse and specific situations. Finally, he advised: "Patience is always the best medicine to heal this rash in the relations, caused by misunderstanding and preventive distrust on the one side and unproper [sic] conduct on the other."[114]

Despite their attempts to overcome cultural misunderstanding and foster a sense of goodwill on the part of the Vietnamese, members of the MSU group found that their relationships with local officials did not improve significantly. More importantly, the Americans learned that Vietnamese leaders often responded to MSU advice in unexpected ways and sometimes adapted the group's assistance to fit their own needs. For example, a small group within the police team traveled around the country and administered surveys to determine what material aid local police organizations required. However, they encountered many officials who simply refused to cooperate in completing the survey. They concluded that, by conducting the evaluations, the Americans actually succeeded in increasing antagonism on the part of Vietnamese police officers and the general population. Furthermore, officials frequently changed the ultimate destination of certain aid materials, such as communications systems and police equipment, and used the resources for purposes that differed from the Americans' original intent.[115]

One member of the MSU police team who conducted an exploratory field trip to Central Vietnam reacted with surprise when he discovered how police officers in the region's ten provinces dealt with questions about the insurgency. According to the report he filed, none of the local authorities admitted to having any problems with National Liberation Front members or sympathizers, despite the proximity of this region to the DRV. Ironically, the report indicated: "The closer one approaches the 17th parallel the more emphatic [the police officers] are in their denials of any Viet Cong activities or members." The local leaders' responses did not tell the whole story, however. During his trip, the MSU police adviser also learned that police had performed over twelve hundred illegal arrests of suspected Communists in Bao An Province alone. According to Vietnamese employees of the civil guard corps stationed in Hoi An (Faifo), officers from district posts arrested any individuals who had been accused by neighbors of supporting the insurgency without investigating the suspects or acquiring evidence to substantiate the accusations.[116] Despite the large number of arrested and suspected Communists being held in prisons, the local police chiefs probably denied Viet Cong activity in their jurisdictions in order to protect their own jobs. If it appeared to the GVN that certain chiefs could not defend the inhabitants of their districts or eliminate Communist insurgents, it might be tempted to replace those chiefs with others it deemed more capable or loyal.

## Bureaucratic Rivalries

In addition to the difficulties it experienced in dealing with Vietnamese police officers, the MSU police team also found itself at odds with many of the other American agencies in Vietnam. Disputes over the civil guard had severely damaged relations between the university group and MAAG. Perhaps as a result of its unrealistic approach to security issues in Vietnam and its disagreements with policy makers in Saigon, officials at the US embassy distanced themselves from the MSU group. Furthermore, Americans working for USOM attempted to solidify their agency's position in Vietnam and in doing so sometimes asserted their authority over MSU participants. "There was always a lot of tension between the MSU group and the aid mission," Ralph Smuckler later explained, and both sides bore some of the blame.[117]

In 1959, USOM established its own bureau for police administration, the PSD. The PSD assumed many of the university group's responsibilities and quickly replaced MSU's police team as the most influential advisory body on civilian law enforcement in Vietnam. The bureaucratic rivalry that had always characterized relations between USOM and MSU grew more intense with the creation of the PSD. As the responsibilities of the two organizations overlapped, open conflicts emerged. For example, USOM and MSU held opposing views over whether to establish a complex telecommunications system throughout South Vietnam. Because the MSU group disagreed with USOM about the value of such a system, two USOM communications specialists refused to associate or cooperate with Jerome Hemmye, MSU's communications adviser. Eventually, the ICA sided with USOM by awarding the PSD full control over the project and eliminating MSU's role in the police communications program.[118]

MSU's loss of authority over police communications in particular and law enforcement in general reflected a basic shift in US efforts to improve internal security in Vietnam. By 1957, when the US government suspended funding for MSU's assistance to the civil guard, policy makers in Washington, DC, had demonstrated their misgivings regarding the MSU group's ability to improve security in South Vietnam. American officials may have preferred dealing with USOM rather than MSU because they enjoyed a greater degree of control and oversight regarding the aid agency than they did regarding the more independent university group. At the same time, US policy makers confirmed their mounting commitment to using military force to solve the country's problems.

To their dismay, the MSU group discovered that Diem and his closest advisers embraced the approach set forth by US military leaders. Members of the police team repeatedly expressed their frustration over Diem's refusal to implement their recommendations. In June 1957, Ryan told Fishel that Diem had not accepted or adopted any of the group's proposals for improving law enforcement in Vietnam. Ryan attributed the lack of progress not only to Diem's own stubbornness but also to more general problems of leadership and authority in the country. According to Ryan, provincial chiefs and other local leaders often interfered in matters that should have been managed by the VBI while the Ministry of the Interior

insisted on handling more minor decisions that should have been del-
egated to police administrators at lower levels.[119] Similarly, in a personal
letter written in October 1957, Howard Hoyt complained to his family
and friends that Diem had no intention of going along with any MSU
plans. Rather, the president aimed to "militarize the main police force
and make it a hard striking force . . . where a one-man regime tries to
impose its wishes on the masses." On another occasion about a year later,
Hoyt pessimistically explained the ramifications of Diem's approach: "He
believes strongly in military forces rather than civilian forces in ruling a
country. He is losing popularity among his own people fast."[120]

Most MSU police advisers offered their recommendations to Diem
through official channels. However, Wesley Fishel attempted to use his
personal relationship with the president to convince him of the merits of
the university group's advice. Even after his tenure as chief adviser of the
Vietnam Project had ended, Fishel continued urging Diem to respond to
American and Vietnamese critics by addressing their concerns through
meaningful reforms. Writing from East Lansing in early 1960, he suggested to Diem that the GVN should delegate specific authority and
responsibility to each law enforcement organization. He referred to the
government's "fatal delay" in responding to insurgents' attacks while the
authorities decided which civilian or military group to dispatch. He also
advised Diem that his "seeming reliance on 'repression' in trying to solve
the problems of government in the field" alienated his supporters both in
Vietnam and in Washington, DC.[121] Later that year, Fishel warned Diem
that, as a result of their conversations with Vietnamese people, many
Americans working in Vietnam believed there to be a "distinct lessen-
ing of popular confidence in the ability of [Diem's] government to extend
adequate protection to the population outside the cities." In addition, he
once again shared his concerns with Diem about the Vietnamese government's increasingly authoritarian rule.[122]

Despite his close friendship with Fishel, Diem refused to accept either
the university group's recommendations or Fishel's appeals. At one time,
in the mid-1950s, Fishel had been one of the few Americans who enjoyed
almost unlimited access to Diem. In fact, the cozy relationship between the
two and Fishel's position within Diem's inner circle of advisers caused considerable envy and resentment on the part of other Americans in Saigon as
well as among many Vietnamese officials.[123] By the early 1960s, however,

Diem stopped listening to Fishel and other Americans who had formerly been his most trusted confidantes. Instead, he turned his attention to American advisers whose views about defeating the insurgency matched his own. When Fishel visited Saigon for four weeks in early 1962, the Vietnamese president declined to see him, despite Fishel's repeated requests for a meeting.[124] Immediately following this incident, Fishel sent a letter to MSU president John Hannah in which he expressed deep misgivings about the future of South Vietnam and discussed the "profound and distressing deterioration there, politically, socially, and psychologically." He wrote: "The hopes and aspirations of 1954 and 1955 have been allowed to die, and a miasma of apathy pervades the atmosphere." The letter continued: "The commendable programs which were begun a few years ago have been allowed in many instances to lose their momentum by reason largely of a failure on the part of the Central Government to follow through on initial decisions and acts."[125] Fishel's report on conditions in Vietnam eventually reached the highest levels of the US government, including President John Kennedy.[126]

In retrospect, Fishel's doubts and admonitions seem prescient, although perhaps they came too late to reverse the damage done by flawed US and GVN policies. Unfortunately, neither Diem nor high-level officials within the US government were prepared at the time to deal with Fishel's criticism. Diem refused to acknowledge that increasingly repressive authoritarian rule did not win him any friends in the Vietnamese countryside or in Washington, DC. Instead, he dug in his heels and relied increasingly on intimidation and violence to maintain control. Similarly, American policy makers continued to believe that South Vietnam's problems could be solved by an intense military campaign. As a result, in the early 1960s, the Kennedy administration called for a dramatic increase in the number of American military advisers in South Vietnam. Most US officials demonstrated little understanding of the disastrous effects that militarization had on Vietnamese views of the United States and on the ability of American civilians to provide effective technical or development assistance to the Vietnamese people.

## "A Basic, Irreconcilable Difference"

Ultimately, the MSU and USOM police advisory programs had little lasting impact on Vietnam. The university police group achieved a modest degree of success through its various training programs, which many Vietnamese championed. Although the long-term effects of MSU training activities are difficult, if not impossible, to measure, the large number of Vietnamese policemen who received instruction in weaponry, communications, identification methods, and English indicates some of the immediate results of the program. Despite these limited accomplishments, however, the police team met with disappointment when it came to implementing a fundamental restructuring of Vietnamese law enforcement organizations or creating a comprehensive intelligence agency. MSU's efforts in these areas were futile because they did not address Diem's lack of legitimacy, his authoritarian rule, or the nature of the insurgency that threatened to drag the country into a civil war. Furthermore, the university group's vision for these endeavors proved divisive and failed to win the support of either Vietnamese or American officials.

According to the university group's final report: "A basic, irreconcilable difference between the Government of Vietnam and [the MSU group] precluded the project's continuation for an optimum period."[127] Although this statement refers specifically to the disagreement between Diem and MSU over academic freedom and the publications of former participants in the Vietnam Project, it could easily be applied to the MSU team's overall experience in Vietnam. Police advisers from the university group and Vietnamese government officials disagreed over the nature of law enforcement in Vietnam and how the United States could best help Diem's regime achieve internal stability. When coupled with the escalating civil war and US government policies that favored using the military to fight political subversion, the irreconcilable differences among GVN officials, American military personnel, and university advisers proved too great to overcome. As antigovernment violence increased, the MSU group appeared less suited to help ease South Vietnam's security crisis. By the end of the 1950s, when USOM introduced its PSD, MSU had effectively been replaced by an organization willing to implement the Ngos' and American policy makers' military agenda. In the end, MSU's police team failed to establish in Vietnam the foundation for a modern, transparent, and democratic law enforcement system, largely because it never came to grips with the nature and depth of Saigon's political and security problems.

# 5

# Teaching Loyalty

## Educational Development and the Strategic Hamlet Program

The things which will, in the long run, probably determine whether or not the strategic hamlet program is a successful one are not the barbed wire, alarm systems and militia but rather the Economic and Social developments within the hamlets.
—Willie Meyers (1963)

American nation builders believed that educational development offered an important avenue for bolstering the state of South Vietnam and for improving the lives of its people. Most aid workers had an idealized vision of the transformative effects of education. They believed that American education models, which emphasized scientific methods and English-language acquisition, could help modernize Vietnamese society, which they viewed as backward and traditional. They also believed that a Western education system might promote stability and economic development in South Vietnam. Such grand ideas about the power of education mirrored the goals of education reform in colonial settings. Like colonial administrators in earlier decades, American nation builders advocated using education as a means of uplifting a foreign population.

Despite the lofty ambitions articulated by aid workers, however, US and South Vietnamese policy makers had pragmatic, strategic, and political reasons for installing American teachers in South Vietnamese schools and for reforming the country's education system. As the number of US military advisers and soldiers dramatically increased during the late 1950s and early 1960s, Americans needed more Vietnamese people to speak English in order to work with them. Although most US officials considered educational development to be a lower priority than nation-building projects such as public and police administration, many believed that reforming South Vietnam's education system might complement other efforts to strengthen the state while simultaneously countering the appeal of communism. They hoped that, by modernizing South Vietnam's education system and increasing access to it, they could help raise living standards and also train administrators and laborers who might work in service of the state. At the same time, they assumed that education might also contribute to their counterinsurgency efforts. In essence, many US officials thought that Americans could teach Vietnam's population to support the Government of Vietnam (GVN) and, by association, the American intervention. Aid workers at the US Operations Mission (USOM) and volunteers from International Voluntary Services (IVS) shared this conviction and eagerly offered their services.

Education advisers from USOM and especially IVS assumed an explicitly political role and served to implement US and GVN policies to a far greater degree than most other American aid workers in the country. IVS promoted a bottom-up, grassroots approach to development that differed significantly from the high-modernist emphasis of most leaders in Washington and Saigon. However, most IVSers generally supported the broad goals of US assistance. According to an internal history of the IVS mission in Vietnam, the volunteers "accepted the purposes of the U.S. government's association with Vietnam as set forth in the Truman Doctrine."[1] As a result, their efforts often proved counterproductive— by strengthening the authority of the repressive South Vietnamese state, they contributed to opposition to the undemocratic regime in Saigon. Although many volunteers eventually came to appreciate that their close association with both the US and the South Vietnamese governments might alienate them from local communities, they were unable to distinguish themselves from the two governments in the eyes of the Vietnamese people. Instead, their work exacerbated tensions between the population and the two governments.

The IVS education volunteers' activities, and particularly their work in the strategic hamlets, reinforced misguided policies and resulted in increasing political polarization within South Vietnam. By agreeing to participate in the hamlet program, the IVSers became the vanguard in US and South Vietnamese efforts to wage unconventional warfare in rural parts of the country. As a result, they contributed directly to the implementation of one of the most politically destructive and unpopular programs introduced in South Vietnam. Their involvement in the strategic hamlet program also underscores how counterinsurgency efforts subsumed all other development goals by the early 1960s. The story of the IVS education team reveals the devastating effects of the organization's participation in the flawed nation-building experiment as well as the aid workers' complicity in American military escalation in Vietnam.

## USOM and Educational Development in the 1950s

Even before the French had granted Vietnam independence, American officials identified education as a prime area for foreign investment and development assistance. They believed that introducing an American-style education system to Vietnam offered significant strategic benefits that would translate into increased support and loyalty to the Saigon government. In the early 1950s, while the First Indochina War still raged, US policy makers entered into a trilateral arrangement with the French and Emperor Bao Dai's government to provide financial aid to the State of Vietnam's small number of technical-vocational schools. Following the French defeat and the partitioning of the country, American aid workers expanded their efforts to assist the fledgling state in southern Vietnam in educational development and reform. By 1956, USOM had assumed sole responsibility for administering material assistance to all South Vietnam's technical-vocational schools. The following year, the US government and the GVN formalized their commitment to these schools and other education institutions, and USOM began providing the funding for and overseeing the construction of new polytechnic schools. Also in 1957, Ngo Dinh Diem's regime began sending students attending those schools to the United States and other countries for intensive training.[2] These efforts and others in the field of educational development produced dramatic results and led to increasing American involvement in South Vietnam's education system as well as other social and economic-development programs.

During the second half of the 1950s, the United States increased its commitments and levels of nonmilitary aid to the GVN significantly. American education aid efforts grew during this period and achieved measurable results. By 1961, aid workers at USOM's education team could boast of their contributions to soaring enrollments in both traditional and vocational schools, to the construction of new education facilities, and to developing teacher training programs throughout South Vietnam. Rising enrollments offered perhaps the most dramatic illustration of these accomplishments. According to a USOM report, in 1955, 601,862 pupils were enrolled in elementary schools in the country. Nearly 12,000 teachers taught those students. Five years later, those figures had more than doubled, with an estimated 73 percent of elementary school–aged children attending school regularly.[3] Similarly, between 1955 and 1960, enrollment figures for high school jumped from 53,501 to 169,581 students.

But boosting school enrollments required that the state provide enough resources and schools to support the growing student body. As a result, USOM also devoted substantial funding and energy to increasing the number of classrooms and education institutions in South Vietnam. According to American aid workers, enrollment at secondary schools would have been even higher had there been enough classrooms to accommodate all the students who wished to attend high school. USOM reported that only one in five qualified elementary graduates could enroll in high school because of severe classroom shortages. In an attempt to address this problem, USOM and the Department of National Education (DNE) of the Republic of Vietnam (RVN) prioritized classroom construction. As a result of their efforts, in the second half of the 1950s, the number of elementary classrooms doubled while the number of high school classrooms tripled. USOM and the DNE also worked together to build high school laboratories in which secondary students could study physics, chemistry, and biology. Before the introduction of USOM's education team, South Vietnam had no adequate science labs in its secondary schools. Many of these construction projects depended on cooperative arrangements or self-help initiatives, on which the local community or provincial officials and USOM worked together and supplied equal amounts of funding.[4]

In addition to financing elementary and secondary schools for Vietnamese youths, USOM provided funding for the construction of normal schools where local elementary school teachers could receive training.[5] The first of these institutions, the National Normal School in Saigon, was constructed in 1955. Within the next five years, the DNE and USOM oversaw the creation of eight additional normal schools in provincial capitals throughout South Vietnam. American aid workers not only delivered funding for these schools but also worked with officials in the RVN to plan the sites, design curricula, select and order equipment and supplies, and provide training for the teachers enrolled in normal schools. Teacher training figured as a particularly important aspect of US educational-development efforts because it allowed the American system and models to perpetuate and continue, even after the departure of US aid workers.

American nation builders also prioritized the creation of new and improved technical and vocational schools. Aid workers believed that developing countries in particular needed a strong base of skilled workers and technicians. In fact, they saw well-trained, skilled laborers as the critical element necessary to establish new industries, modernize the agricultural system, expand commercial relations, and maintain existing facilities and factories in southern Vietnam. As a USOM report explains: "The expansion and improvement of technical and vocational training programs is basic to the success of other types of economic-development projects."[6] Many South Vietnamese officials, including those at the DNE, agreed with this assessment.

In order to implement their ambitious educational-development plans, the DNE and USOM contracted out some of the work to other organizations and university groups. For example, a team from Southern Illinois University served as consultants to the National Normal School in Saigon and two of the rural normal schools as well as the USOM-sponsored Phu Tho Polytechnic School, providing in-service training for teachers. Similarly, USOM enlisted a small contract team from Ohio University to assist faculty in the Pedagogy Department at the University of Saigon as they developed a comprehensive program for training secondary teachers.[7] The USOM education team's most important affiliation, however, was its partnership with IVS.

IVS had been active in South Vietnam since 1956, and members of the USOM rural affairs team had established good working relationships with IVS agriculture volunteers. As a result, when the DNE and USOM required additional support for their education programs, especially in rural areas, they looked primarily to IVS. By the early 1960s, DNE and USOM officials faced pressure to meet the increasing demand within South Vietnam for English-language instruction. As more American military personnel and civilian advisers arrived in the country, the need for Vietnamese who could communicate with those foreigners rose exponentially. In late 1961, Herbert Walther, one of USOM's education advisers, wrote to the director of USOM, requesting more Americans to teach English in order to "keep pace with demand." In his letter, Walther specifically mentioned the possibility for collaboration with IVS or the newly created Peace Corps. He explained that South Vietnamese policy makers also supported USOM's bid for assistance. He cited an appeal from Phan The Roanh, the GVN deputy director general of instruction at the DNE, who called for more American aid workers to teach English.[8]

Shortly after Walther wrote about USOM's need for assistance, IVS agreed to introduce an education team to South Vietnam. The first group of education volunteers arrived in South Vietnam in the spring of 1962, thereby expanding the mission and services of IVS in the country. Initially, the IVS education team consisted of eleven volunteers, but the group grew quickly, eventually outnumbering the organization's agriculture team. Education IVSers lived in both urban and rural areas, and they provided courses in English, science, home economics, and other subjects to the local population. In addition to addressing the demand for increased English-language instruction, the introduction of the IVS education team reflected the organization's faith in the important role of education in international development.[9]

## IVS Volunteers and the Ideology of Education

The IVS education team's vision for how their work might contribute to nation-building efforts in South Vietnam stemmed from the volunteers' experience coming of age in the wake of the Second World War and their assumptions about development, foreign aid, and the Third World. Like their counterparts in the IVS agriculture team, members of the education team generally accepted the official rationale behind President Truman's Point Four Program, which linked American security interests with economic assistance in the developing world.[10] In addition, the education IVSers, who all volunteered after John F. Kennedy had taken office, found the young president's appeal for public service particularly persuasive.

Kennedy's January 1961 inaugural address deeply influenced many members of the IVS education team. In it, the president challenged Americans to embrace their duties and responsibilities as citizens of the United States with his famous pronouncement: "Ask not what your country can do for you; ask what you can do for your country."[11] Many young Americans responded with enthusiasm to Kennedy's call for public service by volunteering for organizations like the newly constituted Peace Corps and its predecessor, IVS. In explaining their reasons for joining IVS, several education team members referred directly to the president's inaugural or the idealism that Kennedy espoused. One teacher, John Sommer, wrote to his family and friends: "Never have the words for [Kennedy's] Inaugural Address rung so true as here in Viet-Nam now." Sommer then cited the passage from the address that he found most influential and relevant to his own experiences. He wrote, quoting Kennedy: "Now the trumpet summons U.S. again—not as a call to bear arms, though arms we need—not as a call to battle, though embattled we are—but a call to bear the burden of a long twilight struggle, year in and year out, rejoicing in hope, patient in tribulation—a struggle against the common enemies of man: tyranny, poverty, disease, and war itself."[12]

Although many IVS volunteers saw their work as a novel way to address the uncharted problems of the "New Frontier," as their president had eloquently described the challenges facing the world, educational development in Vietnam was reminiscent of earlier colonial endeavors. In particular, the IVS program closely paralleled the establishment of Indian boarding schools in the United States as well as American education reform in the Philippines. Beginning in the late nineteenth century, as part of an effort that some scholars have described as *internal colonization*, the US Bureau of Indian Affairs created boarding schools for Native American children. The government often built these schools in remote areas far removed from the ancestral lands of the populations whose children attended. The program removed Native American children, often forcibly, from their families and communities and compelled them to adopt the English language and other dominant cultural practices. It constituted an overt attempt to eradicate cultural traditions that differed from those of the white majority and assimilate native people into mainstream American society.[13]

In the early twentieth century, US officials began to export the model of educational development first used in Native American communities. Colonial administrators introduced an American-style school system and established English as the primary language of the educated classes in the Philippines, which the United States had recently acquired as a result of its victory in the War of 1898 and subsequent defeat of Filipino nationalists.[14] In fact, IVS had a direct link to the American colonial project in the Philippines. John Noffsinger, one of the founding members of the organization and later a central adviser for Kennedy's Peace Corps program, began his career as a teacher in the Philippines. According to the historian Paul Rodell, Noffsinger's early experiences teaching in Manila influenced his views on the role of English-language training and education in international development and inspired IVS's institutional approach of exporting American education models abroad.[15]

Even before IVS introduced its education team in 1962, its agriculture volunteers had participated in "nonformal" educational activities. For example, many IVSers taught English to their neighbors and the local farmers with whom they worked in Vietnam.[16] IVS's decision to add an education team to its program in Vietnam stemmed in part from the perceived success of these informal teaching arrangements. According to its final report for its Vietnam mission, IVS "justified the formal education enlargement on the grounds that it enabled IVS to establish community contacts, developed and strengthened the nation's educational system, and trained Vietnamese leadership." Like aid workers at USOM, IVSers saw Vietnam's education system as "inadequate," and they expressed confidence that they could play an important role in improving it. IVS considered the system, which was patterned largely on the French model, to "[overemphasize] examinations at the expense of learning." The IVSers believed that they could contribute to modernization and economic progress in Vietnam by teaching English, by introducing scientific methods, and by assisting local teachers in their classroom preparation. As the organization's final report stated, in these ways the volunteers "sought to relate 'education' and 'development.'"[17]

The majority of IVS education volunteers lived and worked in cities and towns throughout South Vietnam, while about a quarter worked in the strategic hamlet program in more rural areas of the country. Most volunteers in both settings taught English, and a handful offered courses in the life and physical sciences. Some IVSers supplemented their English or science instruction with courses in home economics, music, auto mechanics, and other practical or applied fields of study. The first team of education volunteers, who went to Vietnam in 1962, consisted of eight English teachers and two science instructors. Two years later, the team had grown to a total of thirty-five volunteers, with twenty teaching English, eight teaching science, and seven working as education advisers in the strategic hamlets.[18]

Although they worked for the same organization and their efforts constituted part of the broadly defined mission to provide development assistance to Vietnam, members of the IVS education and agriculture teams differed significantly. The agriculture volunteers were all men, but the education team consisted of both men and women. Some of the female volunteers were single, while others went to Vietnam with their husbands. Several married couples volunteered together for the education team, and a few female IVSers taught in Vietnam while their husbands worked in the IVS agriculture or public health programs.[19]

For the most part, volunteers on the agriculture and education teams lived and worked in fundamentally different settings. With the exception of a handful of volunteers at the Tan Son Nhut experimental farm in Saigon, most agriculture team members were stationed in rural areas or small villages. On the other hand, many education volunteers lived and worked in larger towns and cities, including Hue, Nha Trang, Ban Me Thout, and Saigon. High-level American officials, including US foreign service officers and military advisers, tended to operate out of South Vietnam's cities and rarely spent extended periods of time in the provinces. As a result, education volunteers had relatively more contact with other Americans in Vietnam at the time than did most IVSers working on agriculture programs. In addition, because IVS teachers instructed students in various classes, the nature of their interactions with local people differed from the relationships forged by agriculture volunteers, who often developed close associations with the handful of farmers with whom they worked on the experimental stations. As the IVS terminal report for Vietnam explains, the introduction of the education team fundamentally altered the character of the mission. When the education volunteers arrived, the size of the

IVS group increased dramatically, the organization's focus shifted from rural areas to towns and cities, and the emphasis on person-to-person assistance diminished as the new teachers concentrated on training large groups of students.[20]

Volunteers in the IVS education team taught at a range of venues, including public high schools, Buddhist monasteries, and normal schools. A handful of them developed mobile science laboratories that traveled from village to village. Through the use of these laboratories, the Americans hoped to introduce scientific methods to students living in more rural communities, where local schools could not afford modern lab equipment. The IVSers' emphasis on scientific method and experimentation reflects their conviction that science and objectivity distinguished modern societies from traditional ones. Because the volunteers viewed the acceptance of scientific principles as intricately linked with modernization, they promoted science as a central element of their vision for education reform in Vietnam.

IVSers kept busy, even when they were not teaching in the classroom. Most members of the education team participated in a host of informal educational pursuits outside their official duties. IVSers organized and took part in various activities during their summer vacation period, when the local schools were not in session. In addition to preparing instructional materials for the following academic year, they developed new projects and assisted in other types of development work. For example, during the summer of 1963, IVSers stationed in Hue provided instruction in swimming and crafts to elementary school–aged students, helped establish a local radio program in conjunction with the US Information Service (USIS), and organized a science workshop. Volunteers working in other areas of the country supervised school construction projects, taught sewing classes, promoted USIS film programs, and set up libraries. Others joined forces with IVS agriculture volunteers to establish pig and chicken programs or plant demonstration gardens. Still others helped public health advisers launch medical clinics, dispense medicine, and organize basic sanitation workshops. Finally, nearly all IVSers continued offering English-language instruction to a range of individuals from a broad cross section of Vietnamese society. For example, one IVSer taught English to art teachers in Hue, another provided instruction to the director of the Qui Nhon Polytechnic School, and another taught students at a nursery school.[21]

Phyllis Colyer, a member of the International Voluntary Services education team, teaches English in South Vietnam. Courtesy International Voluntary Services Records, 1952–2003, Photographs, Vietnam/Laos, 1959–1962, XI-14, box 58, folder 8, Mennonite Church USA Archives—Goshen, Goshen, IN.

As they spent time in Vietnam, the volunteers' experiences tempered their initial optimism. Many volunteers came to recognize that the successful implementation of their programs required the support and trust of the Vietnamese population. Some demonstrated a nuanced understanding of the challenges undermining their projects. These volunteers cited cultural and philosophical reasons to explain why Vietnam's people resisted change to their education system or why social and economic development did not necessarily translate into political support for the South Vietnamese government. More specifically, many volunteers understood that the primary weakness of their program stemmed from the fact that the majority of Vietnamese identified IVS with the US government and American military forces and, by extension, with the repressive and unpopular Diem regime. The Vietnamese population's overwhelmingly negative perception of the GVN and the US government prevented many people from embracing any aid projects associated with them. However, despite their appreciation of the problems posed by their relationship with the US government, the volunteers could not adequately resolve this issue as long as they continued to implement GVN and US government policies.

In their letters to families and friends, many volunteers wrote about the serious mistakes made by the South Vietnamese government. They also expressed concern over the close relationship between politicians in Saigon and Washington, DC. Members of the IVS education team enjoyed an important vantage point from which to judge the deficiencies of the GVN—they saw firsthand the effects of repressive policies and had ample opportunity to speak with local people about their reactions to those policies. Moreover, IVSers worked closely with students and youth groups, who were some of the most outspoken and organized opponents of the government.

In attempting to explain why Diem's regime did not inspire popular support, the IVS volunteer William Forest Gerdes argued: "More than anything else, the intransigent self-righteous attitude of the government, together with unfair practices and poorly restrained use of force, has alienated the Vietnamese people." In 1963, during the major anti-Diem demonstrations staged by Buddhist monks and students, Gerdes was in Hue, the focal point of the protests. He criticized the tactics that Diem's antiriot squads used to discourage the demonstrations, including tear gas, barbed-wired barricades, and heavily armed soldiers stationed on street corners. Encounters between Diem's forces and the demonstrators occasionally erupted into outright violence. According to Gerdes, many Vietnamese responded to Diem's heavy-handed methods for dealing with opposition by "focusing their attention on the instrument of their repression." Revealing an impressive amount of foresight, Gerdes advised his friends at home that the success of American efforts in Vietnam depended on the nature of the association between the two governments. He cautioned: "One thing is sure, what the relationship of the United States to the government is will make a great deal of difference. My friends have said that our country will look bad unless we stand for liberty."[22]

As Gerdes and other IVSers learned, however, neither the Vietnamese government nor its American supporters insisted on liberty and democracy. Instead, consumed by their efforts to defend Diem, American officials turned a blind eye to GVN abuses. Owing to their ideological sympathy for and financial dependence on the US government, the IVS volunteers inadvertently assumed the role of vital players in this struggle to preserve South Vietnam.

## Hearts and Minds

Although many IVSers recognized the devastating effects of GVN repression and understood why the government enjoyed such limited popular support, they were unable (or perhaps unwilling) to address these problems. Because they accepted the basic philosophical and ideological underpinnings of American intervention in Vietnam, they rarely questioned the political implications of their own work. Instead, many blamed GVN and US failures on poor implementation of sound policies rather than on fundamental flaws in the policies themselves. Gloria Johnson, a female volunteer who spent two years working on education programs and then returned to Vietnam as an IVS team leader, wrote about what she characterized as the gap between ideals and action. In December 1964, just a few months before the first American ground troops landed in Da Nang, she told her family and friends:

> This war is an important thing and it's vital that we win it, although I cannot report that there is a general atmosphere of optimism at this particular point. This war here will not be an easy one to win, either, in my opinion. The Viet Cong are certainly not well-equipped militarily, but they are extremely well-trained and they have an ideal that makes them willing to withstand all kinds of hardship, even death. And therein lies the problem: how is it possible to instill within the South Vietnamese the same unfaltering idealism regarding democracy as the Communists have instilled in the North Vietnamese Viet Cong? If we knew the answer, then our arms and our economic aid would do a vast amount of good. Saying you believe in an ideal is one thing, but being willing to fight and die for it is another. It's a question that many Americans never have to face, but almost every Vietnamese will have to ask himself the question and then answer it with action. And many other peoples of the world will have to do the same. If the Communists manage to win in Vietnam and other countries that they are now threatening, Americans may well have to ask themselves this same question some day.[23]

Johnson's reference to the "North Vietnamese Viet Cong" suggests the power and pervasiveness of Cold War ideology. Although she would have been intimately familiar with the political situation in South Vietnam, Johnson nevertheless repeated the official line that the National Liberation Front (NLF) was a North Vietnamese entity rather than a distinct southern insurgency. Such simplistic and inaccurate characterizations of the NLF were commonplace among US and South Vietnamese policy makers, who emphasized the external threats to the RVN's existence. But Johnson's description of the "North Vietnamese Viet Cong" illustrates the profound degree to which official thinking and Cold War assumptions colored aid workers' views and their approach on the ground.

In addition, such observations pointed to a fundamental dilemma at the heart of the IVS mission in Vietnam. Johnson saw the basic problem facing Americans as how to inspire idealism among South Vietnamese people, and she accepted the wisdom of fighting a war on behalf of the South Vietnamese state. However, she failed to acknowledge that neither the GVN nor the United States actually pursued the ideal of democracy in South Vietnam. Instead, both governments endorsed highly undemocratic methods for protecting the authoritarian regime in Saigon.

Other education volunteers made similar observations about the challenge of winning hearts and minds in order to ensure South Vietnam's political survival. Terence Murphy, a volunteer teaching English at a normal school in Qui Nhon Province, argued that the primary goal of the United States should be to help establish a cohesive civil government "which can command the allegiance and obedience of the majority of the people" in South Vietnam. He saw this task as equally important to a military defeat of the Communist insurgency. In his estimation, most Vietnamese preferred to "remain aloof from the political struggle if they could." However, he argued that, when forced to choose, Vietnamese peasants tended to support those who addressed their basic needs and interests—in this case the NLF. According to him, the South Vietnamese government's inability and refusal to dissociate itself from past regimes that limited the freedom of farmers and exploited their labor caused many people to distrust the new government. He believed that the GVN faced the overwhelming tasks of uniting the population, developing a strong and honest government, locating a leader capable of inspiring sacrifice, and promoting a cause that people considered worth fighting for.[24]

Johnson and Murphy articulated concerns that many education volunteers expressed regarding the barriers to American nation-building efforts. According to Murphy, the NLF promised a bright future for many people, while the government protected the status quo. He explained the ramifications of this dilemma with a simple but critical question: "And why should anyone be satisfied with one bag of rice and a little security today when he can have two bags of rice and complete freedom tomorrow?"[25] This question suggests that Murphy understood that many Vietnamese viewed their struggle as a continuation of the war for liberation rather than an extension of the global Cold War conflict. Like Johnson, however, he never fully grappled with the fact that, by advancing official US policies, IVSers only bolstered an unpopular regime that depended on foreign support for its survival.

Unfortunately, the education team's work reinforced precisely those GVN and US policies that drew the most popular contempt. The IVS education team, many of whose members volunteered with the intention of helping people in need, actually served to strengthen the power of political elites in Saigon and help extend the authority of the state. Nowhere were the unintended but devastating consequences of IVS education work more evident than in the group's involvement in the strategic hamlet program. The volunteers' participation in this program illustrates clearly how IVSers implemented flawed policies to advance the GVN and US agendas and, in so doing, severely curtailed their own ability to provide aid that might benefit Vietnam's people.

## Strategic Hamlets and Counterinsurgency Tactics

The arrival of the IVS education team corresponded with the introduction of the strategic hamlet program and a critical transformation in nation-building policies in South Vietnam. Beginning in the early 1960s, the emphasis of nation building shifted from creating institutions that would strengthen and modernize the state and society in South Vietnam to supporting counterinsurgency efforts and defeating the NLF. As a memo produced by the US Agency for International Development (USAID) in March 1962 explained: "The warfare in Vietnam is at a very critical stage in which the next few months could be decisive. The [US]AID program has a major role to play in this unorthodox warfare where military operation cannot succeed without a great deal of civilian support, particularly from the people at whom much of the [US]AID program is aimed."[26] Over the next several years, counterinsurgency remained a top priority of American involvement in South Vietnam. According to a USOM report issued in early 1964: "The overriding purpose of all U.S. programs in Vietnam is to help the GVN achieve an early victory over the Viet Cong."[27]

Launched in early 1962, the strategic hamlet program was the centerpiece of GVN counterinsurgency plans. The brainchild of Ngo Dinh Nhu, Diem's younger brother, it served as a heavy-handed effort to defeat antigovernment guerillas and solve security problems in rural areas. At the same time, the Ngo brothers viewed the program as a model for the radical transformation of South Vietnamese society along the lines of the personalist revolution, which they had been pursuing for years.[28] The program's basic objective was to separate citizens considered loyal to the GVN from antigovernment insurgents, thus making it easier to distinguish and eradicate opponents.[29] The hamlets' inhabitants would provide their own defense against guerilla attacks, thereby removing the need for a large occupying force to be stationed in rural villages.

To implement the program, the GVN sent teams of specialists to rural villages, where they required peasants to help construct heavy fortifications. They then separated the population by gender and age and issued identification cards to everyone residing within the hamlets. Inhabitants were compelled to organize self-defense corps to guard their hamlets. These self-defense corps, which functioned like local militias, were also expected to patrol outside the perimeter of the hamlets and match NLF strategy with their own low-level, guerilla tactics. As the historian Edward Miller explains: "In the role reversal Nhu imagined, the inhabitants of strategic hamlets would actually become guerillas."[30] According to Nhu's vision, this system would not only shift the dynamics of the war against the NLF but also contribute to the broader GVN goals of remaking and modernizing Vietnamese society.

Securing the countryside and creating easily identifiable pacified regions had been priorities of the South Vietnamese government since the mid-1950s. Shortly after taking office, Diem began trying to consolidate his hold over the rural areas of South Vietnam. He recognized that most of his supporters resided in Saigon and other large cities. He understood that, in order to maintain his position, he would have to encourage the cooperation and allegiance of peasants, who constituted the majority of South Vietnam's population. Assuming that he could best assert his authority by bringing those peasants into the national body, he introduced highly centralized political, administrative, and economic reform programs. For example, he issued decrees on March 3, 1955, and October 24, 1956, that effectively abolished self-rule and autonomy in the provinces.[31] When early reform efforts failed to produce widespread support for the GVN, and as attacks on government officials escalated, Diem's regime enacted more extreme measures to bring rural populations under its control.

The GVN's 1959 agroville program was a significant component of this approach.[32] The program was created in direct response to the rising number of attacks against local administrators in the provinces and the increasing appeal of the antigovernment movement throughout the countryside. The GVN established protected villages called *agrovilles* and forced peasants to leave their homes and move into them. It expected the two to three thousand inhabitants of each agroville to build new houses using materials from their old residences. In exchange for relocating and providing forced, unpaid labor, the agroville residents were promised basic social services such as schools, medical facilities, electricity, and collective security. The promised amenities rarely materialized, however, and Diem demonstrated little interest in improving the social and economic conditions of rural Vietnamese.[33] At the same time, the agrovilles were explicitly intended to prevent villagers from supporting or joining the antigovernment movement. They allowed GVN officials to keep a closer watch on the inhabitants and ensure that they did not support the insurgents by paying taxes to Communist authorities or by providing food, clothing, weapons, or shelter for local cadres. According to the scholar George Kahin, the agrovilles functioned as "fortified concentrations where [Vietnamese peasants] could be both more easily controlled and better insulated from contact with ex-Vietminh and others who resisted Saigon's authority."[34]

The agrovilles attracted few enthusiasts among the Vietnamese people, who resented being forcibly relocated and compelled to perform unpaid labor for the construction and defense of the villages. The American journalist Stanley Karnow visited several agrovilles in the Mekong delta during the late 1950s. According to Karnow, the agrovilles "were built and managed in such a way that they alienated peasants." He explained: "Peasants assigned to the agroville had been uprooted from their native villages and ancestral graves, and their traditional social pattern disrupted."[35]

Although most contemporary observers considered the agroville program to be ineffectual, GVN policy makers seemed to rely heavily on that earlier model as they devised the strategic hamlet program.[36] In fact, the strategic hamlets of the early 1960s were strikingly similar to the agrovilles of the late 1950s. Not only did the two programs share a vision for how to win political support by providing services to the rural population; they both relied on forced relocation and heavy-handed methods for protecting inhabitants. As a result of these deliberate and repressive attempts to divide people into friend or foe, both the agroville and the strategic hamlet programs were counterproductive in that they drove an even deeper wedge between the South Vietnamese regime and the majority of the country's population.

Recent scholarship by Philip Catton and Edward Miller has challenged the conventional wisdom that the strategic hamlet program borrowed from earlier British and American models. However, the Vietnamese program bore a significant resemblance to counterinsurgency efforts in postcolonial Malaya and the Philippines.[37] As the historian Michael Latham explains, the strategic hamlets did not introduce new concepts but simply revised older ideologies and techniques of state control.[38] Even if Nhu explicitly rejected key aspects of the British and American models, as Miller asserts, the perceived successes of those earlier attempts likely contributed to American policy makers' support for the hamlet program.[39]

Along with the GVN, a number of American agencies, including the CIA, the State Department, and USAID, played a central role in implementing the hamlet program. Although some Americans expressed concern over the more draconian aspects of the program, most US policy makers were willing to support the basic outlines of the strategic hamlets. Their support likely derived from their own views about unconventional warfare and counterinsurgency. During the Korean War, the US military and civilian intelligence agencies experimented with new techniques for defeating the Korean Communists through unconventional methods, including psychological warfare and the extensive use of propaganda. A 1951 army manual titled "Operations against Guerilla Forces" laid the foundation for US counterinsurgency doctrine in the following decades.[40]

That doctrine argued that the best strategy for defeating a popular revolution was, as the scholar Michael McClintock put it, to "[fight] like with like" by employing "mirror image attacks" and using the methods and techniques of the insurgents in order to crush them. According to this view, which dovetailed with Nhu's vision for how the hamlet militias would function, guerillas were best fought by individuals who employed similar tactics. McClintock has explained how this principle guided counterinsurgency experts' efforts at population control and forced relocation: "In a revolutionary insurgency, where the insurgents are of and among the people, the counterinsurgent's attempts to isolate the insurgents from 'the people' must almost inevitably take on the same characteristics as the tactics of an occupation force in conventional warfare."[41]

In describing the potential merits of the strategic hamlets, both Vietnamese and American officials emphasized the nonmilitary goals of the program. Nhu, in particular, argued that social and political development ranked high among its aims. He envisioned a "triple revolution" and maintained that the strategic hamlets advanced social progress and democracy in a distinctly Vietnamese manner, one conforming with the personalist revolution the Ngos promoted.[42] He claimed that peasants would recognize the protection afforded them by the hamlets even though security factored as just "one consequence of the social and political revolution contained in the strategic hamlet philosophy."[43] In fact, the strategic hamlet program provided a clear means for the Ngo brothers to advance their ideas about social engineering and rural reorganization.[44]

American officials also embraced this rationale. For example, in a letter to Diem, John F. Kennedy praised the strategic hamlet program's goal of "bring[ing] lasting social and economic benefits to the people in the countryside." In his response, Diem wrote: "I deeply appreciate the fact that you made a special reference to our strategic hamlets and described them as an institution designed to help us rapidly attain the essential objectives of our policy, which are respect for the human person, social justice, and the creation of true democracy."[45]

Such rosy descriptions of the program's nonmilitary objectives did not reflect a serious assessment of the strategic hamlets' actual purpose or their potential effects on Vietnamese society. Fundamentally, the hamlets served as a counterinsurgency weapon to reinforce Diem's control over the population and defeat the NLF. As one US report explained: "The basic aim is, of course, to separate the people from the [Viet Cong]."[46] The Ngo brothers and their American advisers believed that the strategic hamlets offered "the easiest and most promising course" for defeating the insurgency.[47]

Guided in particular by Nhu's enthusiastic support, the South Vietnamese government fervently pursued the strategic hamlet program, and it quickly became one of the regime's most expensive and ambitious projects. Diem and Nhu first introduced the program to the Mekong delta region in March 1962. They directed the South Vietnamese army to begin building stockades and hamlets as quickly as possible. In July of that year, the CIA reported that two thousand hamlets had already been constructed and that the GVN had drawn up plans for another seven thousand.[48] Like the Americans at the CIA and the Pentagon, Diem and Nhu became obsessed with the numbers and statistics surrounding the program. At the end of September 1962, the GVN released a report claiming that 4,322,034 people, or 33 percent of the population, had been moved into strategic hamlets.[49] In November of that year, the US military reported to Secretary of Defense Robert McNamara that, of the GVN's projected total of 10,971 hamlets, 3,353 had been completed.[50] GVN's and US officials' fixation on such numerical data as a means of measuring the progress of the hamlet program not only masked the fundamental problems of their policies but also foreshadowed their obsession with statistics and body counts as the war escalated in the following years.

Despite the impressive numbers of hamlets constructed, American officials harbored some concerns about the actual accomplishments of the program. In late 1963, General Maxwell Taylor, chairman of the Joint Chiefs of Staff, reported to McNamara that only about 600 of the 3,353 completed hamlets could be considered as "fulfilling the desired characteristics in terms of equipment, defensive works, security forces and, possibly most important, government." Taylor argued that the GVN demonstrated "little planning and less coordination" in its efforts to implement the strategic hamlet program.[51] Similarly, the State Department official Roger Hilsman concluded: "In many [hamlets], nothing seems to have been done but to construct a barbed wire or bamboo fence."[52]

Although Taylor, Hilsman, and others expressed frustration with the way in which the Vietnamese government executed the program, in 1962 and early 1963 few American officials questioned the wisdom of the basic premise of strategic hamlets. In discussing the shortcomings of the program, Taylor stated: "A basically sound idea got off to a weak start."[53] Hilsman criticized the Diem regime's handling of the hamlets. He claimed: "The GVN failure to emphasize political, social and economic reform at the outset may deprive the entire effort of much of its impact. Much depends on the ability of the government to show convincing evidence of its intent to improve the lot of peasants. Instead, government efforts appear to be aimed largely at increasing government control over the peasants."[54] Such military and political objectives superseded any other incidental benefits that the hamlet inhabitants might have received.

The strategic hamlet program was a direct response to escalating warfare and the failure of previous GVN attempts to secure the loyalty of Vietnam's rural population. By the early 1960s, the antigovernment insurgency had become a full-scale civil war that disproportionately affected rural inhabitants and negatively affected even those people who sought to remain uninvolved in the conflict. Because of the military context and emphasis, the program strained relations between the Vietnamese population and Americans working in the country. American involvement in the program inspired doubts among many Vietnamese regarding the true objectives of the United States in their country. Through their financial and logistic support of new hamlets, American aid workers became highly visible participants in the program. American aid money helped fund the creation of these hamlets and cover the costs of relocating tens of thousands of people to live in them. Aid workers from organizations such as USOM and IVS took part in construction efforts and then continued working in hamlet medical clinics and schools.

## Aid Workers and Strategic Hamlets

An examination of American aid workers' participation in the strategic hamlet program helps explain how and why US nation-building efforts not only failed to accomplish their specific objectives but also contributed to the widespread belief among the Vietnamese people that neither their own government nor its American supporters had their best interests in mind.

Poor security and warfare had a direct impact on schools, students, and teachers in rural as well as urban parts of Vietnam. According to statistics released by the DNE, during 1962, as a result of the civil war, 50 schools were burned, 1,641 classrooms in 574 schools were closed, 1,308 teachers were displaced, 39 teachers were killed by insurgents, and 91 teachers were captured. The DNE estimated that during 1962 alone warfare caused 69,324 students to be "deprived of education."[55] In order to escape the violence, many families moved from the countryside to cities. The influx of these displaced populations strained schools in urban areas, where the shortage of classrooms and exceedingly high enrollment figures meant that many students received, at most, two hours of instruction per day.[56]

In an effort to address these issues, USOM called for "concerted action to assist rural education." American aid workers emphasized the value of bolstering elementary education in strategic hamlets, including converting "regular" schools to community ones and building new schools in the hamlets. They argued that "improved security and the placement of new schools within strategic hamlets will markedly improve educational opportunities."[57]

American aid workers adopted an ambitious plan for educational development in the strategic hamlets. In the first phase of the program, USOM proposed that American aid workers and hamlet residents construct and furnish 660 new elementary classrooms in twenty provinces. Construction of new classrooms would occur only in hamlets that currently lacked schools or were far from other local schools. Furthermore, aid workers offered investment in educational development as an incentive for communities that supported the hamlet program. According to official USOM policy, classroom construction would be limited to hamlets that "enjoy[ed] full security, and which have done their share in promoting the National Strategic Hamlet Program." In addition to constructing classrooms, during the first phase of the hamlet program American aid workers would train 440 new teachers and 200 principals. USOM would also provide money to cover one year of those teachers' salaries as well as supplies and instructional materials. Plans for the second phase of the program called for an extension of those same basic provisions to strategic hamlets in fourteen additional provinces.[58] In fact, American aid workers exceeded their goals. In July 1963, USOM reported that they had already provided training to 820 Vietnamese teachers in three-month-long sessions. Those instructors would then be responsible for teaching more than thirty-three thousand students in strategic hamlets.[59]

While aid workers from USOM oversaw hamlet school construction and teacher-training programs, IVS education volunteers provided grass-roots-level assistance to Vietnamese instructors and served as teachers in the strategic hamlets. They accepted this position without questioning the implications of the military objectives driving the program. In fact, many IVSers believed that the creation of strategic hamlets would actually simplify their goals by providing them access to a concentrated group of people within a secure area. At the same time, the volunteers almost uniformly disregarded the devastating consequences of the program for the people who were forced to move to the hamlets. The volunteers' vision of helping Vietnam's people was incompatible with the counterinsurgency goals of the strategic hamlet program. Moreover, the IVSers' involvement in the program represented the degree to which even civilian aid workers had come to rely on military solutions to advance their nation-building agenda in Vietnam.

The volunteers' initial attitudes about the strategic hamlets reflected the idealism that motivated these young men and women to join the mission. The ruminations of one volunteer, Walter Robertson, illustrate the assumptions that IVSers brought to their assignment of working in the hamlets. Although Robertson had a different background from many of his IVS colleagues, his eagerness to participate in the hamlet program mirrored that of many other volunteers. When he joined the organization and traveled to Vietnam, Robertson was older than most other IVSers. After serving in World War II, he had lived and taught on the Navajo Reservation in Arizona for five years. In a letter written to his friends just after his arrival in Vietnam, he described IVS's role in educational development in the strategic hamlets. He explained that he would be working in hamlets with the "mountain tribes" of the Southern Highlands and wrote with enthusiasm: "My own assignment is one I am looking forward to."[60]

Robertson's excitement about his assignment stemmed from his desire to work with people "in an underdeveloped area where many changes have not yet been made." He referred to his "rewarding" experiences on the Navajo Reservation but claimed that he had become frustrated with his inability to continue aiding the Navajo once their society had reaped the benefits of oil and mineral discoveries. With their resultant wealth, they "had undergone many changes" and no longer required assistance in the same way they once had. Robertson reflected: "Fine roads opened up much of the reservation and some of the feeling of being there was lost to me in the process." In his assessment, paved roads symbolized the achievement of economic progress for the Navajo people and the culmination of his own efforts to bring material advancements to them. As he saw his utility on the reservation drying up, he looked for other opportunities to introduce social and economic progress to underdeveloped societies.[61] Robertson's glorification of Navajo society was not unusual—other IVSers idealized premodern societies, including Vietnam, in their letters home.

The IVS education team's enormous commitment to the strategic hamlets matched the scope of the program itself.[62] In 1962, IVS assigned seven new education volunteers to work in the hamlet schools. Initially, these volunteers visited primary schools that had already been built in the hamlets. They consulted with the teachers and demonstrated teaching methods. According to IVS's terminal report: "The establishment of primary schools in each of the units [hamlets] was a pivotal part of national policy."[63] Intended to serve as community centers as well as learning institutions, the schools occupied a central location in each hamlet, and houses were grouped around the school building. The GVN and US governments placed a high priority on hamlet schools since, as one American official explained, they considered "education as key to vertical mobility for many Vietnamese." By establishing a good primary education system within the hamlets, the GVN hoped to "capture the loyalty of those young Vietnamese who might otherwise seek to shoot their way to position and prestige with the Viet Cong."[64] The IVS report stated: "IVS, because it was a rural operation and related to the villagers, was particularly suited to perform this service."[65]

The volunteers' primary mission in the hamlets was to inspire a "desire for education" among the local population. They strove to accomplish this goal through "the mental conditioning of villagers to accept change and development."[66] They secured books, supplies, and audiovisual materials and distributed them to the hamlet schools. They encouraged Vietnamese hamlet teachers, who earned about eight dollars per day, to plant small gardens in the schoolyards to supplement their incomes and demonstrate farming techniques to their students. They also urged teachers to improve their pedagogical skills by attending provincial and district-level workshops.[67]

After the IVSers had visited fifty schools and advised many of the teachers already working in hamlet classrooms, they turned their attention to constructing new schools and training more teachers. According to one volunteer, their initial job was to work with their Vietnamese counterparts or interpreters and oversee the construction of 660 classrooms. Those classrooms would be built throughout two hundred hamlets in over twenty provinces. This assignment was ambitious, especially given the relatively small size of the IVS hamlet education team. In addition, the volunteers would help establish fourteen teacher-training centers in rural locations near strategic hamlets. IVS expected 440 new teachers to participate in one-month-long in-service training programs during this first phase. Following their training sessions, these teachers would be responsible for instructing over thirty thousand students in hamlet schools.[68] During the subsequent phase of assistance, IVS planned to construct an additional 462 classrooms in fourteen provinces and train 440 more teachers.

Even after the classrooms had been built and the teachers trained, the volunteers would continue working on the hamlet education program. At that point, they would distribute books and supplies, demonstrate additional ways in which the teachers could use local materials in their instruction, and, as Robertson explained, "in general, make use of anything and everything that we [had] to offer."[69]

The IVS volunteers assigned to the strategic hamlets initially supported the program and displayed little concern over their involvement in the enterprise. Their attitudes about the benevolent forces of modernization on display in the hamlets echoed the rhetoric of US officials. For example, the IVS volunteer Willie Meyers emphasized the nonmilitary aspects of American aid to strategic hamlets. Shortly after accepting his position as an education team leader in one of the hamlets, Meyers wrote: "The things which will, in the long run, probably determine whether or not the strategic hamlet program is a successful one are not the barbed wire, alarm systems and militia but rather the Economic and Social developments within the hamlets."[70] This observation mirrored the predictions made a few months earlier by Roger Hilsman, the State Department's intelligence chief, who argued that US objectives in Vietnam could be met only if social, economic, and political progress accompanied military operations.[71] Another adviser to President Kennedy, Eugene Staley, argued for a link between economic advancement and state power in South Vietnam. He claimed: "You've got to do something on the economic-social side to improve the spirit of the people and show that things will move ahead under the present government."[72]

Many IVSers who worked in strategic hamlets focused on self-help projects and celebrated the merits of teaching hamlet residents to help themselves. Meyers earnestly described the value of local self-help projects and explained to his family and friends that IVS encouraged people to improve their own lot in life rather than impose foreign ideas on them. According to Meyers, self-help projects allowed local people to choose an area that needed improvement or a project that would benefit the community and required them to provide the labor for the job. USOM would then supply necessary materials and funding in order to see the projects through to completion. Self-help projects promoted teamwork among villagers, which, as Meyers noted, "they are not accustomed to doing." Such projects also made the services of the South Vietnamese government and American aid agencies responsive to the Vietnamese people's needs, improving social and economic conditions in rural areas, and "[giving] the hamlet person something which he feels is worth defending." However, despite the lofty ambitions of self-help programs, Meyers admitted that such goals constituted an "optimistic view" and did not necessarily represent actual experiences within the hamlets.[73]

Other volunteers also expressed confidence in the US policy of funding hamlet self-help projects. William Forest Gerdes, an IVSer whose primary job was teaching at a normal school in Vinh Long, spent part of his summer vacation working in strategic hamlets in the northwestern part of the country. When he learned of the need for an IVSer to work temporarily in Quang Tri Province, which bordered North Vietnam, Gerdes volunteered to assist with self-help projects in strategic hamlets. He felt "glad to be part of a program that [recognized] that ammunition alone will not win this war." He visited a number of hamlets, sometimes six in one day, and discussed with local leaders their plans for projects such as building irrigation dams, bridges, and water pumps or purchasing a herd of cattle for the community to own jointly. He approved nearly every project he inspected and offered advice on how much material a given project would likely require. He believed that the hamlet residents would demonstrate a newfound devotion to the Saigon regime as a result of these projects.

When he reflected on his experiences working in the strategic hamlets, Gerdes voiced his general enthusiasm for self-help projects, arguing: "For many [this] is the first time they have even known their government to contribute anything material to the local life."[74] However, he did not give any examples that illustrated how the residents' view of the government manifested itself in their behaviors or attitudes.

Many other volunteers conveyed optimistic attitudes similar to Meyers's and Gerdes's. Few voiced any criticism of the strategic hamlet program or the problems stemming from their association with it until months after they actually began working in the hamlets. Eventually, a number of them expressed disillusionment over their failure to implement positive education reform or improve the lives of hamlet residents in any measurable way. In particular, IVSers working in hamlets with non-Vietnamese populations became frustrated by their inability to carry out their vision.

## IVS Aid for Ethnic Minorities

A number of volunteers participating in the strategic hamlet program focused on providing educational-development opportunities for ethnic minority communities, such as the Rhade, Jarai, and Raa groups. Ethnic minorities occupied an important position in South Vietnam's political landscape as the GVN and US officials struggled to form alliances with and ensure the loyalty of non-Vietnamese populations. The US and South Vietnamese governments had strategic as well as political reasons for targeting the minority groups, to which they often referred as *Montagnards*.[75] Most of Vietnam's ethnic minorities lived in upland areas, along the border with Laos and Cambodia. As a result of their geographic and economic position, these groups found themselves caught in the middle of the civil war in Vietnam. At times, this position benefited them—the GVN and US governments targeted them for development projects and dedicated significant aid money to their communities. However, this position also rendered them vulnerable to the whims of the more powerful states around them and challenged their autonomy.

Beginning in the early 1960s, advisers from the People's Army of Vietnam (PAVN) traveled south to support the southern insurgency. After 1964, when the Vietnamese Workers' Party (VWP) approved the deployment of regular PAVN units, North Vietnamese soldiers joined the

NLF forces in their war.[76] Many of those North Vietnamese forces circumvented the demilitarized zone at the seventeenth parallel and instead traveled south through Laos and northern Cambodia, along the infamous network of roads and paths known as the Ho Chi Minh Trail. When they crossed into South Vietnam, PAVN advisers and troops frequently traveled through territories populated by ethnic minorities and only loosely controlled by the GVN. As a result, northern forces along with NLF cadres operating in the highlands relied on minority communities for shelter, provision, and other types of assistance. In response, South Vietnamese and American policy makers looked to cultivate support from minority groups as a counterweight to cooperation between minorities and insurgents or PAVN troops. They hoped to enlist the assistance of minorities to prevent northern forces from streaming into South Vietnam or at least ensure that the Montagnards did not help them by providing safe haven or material support.[77]

In addition to these strategic and military objectives, Vietnamese and American leaders had political reasons for targeting non-Vietnamese communities for development assistance. They believed that, like Catholic refugees from North Vietnam, ethnic minorities potentially offered a supportive constituency for GVN and US policies. This assumption stemmed from the historical collaboration of some minority groups with outsiders such as the French.[78] Diem considered ethnic minority groups a prime target for his attempts to consolidate central state authority. He also regarded the lands they had traditionally occupied as offering a solution to the problem of overpopulation in the coastal lowland areas.[79] The GVN sent northern Catholics into regions controlled by these groups in order to undermine their local autonomy. For their part, American aid workers believed that the minorities would be open to development schemes and foreign aid as an antidote to the negative effects of poverty in their communities.

In the eyes of American and Vietnamese observers, South Vietnam's ethnic minorities were even more poor and backward than their Vietnamese neighbors. As discussed in previous chapters, many ethnic minorities lived in Vietnam's Central Highlands, depended on swidden agriculture and a subsistence economy, had distinctive social and political organizations, and practiced substantially different cultural traditions from the lowland Vietnamese.[80] Americans tended to view minority people as primitive, and many aid workers believed that their development efforts would be particularly well received within their traditional societies. The IVSers' comments about minority people, which relied on stereotypes and cultural distinctions between themselves and the minorities, reveal their assumptions about the superiority of modern American society. As Walter Robinson put it, minority communities were places "where the loincloth is still worn." Given the IVS volunteers' emphasis on assisting the most impoverished and underdeveloped people of Vietnam, introducing programs to the highland region, with its "primitive economy" and traditional cultures, figured as one of their highest priorities.[81]

Working with ethnic minority groups posed a distinct set of challenges for the IVS education volunteers. Few minority people spoke English, and many did not even speak Vietnamese. In order to assist them, IVSers required two interpreters—one to translate between English and Vietnamese and one to translate between Vietnamese and the local minority language.[82] To further complicate the situation, the minority groups targeted by the GVN and US government, which included the Rhade, Jarai, Cham, and others, were extremely diverse. Each group, and sometimes each community or clan within a group, had its own language, traditions, and practices. Overcoming and understanding these differences proved difficult for the American volunteers.

John Sommer, a volunteer stationed in Dalat, served as an education adviser to hamlet communities of ethnic minorities in Tuyen Duc and Lam Dong Provinces. Initially, Sommer conveyed his enthusiasm for the project, exclaiming: "Now I wouldn't exchange my new assignment for a plain teaching job for anything!" Echoing the arguments of American and Vietnamese policy makers, he explained the logic behind the strategic hamlet program in upland areas. Describing the hamlets, he wrote: "Here the people can be both watched for loyalty and also defended better, as well as being settled in some organized framework through which might be better approached such problems as economic development and education in its broadest sense." In the early stages of his time in Dalat, Sommer pointed to bad weather and violence as two of the most pressing challenges he faced in implementing education programs. Heavy rains during some parts of the year made construction projects nearly impossible. In addition, aid workers had difficulty traveling through insecure areas or along unprotected roads, which hindered their ability to transport supplies and building materials.[83]

After he had been in Dalat for several weeks, Sommer discovered other obstacles. He noted the basic problem of hamlet communities not having enough money to meet their residents' basic needs. He explained that, as part of the American aid package, each hamlet received funding to construct a school. Officials then expected the hamlet's residents to provide the salaries for the school's teachers once those schools had been built. Such expectations, which required capital that local communities usually lacked, paralleled the IVS agriculture volunteers' assumption that farmers could afford the maintenance and operating costs of new technologies. Because many of the hamlets' inhabitants were simply too poor to support the teachers, Sommer and other aid workers searched for ways to generate money for the hamlets' inhabitants, for example, by planting school gardens or introducing livestock.[84]

By Sommer's estimation, however, poverty constituted only one of several impediments to aid projects in strategic hamlets. He believed that cultural differences among the Vietnamese, minorities, and Americans also limited the effectiveness of American educational assistance in the strategic hamlets. According to Sommer, many Vietnamese officials' bigotry toward ethnic minority people posed a hurdle for anyone hoping to help both groups. He claimed: "The discrimination of the Vietnamese against the Montagnard is probably more evident than that of white Americans against Negroes, and I've heard more than one government official raise his hands in despair and wail that the 'prehistoric' Montagnard are hopeless cases."[85]

Although Sommer and other IVSers criticized the openly racist views of Vietnamese officials, many of them nevertheless resorted to stereotypes when discussing Vietnam's ethnic minority people. A number of volunteers described minorities as *primitive* and compared them with American Indians. While such labels may not have carried the same hostility as expressions of overt racism, the IVSers' tendency toward superficial assessments of ethnic minority societies reflected their sense of superiority and their assumption that these communities could not take care of themselves. Their patronizing attitudes also led them to dismiss any individual's suspicions about the GVN or US government as culturally determined superstitions. By seeing all decisions through the lens of culture, they excluded the possibility that the hamlet residents were motivated by alternative considerations, such as class, political interest, or self-preservation. Their hubris as well as their fixation on race and cultural explanations for behavior prevented many IVSers from thinking critically about their organization's relationship with the US government or from questioning the political implications of their involvement in the strategic hamlet program.

The observations about the difficulties John Sommer encountered working with minority communities illuminate the assumptions driving American and Vietnamese policies. He argued, without mentioning the official GVN strategy of civilizing highland people by forcibly relocating them to hamlets: "Most have fled their native mountain hideouts to escape the Viet Cong, and they have fled with virtually no earthly belongings." He explained that the minorities' "mental processes are very different from ours" and opined: "I think they really are not very sure just what a school is." When he asked a hamlet chief what his people needed, the leader replied that he would accept anything Sommer would give him. According to Sommer's interpretation of this exchange, the chief was "either too timid or too unimaginative to think of something." Sommer failed to consider, however, that the chief's response may have been quite deliberate and pragmatic. For example, he may have hoped to obtain as many resources for his community as possible or protect the community from NLF retaliation for cooperating with Americans. In response to questions about whether IVSers had the right to "bother these poor people," Sommer argued that at some point ethnic minorities would have to change and that "now is the most painless time to do so, before the gap becomes hopelessly great, and before they become helpless prey to some malevolent force."[86]

Other volunteers made similar observations about the ethnic minorities with whom they worked in strategic hamlets. For example, a female IVSer described the "primitive" tribes and the difficulties moving to the hamlets. Gloria Johnson, who worked with the Rhade people in strategic hamlets near Ban Me Thuot, discussed the implications of the fact that the Rhade could no longer rely on their traditional nomadic lifestyle. She wrote: "The way of life of the Montagnard will need to be drastically changed, since he will be permanently settled in his strategic hamlet." As this would likely be a difficult task, "IVS, USOM, and the Vietnamese government [would] work to help the mountaineers re-establish themselves."[87] Johnson failed to appreciate the fact that the GVN and the US

The International Voluntary Services volunteer Gene Stoltzfus with local leaders, including the village chief (*center*) at a "Montagnard" strategic hamlet. Courtesy Gene Stoltzfus Papers, 1940–2012, HM1-101, Photographs: Vietnam, International Voluntary Service, 1963–1967, box 4, folder 2, Mennonite Church USA Archives—Goshen, Goshen, IN.

government had created the very problem she now attempted to solve: the Rhade required public assistance and could no longer support themselves largely because the two governments' policies had forced them off their lands and into strategic hamlets.

Johnson's primary responsibility consisted of working with a six-member team of Rhade men and women who offered their communities instruction in agriculture, sanitation, nutrition, child care, and basic health. After spending some time working with the group, Johnson expressed cautious optimism about her ability to help them: "At this point, I'm hoping like heck I can accomplish something here but am not sure of a thing. At any rate, it should be tremendously interesting."[88]

Within six months, this optimism gave way to frustration. Johnson described her "sagging spirits" when she realized that any "accomplishment seemed next to impossible." She realized that the basic structural problems of poverty made it almost impossible for her or other volunteers to help assimilate the Rhade people into a more modern society. According to her, many Rhade women were receptive to the child-care, cooking, and sewing demonstrations that her extension team conducted. However, they could not afford the basic materials required to implement the projects that the volunteers introduced, and Johnson could not secure more funding for the program. She wrote: "In every case [the Rhade women] reported to us that they did not have enough money to buy even the simplest items which it might be necessary to add to their household in order to do things as the girls demonstrated them—and our equipment was simple."[89]

In order to introduce the type of transformations to Rhade society that both the GVN and the American aid workers deemed vital, either the United States or South Vietnam needed to invest much more money in the programs and ensure that funds were distributed among the people. However, neither government considered such an investment a priority. The GVN and US government's inaction underscored the fact that security and control remained the central elements of the hamlet program, rather than a genuine commitment to development. As Johnson explained, the Rhade "are almost self-sufficient in natural resources and need little money to get along as they are, but improvement of family life would definitely require additional money in the family, which just isn't available now."[90] After struggling to make progress with the Rhade, Johnson moved on to other projects, including teaching at a high school in Ban Me Thuot and working in "new life hamlets" in the Mekong delta town of Tan An. Although she considered these projects to be more enjoyable and successful, owing in part at least to the fact that the programs received enough material support from USOM and that the Vietnamese people with whom she worked were not as poor as the minorities, she still questioned the significance of her efforts.

Ultimately, Johnson reflected on her time in Vietnam with a sense of disappointment over the shortcomings of her work. Her regrets and frustration appear to have resulted largely from her demoralizing experiences with the Rhade people in strategic hamlets. She wrote to her family six months after leaving Ban Me Thuot and completing her work with the Rhade that she was "sorry to report . . . that it was not successful in terms of my original objectives."[91] In her final letter before departing Vietnam, she wrote: "I cannot say that Viet Nam has benefited from my stay here. I wish I could point with pride to some real achievement, but I cannot."[92]

Despite all this, Johnson returned to Vietnam in 1966 as a team leader because she still believed in the mission of IVS. Explaining her reasoning, she argued: "The war cannot be won militarily only, which is why so many Americans are here." She claimed that she looked forward to the challenge of finding "the key to understanding and solving 'people problems'" in Vietnam.[93]

## From Enthusiasm to Defeat

Although most members of the IVS education team shared with Sommer and Johnson an initial sense of optimism about their efforts, nearly all the volunteers soured on the endeavor once they saw firsthand how the strategic hamlets functioned and learned about the profound limitations on their assistance programs. Eventually, their association with the US government disillusioned most IVSers. Many became critical of the way foreign assistance and nation building had become an integral part of the military campaign instead of a means to promote economic development.

One volunteer in particular provided outspoken criticism of US and GVN policies throughout his tour with IVS. Robert Biggers, a member of the education team stationed in Kien Hoa Province along the southern tip of the Mekong delta, became "discontented and disappointed" almost as soon as he arrived in Vietnam. His immediate pessimism and condemnation of IVS education programs was somewhat unusual. In October 1963, he wrote a letter to Dr. Russell Stevenson, then the director of IVS, voicing his many concerns about working in South Vietnam. He threatened to break his contract with the organization if the situation did not improve. He explained: "I want so much to help in some way . . . but I find myself surrounded by restrictions." Among the restrictions he cited, he focused on the negative implications of IVS's association with USOM, the rampant corruption of the GVN, and abuses committed by both the Vietnamese government and the NLF insurgents. Referring to himself as a "frustrated idealist," he expressed his dismay at learning from several USOM officials that IVS was "not here to help people, only to support U.S. foreign policy, and that helping people was only a secondary and unimportant consideration." Most upsetting, however, were the human effects of the war. He cited the South Vietnamese government's draconian intimidation tactics and argued that they mirrored methods employed

by the NLF. After speaking with government officials, Buddhist leaders, students, and peasants, he concluded that the Vietnamese population
"[lived] in constant fear of two enemies" as a result of the "torture, forced
confessions, needless bloodshed, and 'midnight arrests'" propagated by
both sides. Because he believed that US support for the GVN amounted
to implicit approval of such harsh methods, he told his superiors at IVS
that he did not want to take part in the American nation-building enterprise in South Vietnam.[94]

Although he ultimately chose to stay in Vietnam and complete his
tour, Biggers remained critical of US and GVN policies. He faulted
American military advisers for not adequately supporting the "foot soldiers" of South Vietnam—those men who served within the ranks of the
regular army, the civil guard, or the local self-defense corps. These soldiers
received low pay, lacked access to any facilities or amenities, and commanded little respect from South Vietnamese officials. In a letter that
he wrote and expected the IVS staff to type, photocopy, and forward
to his family and friends, Biggers observed that many soldiers received
their monthly stipend late, and he suggested that local officials not only
"dipped their hands into the pie" but also may have prevented investigations into corruption charges. He claimed: "If inquiries are made into
the latter [corruption charges], investigation teams may be 'ambushed,'
supposedly by the Viet Cong." However, next to this sentence, the word
"OMIT" appears in handwriting. Someone, presumably an IVS employee
in Washington, DC, did not want the recipients to read his accusation. As
this incident suggests, even a veiled criticism of GVN tactics issued by a
low-level aid worker in his letter to family may have violated the organization's unflinching support for official American objectives in Vietnam.[95]

As time passed, Biggers's disillusionment turned to cynicism. Following Diem's ouster, he referred in early 1964 to the series of coups d'état as
"Standard Operating Procedure" in Saigon and assumed that whichever
man eventually claimed power would govern as a dictator while paying
lip service to democratic institutions only "in order to appease the United
States or to make justification of U.S. diplomats' recognition and support
easier." He predicted that the South Vietnamese government would institute an even more aggressive campaign of social and economic reforms,
with the help of the United States. He saw clearly that this push for economic aid and social reform constituted a war strategy in which the GVN

sought to "win back the confidence of the people" and, by improving their lives, encourage the Vietnamese to reject the antigovernment movement.[96]

Biggers's interpretation of the situation proved correct. The strategic hamlet program constituted a particularly brutal and repressive approach to counterinsurgency, even though it ultimately proved ineffective. By early 1964, after both Diem and Kennedy had been assassinated, many American officials had abandoned the program and viewed strategic hamlets as a failed military tactic and a waste of US aid dollars. At that point, however, the program had already caused considerable damage and hardship to hundreds of thousands of Vietnamese and minority people by forcing them into hamlets and limiting their economic opportunities. These individuals demonstrated no more loyalty to the GVN than they had before. In all likelihood, the program alienated many people and perhaps even drove them to support the insurgency. Following the November 1963 coup, and for the duration of the war, Vietnamese military leaders seized power in Saigon. After that time, with political forces in South Vietnam in disarray, US policy makers shifted their focus almost exclusively to military campaigns to win the war.

Although their initial idealism obscured the political realities in South Vietnam as well as their role in advancing bellicose policies, most of the education aid workers eventually developed a more sophisticated understanding of the problems facing the Saigon government and posed by American intervention. Their appreciation of the unpopularity of US and GVN policies often proved to be more accurate and prescient than high-level policy makers' evaluations of the situation. Despite the failure of these nation builders to inspire widespread support for Diem's regime, the US government remained undeterred and soon embarked on even more catastrophic attempts to bolster the South Vietnamese government.

As the 1960s wore on, the war consumed all other American efforts in Vietnam. American aid programs increasingly assumed counterinsurgency functions and explicitly advanced military objectives. Through their involvement in flawed policies such as the strategic hamlet program, the American aid workers unwittingly contributed to the escalation of the war. Nearly ten years after the first team of IVS education volunteers arrived in Vietnam, the organization finally admitted the costly mistake of its partnership with the US government and GVN. After a long, slow decline, in late 1971 IVS removed its remaining volunteers from the country. The departure of IVS marked the final blow to civilian nation-building efforts in South Vietnam. Although US officials continued to pay lip service to winning hearts and minds, during the final years of the war they were focused on shifting the burden of fighting to South Vietnamese forces while maintaining enough military and political advantage to secure an acceptable peace settlement.

# Conclusion

# "Ears of Stone"

In March 1963, the former International Voluntary Services (IVS) agriculture volunteer David Nuttle was invited to brief President John F. Kennedy on the situation in Vietnam. The president and his advisers were particularly concerned about the effectiveness of counterinsurgency methods and pacification efforts in the Vietnamese countryside. Drawing on his experiences during three years in Vietnam, Nuttle hoped to convince the president of the "improbability of ever achieving a conventional military solution to the Viet-Nam problem." In his recommendations, he was "most emphatic" about the need to limit the number of US military personnel and refocus on civilian development efforts that provided meaningful services and assistance to the people of Vietnam while protecting them from insurgent attacks. He left the meeting optimistic that the president and his advisers would seriously consider his suggestions and seize the opportunity for a "course correction" in Vietnam.[1]

American policy makers never fully heeded the advice that Nuttle and other civilian aid workers offered once they had developed an understanding of the real problems in Vietnam and the flaws in nation-building projects designed to address those problems. Kennedy was assassinated within eight months of the meeting. And Kennedy's inner circle of advisers, all of whom stayed on to serve in Lyndon B. Johnson's administration, failed either to grasp the limitations of conventional military escalation or to convince the new president of the futility of it. As Nuttle explained when reflecting on his experiences in Vietnam several decades later, the problem confronting American policy makers was not that they lacked experts to consult on Vietnam. Instead, they routinely ignored the advice of low- and mid-level aid workers, either because of the nation builders' junior rank or because they did not like the advice they were given. As Nuttle discovered, at least when it came to Vietnam, American policy makers had "ears of stone" and heard only what they wanted to hear.[2]

Several years after Nuttle's fruitless attempt to persuade Kennedy that the United States was pursuing a flawed approach to Vietnam, a large group of IVS volunteers staged a more dramatic effort to influence US policy. In September 1967, as the war raged and negotiations seemed like a remote possibility, forty-nine members of the IVS team signed an open letter to President Johnson imploring him to change course and end the war in Vietnam.[3] In their letter, the IVSers documented the devastating effects of the war on Vietnam's people, including the development of virulent anti-American sentiment among the local population. They also argued that US assistance and nation building had thwarted real self-determination. Although they did not specifically refer to US involvement in Vietnam as imperialist, the parallels between their description of American advisers and colonial authorities are striking. For example, they described how Americans served as central advisers to all GVN bureaucrats and South Vietnamese military commanders, a role reminiscent of many earlier colonial projects.[4] As the historians Michael Hunt and Steven Levine have recently argued, the US military intervention in Vietnam represented a continuation of other American imperial policies in Asia.[5] Although Hunt and Levine focus on wars and military engagement as they trace the arc of American empire in the Philippines, Japan, Korea, and Vietnam, their analysis might easily have included nation-building exercises in those countries as well. As this study has demonstrated, American nation builders approached Vietnam with distinctly imperial (or neo-imperial) goals—they actively sought to extend US control and influence while promoting economic development and a fundamental transformation of South Vietnamese society.

At the same time they issued this letter, four volunteers, including the director of IVS in Vietnam, resigned from their positions in order to "speak out freely" about the situation. As their letter argued: "To stay in Vietnam and remain silent is to fail to respond to the first need of the Vietnamese people—peace." They also noted the negative consequences of their relationship with the US government and the perception among many Vietnamese that the volunteers' primary goal was to advance American interests. They explained: "Some of us feel that we can no longer justify our staying, for often we are misinterpreted as representatives of American policy."[6]

In a book they wrote two years later, the former volunteers Don Luce and John Sommer suggested that the IVS letter had reached and perhaps influenced a large audience: "The letter and resignations, coming from persons so close to the Vietnamese and so close to the implementation of American policy, made a deep impression in government and non-government circles—and in the world press—for months thereafter."[7] Even if Luce and Sommer were correct that the IVSers succeeded at making an impression, their efforts clearly failed to result in consequential changes to the US approach in Vietnam. Not only did the war continue for nearly eight more years, but American nation-building efforts also persisted, albeit in a form more explicitly linked to the combat efforts. As the historian James Carter's work shows, the focus of nation building during the final years of the 1960s shifted to large infrastructure projects explicitly designed to support military movements and operations that were carried out by private contractors or military personnel themselves.[8] And, despite the handful of resignations, IVS remained in Vietnam until 1971, when the mission finally closed.

The title of Luce and Sommer's book—*Vietnam: The Unheard Voices*—confirms the disconnect between policy makers in Washington and Saigon and people on the ground. Their primary goal in writing the book was to provide a voice for the Vietnamese people by reflecting "the feelings of [their] Vietnamese friends and colleagues." But Luce and Sommer also argue that the voices of American aid workers "were often not heard."[9] Many other aid workers from IVS, USOM, and Michigan State University expressed a similar sentiment, either at the time or in their later recollections.

Although their 1967 letter and resignations strongly condemned US policies, like most other nation builders the IVSers failed to acknowledge the pivotal role that they and other civilian aid workers had played in shaping and implementing those policies. In fact, given the central position they had occupied in executing development projects and advancing US goals in Vietnam, their shift and later critique of American policies appears somewhat ironic. While the nation builders cannot and should not be blamed for military errors (and atrocities) committed during the war, they did bear responsibility for the intensification of US support for an unpopular and authoritarian government in Saigon as well as some of the military escalation that preceded the introduction of ground troops. In key ways, the ineffectiveness of nation-building and development programs—all in service of propping up an unpopular, repressive, and, in the minds of some people, illegitimate regime in the South—led directly to the very war that many aid workers later protested.

The blunders and miscalculations that characterized American intervention after 1965 were a direct outgrowth of the earlier failures of nation-building programs. In the first decade of involvement, US policy makers embraced the idea that Americans—whether social scientists, agricultural volunteers, public health workers, policemen, or teachers—could solve South Vietnam's problems by introducing Vietnamese people to American methods, with little regard for local conditions. This approach, which reveals in stark terms the limitations of both high-level modernization theory and community-development projects guided by foreigners, depended on the assumption that the Vietnamese people would readily accept the advice, vision, and assistance offered by American aid workers. In fact, Vietnamese from all walks of life embraced American nation-building schemes selectively and modified the projects to satisfy their own needs and interests. Even GVN officials challenged or rejected American aid if it seemed to undercut their authority and autonomy or when it did not correspond with their own vision for political, economic, and social development. At the same time, most Americans in Vietnam discounted the historical and political dimensions of the country's revolutionary struggle and insisted on supporting authoritarian and unpopular leaders in Saigon. As an IVS volunteer who served in Vietnam during the war later reflected: "The 'band-aids' marked MADE IN THE USA have been inadequate to deal with the complex, deep-seated problems of this people and country."[10]

The Republic of Vietnam endured for just over two decades. Throughout its short life, it depended on massive amounts of assistance from the United States. The US government made a serious mistake, however, in supporting a nation whose very existence violated an international agreement and thwarted the will and interests of many local people. American officials compounded the situation by insisting on defending that nation at any cost, even as it became apparent that fighting the war would have devastating and long-term effects on the environment, the economy, the culture, and especially the civilian populations of both Vietnams. Given the complex political and economic challenges facing the South Vietnamese leadership, the repressive policies of the GVN, and the widespread populist appeal of the antigovernment insurgency, South Vietnam would probably never have survived on its own. But American policy makers and nation builders alike ignored these conditions and aggressively labored to construct a state favorable to their own interests.

The nation-building experiment in Vietnam not only led to deeper American military intervention there but also had implications for US policies elsewhere. The experience in Vietnam—the failed war as well as the unsuccessful nation-building programs—resulted in a credibility gap and caused many Americans to question the integrity of their elected officials and political institutions. Perhaps more importantly, involvement in Vietnam led to a profound sense of confusion on the part of policy makers and the American public regarding the role of the United States in the world. In the aftermath of the war, many Americans felt more uncertain than ever about how the United States should engage with other people and states. Despite such disillusionment, however, US officials remained fully committed to advancing American interests and hegemony abroad. They simply looked to alternative methods for doing so, which increasingly consisted of covert aid to so-called friendly governments and military forces.

By the end of the Vietnam War, American policy makers had soured considerably on modernization theory and nation building as useful and effective tools in foreign relations. Officials proved reluctant to pursue the type of ambitious modernization projects they undertook in South Vietnam, especially without the cover of international support. Instead, subsequent development efforts relied more on behind-the-scenes military support or economic aid. Sometimes, as through the Iran-Contra arrangement in the mid-1980s, policy makers went to great lengths and violated US laws to conceal this assistance from Congress and the American public. And, even recently, many American politicians felt the need to assure their constituents that they would not pursue nation-building projects.[11]

But despite politicians' public derision, American policy makers continued relying on modernization efforts, albeit in a modified form, to accomplish their foreign policy goals. Subsequent examples of nation building followed the pattern established during the final decade of US involvement in Vietnam, when military personnel largely replaced civilian aid workers in implementing nation-building and development projects. Beginning in the 1960s, and continuing after the end of the Vietnam War, the United States increasingly engaged in what the historian Bradley Simpson has called "military modernization."[12] In Indonesia, Brazil, Iran, El Salvador, and elsewhere, American aid flowed to the local military forces, which promised to promote economic development and political stability. As a result, US policy makers and military advisers supported authoritarian regimes, propped up foreign militaries, and usually subverted democratic development and political inclusion.

In recent years, and especially under the George W. Bush administration, modernization theory came back into fashion, at least temporarily. After the terrorist attacks on September 11, 2001, US policy makers once again argued that Americans could provide a model for how foreign societies should modernize and democratize. In addition to waging war in Iraq and Afghanistan, American officials engaged in modernizing efforts to promote economic development, democratic reforms, and political stability, particularly in the Islamic world.[13] Although some civilian aid workers participated in these endeavors, American soldiers and marines increasingly performed nation building and community development as central components of their operations. As in Vietnam, US policy makers too often failed to pay sufficient attention to local history, culture, and politics, and, as a result, recent modernizing schemes produced mixed results at best. And, in the wake of the Iraq War, many Americans became disillusioned with the prospect of nation building, much as they had after the Vietnam War several decades earlier.

As the examples of Nuttle's meeting with Kennedy and the IVSers' letter to Johnson a few years later show, American officials consistently failed to consider the lessons learned by American nation builders, who represented some of the first casualties of the flawed US approach to Vietnam. Had they bothered to consult and listen seriously to American aid workers who had lived and worked in Vietnam for years, US policy makers might not have continued to advance such poorly conceived policies. Thinking critically about US goals and behavior in Vietnam, however, would have required a reconsideration of the most fundamental aspects of their assumptions about the role of the United States in the world. But American officials proved that they had little interest in the opinions or ideas of low- and mid-level aid workers, let alone of Vietnamese leaders or the Vietnamese people, especially when those ideas challenged the established approach.

American nation builders in Vietnam desperately wanted to believe that they could help Ngo Dinh Diem and subsequent South Vietnamese leaders cultivate popular support and earn political legitimacy by modernizing Vietnam and "improving" it according to their own ideas, values, and models. The historian Greg Grandin has aptly described this impulse as "the United States' self-assigned mission to reform humanity."[14] As a result, American nation builders demonstrated a willful blindness to the appeal of Vietnamese revolutionaries and the devastating effects of the GVN's authoritarian policies, many of which the US government devised or actively encouraged. Had US officials and aid workers fully appreciated the complex political situation in South Vietnam and responded to these conditions with greater flexibility instead of imposing their own rigid agenda, nation building in Vietnam might have produced more lasting achievements. More significantly, the United States might not have committed itself to the unconditional protection of South Vietnam—a strategy that came with tremendous costs and suffering for everyone involved.

# Acknowledgments

During the years that I worked on this book, I benefited from the generosity, wisdom, and support of many friends, mentors, colleagues, and acquaintances. My interest in the US involvement in Vietnam, as well as my decision to pursue an academic career, grew out of several history courses I took from Charles Neu at Brown University. As a graduate student at the University of California, Los Angeles, I had the great fortune of working with several fantastic mentors. First and foremost, thanks to Jessica Wang, who was an excellent instructor and dissertation adviser. Even these many years later, I still rely on Jessica's astute advice and unwavering support. Also at UCLA, Geoff Robinson, George Dutton, and the late Melissa Meyer played a critical role in shaping my understanding of Southeast Asian, Vietnamese, and American history. My thanks to Tony Reid and the staff of UCLA's Center for Southeast Asian Studies, who all encouraged my study of the Vietnamese language and Southeast Asia.

As I conducted research for this book, I relied on the expert advice of a number of archivists. Thanks to Fred Honhart and Carl Lee at Michigan State University as well as the helpful staffs at the National Archives and Records Administration in College Park, MD, and the National Archives II in Ho Chi Minh City. In Vietnam, Nguyen Ngoc Thang and Nguyen Thi Ngoc Hoang served as research assistants. In addition, I am indebted to Anne Shirk, the final executive director of International Voluntary Services, who kindly shared with me a large collection of letters written by former Vietnam volunteers. I am particularly grateful to the MSU and IVS volunteers who shared their experiences with me and helped bring this story to life.

In the course of working on this project, I received a number of fellowships and grants, including several Foreign Language and Area Studies fellowships, a scholarship to the Vietnamese Advanced Summer Institute in Hanoi, Pre-Dissertation and Dissertation Year awards at UCLA, and the Presidential Award at San Francisco State University.

Allison Webster at the University Press of Kentucky believed in this project from the first moment I contacted her, and she patiently guided me through the publication process. The comments I received from two anonymous reviewers helped me sharpen my analysis and produce what I hope is a much stronger book. I would also like to thank Amy Harris, Mack McCormick, Iris Law, Joseph Brown, Ila McEntire, and Pamela Gray.

Since I joined the history faculty at San Francisco State, I have been continually impressed by the dedication my colleagues bring to their scholarship, our students, and our department. Many of my colleagues have provided helpful comments on various sections of this book, and all have shown me tremendous support throughout these early years of my academic career. I feel incredibly lucky to be part of this remarkable community. I would also like to thank my students at SFSU, whose enthusiasm for the study of history and engagement in the world is truly inspiring.

Several colleagues at other history departments have offered advice, feedback, support, and friendship over the years. Thanks especially to Joanna Poblete, Petula Iu, Jessica Chapman, Matt Masur, Amanda McVety, Scott Laderman, Julie Pham, and Asia Nguyen.

My incredible friends and family, near and far, have helped keep me sane, made me laugh, and provided much needed perspective during the long and sometimes lonely process of writing this book. I could not have completed this endeavor (or accomplished much else) without the love, encouragement, and support of my parents, Hank and Darlene Breiteneicher. Sue and Peter Elkind, my in-laws, have always made me feel at home in the Bay Area and have delivered help in large and small ways for me and our growing family. Thanks also to my sister and brother-in-law Laura and Chris Lay and their son Bodhi as well as my brother and sister-in-law Adam and Arianne Breiteneicher. Caleb, Maya, and Sadie, my three amazing children, give meaning to everything I do and make me proud every day. Finally, thank you to my husband, Ethan. In addition to reading every draft of this book and eagerly discussing my ideas, he provides the perfect combination of support, motivation, and diversion. I am extremely grateful to have such a wonderful partner with whom to share this adventure and so many others.

# Notes

The following abbreviations for publications and archival collections have been used throughout the notes:

*FRUS, 1952–1954*, vol. 16 = US Department of State. *Foreign Relations of the United States, 1952–1954*. Vol. 16, *The Geneva Conference*. Washington, DC: US Government Printing Office, 1981.

*FRUS, 1961–63*, vol. 2 = US Department of State. *Foreign Relations of the United States, 1961–1963*. Vol. 2, *Vietnam, 1962*. Washington, DC: US Government Printing Office, 1990.

IVS = International Voluntary Services documents in the possession of Anne Shirk (former Executive Director of IVS), now housed at Goshen College, Goshen, IN.

MAAG = US Military Assistance Advisory Group.

NARA = National Archives and Records Administration, Archives II, College Park, MD.

RG = Record Group.

TTLT-II = Trung Tam Luu Tru Quoc Gia II (Vietnam's National Archives Number II), Ho Chi Minh City.

USAID = US Agency for International Development Library and Historical Collections, Washington, DC.

VPP = Vietnam Project Papers, Michigan State University, East Lansing.

WFP = Wesley Fishel Papers, Michigan State University, East Lansing.

## Introduction

1. President Diem claimed that the foreigners were actually the intended targets of the attack. According to a conversation he had with Diem, Edward Lansdale reported to Leland Barrows: "Apparently, President Diem feels this ambush might have been laid for you and was forced to premature action by the jeep-load of troops." Lansdale to Barrows, "Incident Near Long Xuyen," October 4, 1956, confidential, NARA, RG 469 (AID Predecessor Agencies), entry 1453, box 2. Although as noted the identity of the attackers was never confirmed, there is a strong possibility that they were members of the Hoa Hao forces. The Hoa Hao were one of the politicoreligious sects that challenged Diem's authority and remained active in

the western delta even after government troops had significantly weakened those sects through fighting during the previous year. For more on the Hoa Hao and other southern insurgents, see Jessica Chapman, *Cauldron of Resistance: Ngo Dinh Diem, the United States, and 1950s Southern Vietnam* (Ithaca, NY: Cornell University Press, 2013), and "The Sect Crisis of 1955 and American Commitment to Ngo Dinh Diem," *Journal of Vietnamese Studies* 5, no. 1 (Winter 2010): 37–85.

2. According to scholars who emphasize geopolitics, American policy makers' Cold War concerns and obsession with the doctrine of containment dictated their course of action in Southeast Asia. The Cold War argument, which stresses how the superpower rivalry influenced American decision making on Vietnam, is presented forcefully in two of the standard overviews of the war: George Herring, *America's Longest War* (New York: McGraw-Hill, 1986); and George Kahin, *Intervention: How America Became Involved in Vietnam* (New York: Knopf, 1986). Despite his overall focus on Cold War geopolitics, Kahin devotes more attention to internal Vietnamese politics than do most other scholars. See also David Anderson, *Trapped by Success: The Eisenhower Administration and Vietnam, 1953–1961* (New York: Columbia University Press, 1991); Ronald Spector, *Advice and Support: The Early Years, 1941–1960* (New York: Free Press, 1985); and Marilyn Young, *The Vietnam Wars, 1945–1990* (New York: Harper Collins, 1991). For early examples of the "internationalization" of the Vietnam War, see R. B. Smith, *An International History of the Vietnam War: Revolution versus Containment, 1955–1961* (New York: St. Martin's, 1983), and *An International History of the Vietnam War: The Kennedy Strategy* (New York: St. Martin's, 1986); and Fredrik Logevall, *Choosing War* (Berkeley and Los Angeles: University of California Press, 2001). The trend to consider the international dimensions of the conflict has accelerated in the past few years. Among the best recent examples are Mark Lawrence, *The Vietnam War: A Concise International History* (Oxford: Oxford University Press, 2010); and Lien-Hang Nguyen, *Hanoi's War: An International History of the War for Peace in Vietnam* (Chapel Hill: University of North Carolina Press, 2012).

3. For example, some historians emphasize American concerns about the expanding international influence of the Soviet Union and China. For a thorough account of US-China dynamics, see Qiang Zhai, *China and the Vietnam Wars, 1950–1975* (Chapel Hill: University of North Carolina Press, 2000). For an earlier example, see Melvin Gurtov, *The First Vietnam Crisis: Chinese Communist Strategy and United States Involvement* (New York: Columbia University Press, 1967). Other scholars focus on American leaders' efforts to maintain good relations with France, a key ally of the United States that was struggling to retain its colonial possessions in Africa and Asia, and entice French leaders to support American aims in post–World War II Europe. The most comprehensive account of how Franco-American relations influenced US policy in Vietnam is Kathryn Statler, *Replacing France: The Origins of American Intervention in Vietnam* (Lexington: University Press of Kentucky, 2007). See also Marianna Sullivan, *France's Vietnam Policy* (Westport, CT: Greenwood, 1978).

4. The best early studies of the pre-1960s period are Ronald Spector's *Advice and Support* and David Anderson's *Trapped by Success.* Spector focuses on the US Army's military assistance and does not consider nonmilitary aid to South Vietnam. As the title suggests, Anderson's book argues that the limited success of Eisenhower administration policies laid the groundwork for further US commitments to Vietnam in subsequent years. My study differs in its emphasis on how the shortcomings of early US involvement, particularly nonmilitary assistance, contributed to the later escalation. In addition to considering US–South Vietnamese relations, historians have recently devoted more attention to the antigovernment insurgency in South Vietnam and North Vietnamese policies in the years before 1965. See in particular David Hunt, *Vietnam's Southern Revolution: From Peasant Insurrection to Total War* (Amherst: University of Massachusetts Press, 2008); Robert Brigham, *Guerilla Diplomacy: The NLF's Foreign Relations and the Viet Nam War* (Ithaca, NY: Cornell University Press, 1998); and Pierre Asselin, *Hanoi's Road to the Vietnam War, 1954–1965* (Berkeley and Los Angeles: University of California Press, 2013).

5. For detailed discussions of the US–South Vietnamese alliance, see Philip Catton, *Diem's Final Failure: Prelude to America's War in Vietnam* (Lawrence: University of Kansas Press, 2002); and Edward Miller, *Misalliance: Ngo Dinh Diem, the United States, and the Fate of South Vietnam* (Cambridge, MA: Harvard University Press, 2013). Both Catton and Miller discuss how American and South Vietnamese policy makers differed in their vision and approach toward nation building. Chapman's *Cauldron of Resistance* focuses on the critical period from 1953 to 1956 to explore Diem's rise to power and internal political dynamics in South Vietnam.

6. See James Carter, *Inventing Vietnam: The United States and State Building, 1954–1968* (New York: Cambridge University Press, 2008); William Rosenau, *US Internal Security Assistance to South Vietnam: Insurgency, Subversion, and Public Order* (New York: Routledge, 2005); and John Ernst, *Forging a Fateful Alliance: Michigan State University and the Vietnam War* (East Lansing: Michigan State University Press, 1998).

7. This trend is evident in Edward Miller's examination of the politics of nation building. Miller argues for the "central importance of ideas about nation building and development in both the making and unmaking of the U.S.-Diem relationship." See Miller, *Misalliance,* 17, 13. See also Matthew Masur, "Exhibiting Signs of Resistance: South Vietnam's Struggle for Legitimacy, 1954–1960," *Diplomatic History* 33, no. 2 (March 2009): 293–313.

8. Odd Arne Westad, *The Global Cold War: Third World Interventions and the Making of Our Times* (Cambridge: Cambridge University Press, 2007), 396.

9. David Ekbladh, *The Great American Mission: Modernization and the Construction of an American World Order* (Princeton, NJ: Princeton University Press, 2010), 2. As Westad argues, the United States and the Soviet Union offered competing models of development, and both sides relied on science, technology, and education as central features of their efforts to build modern states. See Westad, *The Global Cold War,* 92–94.

10. The economists Max Millikan and Walt Rostow were among the most influential proponents of modernization theory in the mid-twentieth century. According to them, poverty created the necessary conditions for communism to thrive. Rather than understanding communism as an alternative to the abuses of capitalism, they saw communist systems as a direct consequence of stagnant economies. As a result, in their view, the best hope for controlling communism lay in promoting capitalist economic expansion and in advancing American models for economic, political, and military modernization in the developing world. See Max F. Millikan and Walt W. Rostow, *A Proposal: Key to an Effective Foreign Policy* (New York: Harper & Bros., 1957). See also Walt Rostow, *Stages of Economic Growth: A Non-Communist Manifesto* (New York: Cambridge University Press, 1960). For a critical examination of modernization theory, see Michael Latham, *Modernization as Ideology: American Social Science and "Nation-Building" in the Kennedy Era* (Chapel Hill: University of North Carolina Press, 2000), esp. 1–20. For an excellent discussion of the intellectual history of modernization theory as well as the critiques of modernization theory that began appearing in the late 1960s, see Nils Gilman, "Modernization Theory, the Highest Stage of American Intellectual History," in *Staging Growth: Modernization, Development, and the Global Cold War,* ed. David Engerman, Nils Gilman, Mark Haefele, and Michael Latham (Amherst: University of Massachusetts Press, 2003), 47–79.

11. Michael Latham, *The Right Kind of Revolution: Modernization, Development and U.S. Foreign Policy from the Cold War to the Present* (Ithaca, NY: Cornell University Press, 2010), 3. As Mark Haefele has explained, because Rostow conveyed his ideas about modernization and foreign aid in a clear, direct manner and organized his research around the concerns of policy makers, American officials found his conclusions particularly appealing. Mark Haefele, "Walt Rostow's Stages of Economic Growth: Ideas and Action," in Engerman, Gilman, Haefele, and Latham, eds., *Staging Growth,* 81–103.

12. For overviews of this history, see Curtis Jackson, *A History of the Bureau of Indian Affairs and Its Activities among Indians* (San Francisco: R&E Research Associates, 1977); and Frank Porter, *The Bureau of Indian Affairs* (New York: Chelsea House, 1988).

13. See in particular Walter LaFeber, *The New Empire* (Ithaca, NY: Cornell University Press, 1963); and Emily Rosenberg, *Spreading the American Dream* (New York: Hill & Wang, 1982).

14. Jeremi Suri, *Liberty's Surest Guardian: Rebuilding Nations after War from the Founding to Obama* (New York: Free Press, 2011).

15. Ekbladh, *The Great American Mission;* Nick Cullather, *The Hungry World: America's Cold War Battle against Poverty in Asia* (Cambridge, MA: Harvard University Press, 2010); Michael Adas, *Dominance by Design: Technological Imperatives and America's Civilizing Mission* (Cambridge, MA: Harvard University Press, 2009), and "Modernization Theory and the American Revival of the Scientific and Technological Standards of Social Achievement and Human Worth," in Engerman, Gilman,

Haefele, and Latham, eds., *Staging Growth*, 25–46. For the most thorough discussion of the Tennessee Valley Authority as a model for other development schemes, including in Vietnam's Mekong delta, see Ekbladh, *The Great American Mission*, 48–63, 159–65.

16. Ekbladh, *The Great American Mission*, 4.

17. Gilman, "Modernization Theory," 55.

18. Latham, *The Right Kind of Revolution*, 2.

19. Cullather, *The Hungry World*, 8.

20. Recent scholarship by Nick Cullather, David Ekbladh, Amanda McVety, and others describes in more detail the tension between an altruistic impulse to improve others' lives and American self-interest. See Cullather, *The Hungry World;* Ekbladh, *The Great American Mission;* and Amanda McVety, *Enlightened Aid: U.S. Development as Foreign Policy in Ethiopia* (New York: Oxford University Press, 2012).

21. McVety's *Enlightened Aid* contains a good general discussion of the tensions between self-interest and development.

22. Cullather, *The Hungry World*, 7.

23. Ekbladh, *The Great American Mission*, 2.

24. Westad, *The Global Cold War*, 5. Westad argues that both the American and the Soviet critiques of early twentieth-century imperialism were genuine and deep.

25. Daniel Immerwahr, *Thinking Small: The United States and the Lure of Community Development* (Cambridge, MA: Harvard University Press, 2015), 4, x. For a discussion of alternative or "low-modernist" approaches to development, see also Cullather, *The Hungry World*.

26. For an exploration of the village as a site for Cold War development, see Nicole Sackley, "The Village as Cold War Site: Experts, Development, and the History of Rural Reconstruction," *Journal of Global History* 6, no. 3 (2011): 481–504. Sackley argues: "Village transformation became inextricably tied to projects of state formation, global hegemony, and imperial preservation." Ibid., 482.

27. Rosenberg, *Spreading the American Dream*, 7.

28. Latham, *The Right Kind of Revolution*. For earlier discussions of Americans' responses to revolutions, see Michael Hunt, *Ideology and U.S. Foreign Policy* (New Haven, CT: Yale University Press, 2009); and William Appleman Williams, *The Tragedy of American Diplomacy* (New York: Norton, 1959).

29. In *Embracing Defeat: Japan in the Wake of World War II* (New York: Norton/New Press, 2000), John Dower discusses American nation-building endeavors in Japan and argues that a unique set of circumstances in Japan during the late 1940s and early 1950s allowed the United States to enjoy success in these efforts. For more information on the Marshall Plan, see Michael Hogan, *The Marshall Plan: America, Britain and the Reconstruction of Europe, 1947–1952* (Cambridge: Cambridge University Press, 1987).

30. *Public Papers of the Presidents of the United States: Harry S. Truman, 1949* (Washington, DC: US Government Printing Office, 1957), 112–16. See also Robert Packenham, *Liberal America and the Third World: Political Development Ideas in For-*

*eign Aid and Social Science* (Princeton, NJ: Princeton University Press, 1973); and McVety, *Enlightened Aid*, 83–120.

31. Gregg Brazinsky examines American nation building in South Korea during the Cold War, arguing that US efforts in South Korea led to economic development and democratic politics, largely because of Korean participation in the nation-building process. He demonstrates how Koreans contributed to modernization by infusing the process with their own cultural practices and the belief that modernization need not be the same as Westernization. See Gregg Brazinsky, *Nation Building in South Korea: Koreans, Americans, and the Making of a Democracy* (Chapel Hill: University of North Carolina Press, 2009). For a more focused discussion of how Korean intellectuals used tradition to buttress and inform modernization efforts rather than hinder them, see Gregg Brazinsky, "Koreanizing Modernization," in Engerman, Gilman, Haefele, and Latham, eds., *Staging Growth*, 251–73.

32. Ho Chi Minh enumerated those abuses and articulated specific Vietnamese grievances in his 1945 "Declaration of Independence." Among the excellent scholarship on anticolonialism in Vietnam, see esp. David Marr, *Vietnamese Anticolonialism, 1885–1925* (Berkeley and Los Angeles: University of California Press, 1971), and *Vietnamese Tradition on Trial, 1920–1945* (Berkeley and Los Angeles: University of California Press, 1981). See also William Duiker, *The Communist Road to Power in Vietnam* (Boulder, CO: Westview, 1981); Hue-Tam Ho Tai, *Radicalism and the Origins of the Vietnamese Revolution* (Cambridge, MA: Harvard University Press, 1992); and Peter Zinoman, *Colonial Bastille: A History of Imprisonment in Vietnam, 1862–1940* (Berkeley and Los Angeles: University of California Press, 2001).

33. See David Marr, "World War II and the Vietnamese Revolution," in *Southeast Asia under Japanese Occupation*, Monograph Series no. 22, ed. Alfred McCoy (New Haven, CT: Yale University Southeast Asia Studies, 1980), 125–58, and *Vietnam 1945: The Quest for Power* (Berkeley and Los Angeles: University of California Press, 1995).

34. William Duiker, *Ho Chi Minh: A Life* (New York: Hyperion, 2000), and *The Communist Road to Power*. See also Shawn McHale, *Print and Power: Confucianism, Communism, and Buddhism in the Making of Modern Vietnam* (Honolulu: University of Hawaii Press, 2004).

35. Ho Chi Minh quoted in Duiker, *Ho Chi Minh*, 570.

36. Kahin, *Intervention*, 42.

37. "Agreement on the Cessation of Hostilities in Viet Nam, July 20, 1954," *FRUS, 1952–1954*, vol. 16, pp. 1540–42. George Kahin provides one of the most useful (and critical) discussions of how the United States responded to the terms of the Geneva Agreement. See Kahin, *Intervention*, 50–65.

38. Before leaving Vietnam, Diem had trained at a public administration school in Hanoi and served in the French colonial government as a provincial governor and minister of the interior under Emperor Bao Dai. As one of the youngest provincial officials in Vietnam's history and a member of an elite Catholic family from central

Vietnam, he appeared to have a bright future in politics. But he was a patriot who objected to the French colonial system. An ardent anti-Communist, he also drew the ire of the Viet Minh leadership, especially when he encouraged Bao Dai not to join forces with Ho Chi Minh as the First Indochina War broke out in 1946. He thus occupied an uncomfortable position during that war, in which he offered full support to neither side. He left Vietnam in 1950 to escape this precarious situation and in hopes of garnering international support for his political ambitions.

39. Robert Scigliano and Guy Fox, *Technical Assistance in Vietnam: The Michigan State University Experience* (New York: Praeger, 1965), 1.

40. The Vietnam Lobby was known later as the American Friends of Vietnam. In large measure because of the influence of this loosely organized group, Diem earned the confidence of many American officials and became an important American ally in the Cold War. Among those supporters whom he impressed during his visit to the United States in 1953 were Francis Cardinal Spellman, Senators John Kennedy and Mike Mansfield, the Supreme Court justice William O. Douglas, and the CIA operative Edward Lansdale. See Ernst, *Forging a Fateful Alliance,* 9–11.

41. For one of the most comprehensive accounts of Diem's background and his rise to power, see Miller, *Misalliance,* 19–53. Jessica Chapman's "Staging Democracy: South Vietnam's 1955 Referendum to Depose Bao Dai" (*Diplomatic History* 30, no. 4 [September 2006]: 671–703) contains a detailed discussion of the 1955 referendum and Diem's campaign to depose Bao Dai.

42. Miller, *Misalliance,* 86.

43. See ibid.; Catton, *Diem's Final Failure;* and Masur, "Exhibiting Signs of Resistance." While Ho Chi Minh embraced Marxism-Leninism, Diem gravitated to the French philosopher Emmanuel Mounier's doctrine of personalism, which both Catton and Miller examine in detail. See in particular Miller, *Misalliance,* 43–46. For an interesting, if somewhat outdated, discussion comparing Ho Chi Minh's and Diem's political philosophies, see Neil Jamieson, *Understanding Vietnam* (Berkeley and Los Angeles: University of California Press, 1993), 235–36, 263.

44. Two of Diem's brothers held particularly influential positions within the government. Ngo Dinh Nhu, Diem's younger brother, served as the president's "political adviser" and emerged as the leading ideological and intellectual leader of the GVN. In his position as delegate of the National Revolutionary Movement for Central Vietnam, Ngo Dinh Can enjoyed a great deal of authority over the central provinces. As Jean Lacouture explains, although the official titles of Nhu's and Can's positions suggest that the two played only small roles in governing South Vietnam, maintaining these abstract titles allowed Diem's brothers to function without a great deal of public scrutiny. Jean Lacouture, *Vietnam between Two Truces* (New York: Random House, 1966), 19–20. Nhu and Can created and presided over the Can Lao Nhan Vi Cach Mang Dang (the Personalist Labor Revolutionary Party), a semicovert organization that relied on a massive web of informants throughout the country. According to analysts at the Defense Department: "[They] used [the Can

Lao] to stifle all political sentiment competitive or opposed to Ngo Dinh Diem." *The Pentagon Papers: The Defense Department History of United States Decision-Making on Vietnam*, 4 vols. (Boston: Beacon, 1972), 1:302.

45. As the historian David Anderson argues, Diem's regime placed a higher priority on stability than reform. See Anderson, *Trapped by Success*, 121–33.

46. Kahin, *Intervention*, 96–98.

47. *The Pentagon Papers*, 1:255. See also Kahin, *Intervention*, 96.

48. Chapter 3 below deals with the issue of land reform as well as Diem's limited attempts to address the peasants' grievances and compete with North Vietnamese land-redistribution schemes. See also Kahin, *Intervention;* Douglas Dacy, *Foreign Aid, War, and Economic Development: South Vietnam, 1955–1975* (Cambridge: Cambridge University Press, 1986); and Bernard Fall, *Vietnam Witness, 1956–1963* (New York: Praeger, 1966).

49. The official rationale behind the two decrees (of March 3, 1955, and October 24, 1956) to abolish the village councils and limit autonomy in the provinces appears in a report issued by the GVN, "Tren Dia-hat Hanh-chanh" (In the realm of administration), n.d., Phu Tong Thong De Nhat Cong Hoa (Papers of the president of the Republic of Vietnam), 1955–1963 series, TTLT-II.

50. Kahin, *Intervention*, 98. As many observers and scholars have noted, a popular Vietnamese proverb states: "The power of the king stops at the village gate." This axiom illustrates the widespread perception that local communities had the right to govern themselves.

51. Diem attempted to nationalize the Chinese populations of South Vietnam's cities by pressuring them to give up their Chinese citizenship and adopt Vietnamese nationality. Those who refused to comply with Diem's ultimatum found themselves forced out of profitable occupations such as banking, international trade, and product distribution that had long been the domain of the Chinese in Vietnam. Reinhardt to DOS [Department of State]/Washington, confidential memo, October 14, 1956, NARA, RG 469, entry 461, box 8. For more on the position of Chinese in Vietnam, particularly the disproportionate influence that Chinese had on certain sectors of South Vietnam's economy as well as the historical relationship between the Chinese and the European colonial powers in Vietnam (and elsewhere in Southeast Asia), see Daniel Chirot and Anthony Reid, eds., *Essential Outsiders: Chinese and Jews in the Modern Transformation of Southeast Asia and Central Europe* (Seattle: University of Washington Press, 1997); and Benedict Anderson, *Spectre of Comparisons: Nationalism, Southeast Asia, and the World* (New York: Verso, 1998).

52. Ordinance 53 prohibited foreigners from trade in groceries, coal and oil, fabrics and silk, and iron and copper scraps. Foreigners were also excluded from rice milling, operating pawn shops, serving as commission agents, and transporting goods and passengers by any type of vehicle or water craft. A copy of Ordinance 53, which was issued on September 6, 1956, can be found in NARA, RG 469, entry 461, box 8. Shortly after issuing the ordinance, Diem announced a new decree that required Chinese shops to display all signs in Vietnamese. Although this mandate

was not as destructive as the restrictive ordinance, it did indicate the high degree of institutionalized discrimination against Chinese. As the American ambassador, Fredrick Reinhardt, wrote, the language requirement represented but one of "the minor harassing actions pointing up continued GVN disinclination to modify its anti-Chinese program." Reinhardt to DOS/Washington, confidential memo, October 14, 1956, NARA, RG 469, entry 461, box 8.

53. Gerald Hickey, *Window on a War: An Anthropologist in the Vietnam Conflict* (Lubbock: Texas Tech University Press, 2002), 55–68. Hickey also discusses GVN policies toward ethnic minorities. See Gerald Hickey, *Shattered World: Adaptation and Survival among Vietnam's Highland Peoples during the Vietnam War* (Philadelphia: University of Pennsylvania Press, 1993).

54. Catton provides a detailed discussion of Diem's anti-Buddhist policies and the response from leading Buddhist monks in the early 1960s. See Catton, *Diem's Final Failure*, 185–208.

55. Statler, *Replacing France*, 4.

56. Some scholars use the term *state building* to describe similar endeavors. See in particular Francis Fukuyama, *State Building: Governance and World Order in the 21st Century* (Ithaca, NY: Cornell University Press, 2004); and Carter, *Inventing Vietnam*. However, I have chosen to use *nation building* because it connotes a broader range of activities. I understand *state building* to refer specifically to activities that develop the state apparatus and government institutions (including the military and police forces). While Americans did engage in such activities as a way of bolstering South Vietnam's government, they also focused on assistance in areas that fell outside the traditional purview of the government, including public health and agricultural development.

57. See Miller, *Misalliance*, 12.

58. For description and analysis of similarities and differences in the US government's and the GVN's visions for nation building in South Vietnam, see ibid.

59. As foreign assistance became an increasingly important weapon in the US Cold War arsenal, American policy makers created a new bureaucracy within the government to implement civilian aid programs. This aid bureaucracy took on various incarnations during the 1950s, including the Technical Cooperation Administration, the Foreign Operations Administration, and the International Cooperation Administration. In 1961, President John F. Kennedy issued an executive order creating the US Agency for International Development (USAID). Since its inception, USAID has been responsible for administering all American technical, economic, and humanitarian aid programs abroad. Although USAID is technically an independent body, its officials have worked closely with foreign policy makers in other sectors of the US government, including the State Department and the National Security Council. Originally, the aid agency was also responsible for administering military aid, under the Mutual Security Program. In the mid-1950s, the government reorganized the agency and assigned the task of overseeing international military aid to the Department of Defense. For more on the Mutual Security Program

in Vietnam, see "Mutual Security Program, Fiscal Year 1958 Estimates for the Far East and Pacific," USAID.

60. "International Cooperation Administration Operations Report," June 30, 1957, USAID.

61. Hannah had deep ties to the US government. He served in Truman's administration as a member of the International Development Advisory Board of Point Four from 1950 to 1952. He also served in Eisenhower's administration as the president's assistant secretary of defense for manpower and personnel from 1953 to 1954 and then chaired the Civil Rights Commission from the time of its creation in 1957 through the 1960s. See John Hannah, *A Memoir* (East Lansing: Michigan State University Press, 1980); and Ernst, *Forging a Fateful Alliance,* 5–7. For a detailed discussion of the Cold War alliance between American universities and the US government, see Stuart Leslie, *The Cold War and American Science: The Military-Industrial-Academic Complex at MIT and Stanford* (New York: Columbia University Press, 1993); Rebecca Lowen, *Creating the Cold War University: The Transformation of Stanford* (Berkeley and Los Angeles: University of California Press, 1997); and Noam Chomsky, ed., *The Cold War and the University: Toward an Intellectual History of the Postwar Years* (New York: New Press, 1998).

62. Under Hannah's leadership, MSU established programs in a number of developing countries. By the time the university introduced its aid program to Vietnam, it already had technical assistance projects in Colombia, Brazil, and the Ryukyuan Islands in the Japanese archipelago. In establishing those programs, it joined a growing number of universities, including the University of Michigan, the University of California, and the University of Southern California, in offering economic-development assistance to foreign nations. By the mid-1950s, American universities participated in forty-three technical assistance programs throughout the world. See Ernst, *Forging a Fateful Alliance,* 7. See also Ralph Smuckler, *A University Turns to the World* (East Lansing: Michigan State University Press, 2003).

63. Fishel and Diem shared staunchly anti-Communist political beliefs, and they engaged in long discussions about the history of Vietnam and the Viet Minh's anticolonial struggle against the French. Ralph Smuckler, interview with the author, Washington, DC, April 16, 2004. See also Warren Hinckle, Robert Scheer, and Sol Stern, "The University on the Make (or How MSU Helped Arm Madame Nhu)," *Ramparts Magazine* 4 (April 1966): 11–22.

64. In response to Fishel's personal invitation, Diem traveled to East Lansing in 1953. At the time, Fishel served as the assistant director for the MSU's Government Research Bureau, and he appointed Diem as the bureau's Southeast Asian expert. While in Michigan, Diem became acquainted with John Hannah. By introducing American university and political leaders to Diem, Fishel played a significant role in establishing the foundations of the partnership between the United States and Diem.

65. At one point, Fishel occupied an office in Saigon's presidential palace, and

he often discussed South Vietnam's political affairs over breakfast meetings with Diem. Ernst, *Forging a Fateful Alliance,* 11.

66. The MSU group charged with this task consisted of Arthur Brandstatter, head of the MSU Police Administration School, James Denison, a university public relations specialist, Edward Weidner, chairman of the Political Science Department, and Charles Killingsworth, chairman of the Economics Department.

67. Guy Fox, "MSUG in Vietnam," June 16, 1960, box 657, folder 27, VPP.

68. "Agreement between the Government of the United States, Represented by the Foreign Operations Administration, and Michigan State University," April 19, 1955, box 627, folder 80, VPP.

69. IVS had no official ties to any particular religious group, and the organization prohibited its volunteers from proselytizing while they served abroad. John Noffsinger, one of the creators and early leaders of IVS, eventually used the organization as a model for the Peace Corps. Paul Rodell, "John F. Noffsinger and the Global Impact of the Thomasite Experience," in *Back to the Future: Perspectives on the Thomasite Legacy to Philippine Education,* ed. Corazon Villareal (Quezon City: American Studies Association of the Philippines, 2003), 63–79. Rodell discusses Noffsinger's vision for IVS as well as the development of the Peace Corps according to the IVS model.

70. Robert Zigler to IVS Board, in *IVS Reporter* (1954), IVS. The first group of IVS volunteers was stationed in Iraq, and later missions offered aid in Africa, Asia, Latin America, and other parts of the Middle East.

71. Winburn Thomas, *The Vietnam Story of International Voluntary Services, Inc.* (Washington, DC: International Voluntary Services, 1972), 69, 4.

72. Many volunteers believed that working for IVS gave them a chance to serve their own country, and they took inspiration from John F. Kennedy's appeal to young Americans to perform public service. A number of newsletters, written by IVSers and distributed to their families and friends, contain references to Kennedy's inaugural address or the president's influence. For example, William Forest Gerdes, one of the first IVS volunteers on the education team, explained that he used Kennedy's call to service as a model as he attempted to motivate his Vietnamese students to take responsibility for the future of their country. John Sommer, another education volunteer, assigned the students in his English classes Kennedy's speeches, including his inaugural address. See William Forest Gerdes newsletter, April 1964, and John Sommer newsletter, September 1964, IVS. For young men, volunteering with IVS offered a compelling alternative to military service.

73. "IVS Executive Director's Report," April 25, 1962, IVS.

74. According to the organization's terminal report for USAID, the refugee crisis, with its mass movement of northern Vietnamese to the southern provinces, "created the occasion for IVS" to introduce volunteers to Vietnam. The humanitarian dimensions of the refugee episode seemed perfectly suited to the organization's aims. On arriving in Vietnam, the original group of volunteers, all of whom were male, worked in refugee camps for several months. However, these men were agri-

cultural specialists, and they soon clamored for assignments that would allow them to provide more direct assistance in agricultural development. In 1957, the IVS team stationed at a refugee center in Ban Me Thuot threatened to resign if they were not given more substantial duties in agricultural programs. Soon after, the organization moved those volunteers to other areas of the country, where they began working at agricultural experiment stations. Thomas, *The Vietnam Story of International Voluntary Services*, 2–34.

75. Diem, in particular, proved a difficult partner for the United States. As recent scholarship shows, he asserted his own agenda for modernization and development, and his vision often did not mesh with that of American policy makers. This dynamic played out on the numerous occasions when Diem openly opposed or undercut the efforts of American nation builders. For high-level tensions between Diem and American advisers, see esp. Catton, *Diem's Final Failure;* and Miller, *Misalliance.* Chapman's *Cauldron of Resistance* also discusses some of the points of contention between the partners, and Ernst's *Forging a Fateful Alliance* deals with the split between Diem and various advisers from MSU, especially Wesley Fishel.

76. Bui Duong Chi to Don Schmidt, n.d., in Don Schmidt newsletter, July 16, 1961, IVS.

77. For example, Westad describes the "remarkable consensus as to the immediate aims and means of U.S. policy abroad." Westad, *The Global Cold War,* 9. An important exception to this trend is Cullather, who, in his discussion of agricultural assistance programs in Asia, argues that there was no consensus among American advisers over the best model for rural development. Instead, he demonstrates how "rival ambitions for improving the human condition" played out on the ground in various Asian countries. Cullather, *The Hungry World,* 9. Recent studies by Immerwahr (*Thinking Small*) and Sackley ("The Village as Cold War Site") also suggest that not all Americans involved in development assistance accepted modernization theory and instead offered an alternative, community-oriented approach to foreign aid.

## 1. "The Virgin Mary Is Going South"

1. Walter Mode, "Review of MSUG Field Administration Division Vietnam, July 1955–June 1957," box 1209, folder 21, VPP.

2. Historians have largely echoed this positive assessment of the refugee episode. Most scholars have treated the refugee crisis, as it is often called, as a footnote to the larger story of Diem consolidating his hold on power during the first few years of South Vietnam's existence. Even those scholars who have been most critical of US involvement in Vietnam seem to have accepted the official narrative of success rather than fully exploring how the refugee episode affected either the complex political realities within South Vietnam or the US-GVN relationship. Marilyn Young, e.g., writes of the northern migrants: "In effect they were an imported political resource for Diem, a substantial and dependent bloc of loyal supporters." Young, *The Vietnam Wars,* 45. Similarly, George Kahin argues that Diem saw the refugees as "the most

reliable and effective element in the power base he was establishing." Kahin, *Intervention,* 84. George Herring describes the refugee crisis as "a means of tipping the political balance toward the south and perhaps even winning the 1956 elections." See Herring, *America's Longest War,* 46. And Louis Wiesner, who provides a quantitative and comparative approach to the refugee crisis and one of the most thorough discussions of the period, describes both the southern migration of the refugees and their resettlement as a "tremendous success." See Louis Wiesner, *Victims and Survivors: Displaced Persons and Other War Victims in Viet-Nam, 1954–1975* (New York: Greenwood, 1988), 16.

3. John Osborne, "The Tough Miracle Man of Vietnam," *Life,* May 13, 1957, 156–76.

4. Peter Hansen, "Bac Di Cu: Catholic Refugees from the North of Vietnam, and Their Role in the Southern Republic, 1954–1959," *Journal of Vietnamese Studies* 4, no. 3 (2009): 173–211.

5. For an excellent account of the VWP approach to socialist transformation, including Hanoi's "North-first" policy, see Asselin, *Hanoi's Road to the Vietnam War,* 35–51, 73–85. See also Nguyen, *Hanoi's War,* 34–43.

6. See Chapman, *Cauldron of Resistance,* and "The Sect Crisis of 1955."

7. For Diem's rise to power, see Miller, *Misalliance;* Catton, *Diem's Final Failure;* and Chapman, *Cauldron of Resistance.* Chapman discusses the southern opposition to Diem, particularly among politicoreligious organizations such as the Hoa Hao and Cao Dai, in detail.

8. Kahin, *Intervention,* 76. Kahin estimates that the addition of the refugees brought the Catholic minority to 9 percent in the mid-1950s. Stanley Karnow describes the "political importance" of the refugees, suggesting that their arrival instantly increased the number of staunch anti-Communists in South Vietnam. See Stanley Karnow, *Vietnam: A History* (New York: Viking, 1983), 222.

9. During the 1955 fiscal year, the US government provided $55.8 million to South Vietnam for refugee aid. The following year, the amount dropped to $37 million. This decrease reflected a general cutback of US aid to Vietnam in fiscal year 1956 as well as the perception among American officials that by 1956 Diem's regime no longer required the same degree of financial support. Leland Barrows, "Statement before Vietnam's Committee on Foreign Aid," June 14, 1956, box 649, folder 19, VPP.

10. "Agreement on the Cessation of Hostilities in Viet Nam, July 20, 1954," *FRUS, 1952–1954,* vol. 16, pp. 1540–42.

11. Asselin, *Hanoi's Road to the Vietnam War,* 5.

12. On the Geneva settlement and American policy makers' response, see Kahin, *Intervention,* 50–71, 88–91. See also *The Pentagon Papers,* vol. 1; and Statler, *Replacing France,* 85–99.

13. See Wiesner, *Victims and Survivors,* xvii. In this discussion, I refer to the northerners as *migrants, transplants, émigrés,* and *refugees* interchangeably. Although I am aware of the political implications of using *refugee,* in the interest of avoiding

some repetition and also in keeping with the language used in the American documents, I have not avoided the term. The terminology used in South Vietnamese sources varies from *người di cư,* which translates simply as migrants or people who have moved, to *người tị nạn,* which implies people who have moved under duress or have fled some calamity. This second term, *tị nạn,* parallels more closely the American description of those northerners who moved south in the mid-1950s as refugees.

14. Pierre Asselin cites records of the Canadian International Control and Supervisory Commission, which estimated that 173,900 troops and 86,000 "additional persons" regrouped north between 1954 and 1955. See Asselin, *Hanoi's Road to the Vietnam War,* 18–19. American sources generally provide slightly lower estimates. According to Wiesner, 130,000–140,000 Viet Minh went to the DRV. See Wiesner, *Victims and Survivors,* 3. Kahin estimates that between 130,000 and 150,000 people moved north. See Kahin, *Intervention,* 75.

15. In 1955, the International Commission for Supervision and Control in Vietnam, which consisted of representatives from Poland, India, and Canada, estimated that approximately 893,000 northerners moved to South Vietnam between 1954 and 1955. See *The Pentagon Papers,* 1:290.

16. Quoted in Kahin, *Intervention,* 74.

17. *The Pentagon Papers,* 1:291.

18. Hansen, "Bac Di Cu," 177. According to Hansen, in 1954, there were approximately 1.9 million Catholics in Vietnam. By the end of the transmigration, 1.17 million, or 61.6 percent, of them resided south of the seventeenth parallel.

19. Hansen, "Bac Di Cu," 177.

20. Duiker, *Ho Chi Minh,* 465.

21. Even before the Geneva settlement, the DRV issued an eight-point program to reassure professionals, bureaucrats, and others that the new government would not seize private property unless "imperialists" or supporters of Bao Dai's "puppet authority" owned a particular business. In September 1954, shortly after assuming power, Ho declared that former civil servants would not be arrested unless they took up arms against the government and that those who had previously worked for the French regime could stay in North Vietnam if they pledged allegiance to the new government. Duiker, *Ho Chi Minh,* 465.

22. Hansen, "Bac Di Cu," 187. Although he focuses on the role of the Catholic clergy in inspiring their northern followers to flee, Hansen also discusses many other factors that motivated the émigrés' decision making. See ibid., 182–87.

23. Kahin, *Intervention,* 76.

24. Duiker, *Ho Chi Minh,* 465.

25. *The Pentagon Papers,* 1:248.

26. Karnow, *Vietnam,* 222.

27. Carl Bon Tempo, *Americans at the Gate: The United States and Refugees during the Cold War* (Princeton, NJ: Princeton University Press, 2008), 4.

28. Wiesner, *Victims and Survivors,* 5.

29. MAAG, Coordinators Report of Operations, "Campaign for Freedom," August 8, 1954–September 30, 1954, NARA, RG 469, entry 1453, box 1.

30. Bon Tempo, *Americans at the Gate,* 7. Although Bon Tempo focuses on refugees entering the United States, his discussion of the "ideological continuity" and "procedural consistency" that characterized American-sponsored refugee programs provides valuable insights, even for a study of US involvement with refugee populations overseas.

31. MAAG, Coordinators Report of Operations, "Campaign for Freedom," August 8, 1954–September 30, 1954, NARA, RG 469, entry 1453, box 1.

32. Kahin, *Intervention,* 76–77. Kahin also discusses the "black propaganda" campaign advanced by pro-Diem agents. In the months following the partition, pamphlets and leaflets warning of a possible atomic attack on North Vietnam by the United States were dropped over the northern provinces. For more on the role of the United States in encouraging the refugees to move, see Karnow, *Vietnam,* 222.

33. Edward Lansdale, *In the Midst of Wars: An American's Mission to Southeast Asia* (New York: Harper & Row, 1972), 224 (quote), 226.

34. Kahin quotes a statement made by the deputy secretary general of the International Control Commission, the body charged with overseeing the implementation of the Geneva Accords, suggesting that many northerners were motivated by such fears. See Kahin, *Intervention,* 77.

35. Hansen, "Bac Di Cu," 182–85.

36. Karnow, *Vietnam,* 238.

37. MAAG, Coordinators Report of Operations, "Campaign for Freedom," August 8, 1954–September 30, 1954, NARA, RG 469, entry 1453, box 1.

38. Of those refugees, 6,003 were military personnel and the rest civilians. Ibid.

39. Wiesner, *Victims and Survivors,* 6. The "allied carriers" included French ships and planes and US and British ships, and Wiesner provides a breakdown of how many people each country's carriers transported.

40. A young naval medic, Dooley was sent to the northern port city of Haiphong in 1954 to build health clinics for and provide medical attention to northerners being evacuated on American vessels. He later described attending to people who had been tortured by the Viet Minh or DRV authorities because of their desire to flee the country. See Tom Dooley, *Deliver Us from Evil: The Story of Vietnam's Flight to Freedom* (New York: Farrar, Straus, & Cudahy, 1956).

41. Lavergne to Everett, Adler, and Lauve, "Viet Minh Tactics to Discourage Refugees from Moving South," November 30, 1954, NARA, RG 469, entry 1453, box 1.

42. MAAG, Coordinators Report of Operations, "Campaign for Freedom," August 8, 1954–September 30, 1954, NARA, RG 469, entry 1453, box 1.

43. D. C. Lavergne to Nguyen Huu Chau, May 18, 1956, TTLT-II.

44. Ibid.

45. For a discussion of the perceived benefits of these areas for resettlement, see, e.g., Barrows to Cardinaux, October 5, 1956, NARA, RG 469, entry 1453, box 2;

and D. C. Lavergne, "Special Projects," January 21, 1957, NARA, RG 469, entry 1453, box 5.

46. Miller, *Misalliance*, 160.

47. For more on Diem and Nhu's ideas about personalism and the connections between refugee resettlement and their political goals, see Miller, *Misalliance*, 160–65. See also Catton, *Diem's Final Failure*, 56–59.

48. Bernard Fall, *The Two Vietnams: A Political and Military Analysis* (New York: Praeger, 1967), 291.

49. On Diem's attitudes toward ethnic minorities and their practices, especially swidden agriculture, and his desire to civilize them, see Gerald Hickey, *Sons of the Mountains* (New Haven, CT: Yale University Press, 1982), and *Free in the Forest* (New Haven, CT: Yale University Press, 1982).

50. Hansen, "Bac Di Cu," 193–201.

51. Catton, *Diem's Final Failure*, 60.

52. MAAG, Coordinators Report of Operations, "Campaign for Freedom," August 8, 1954–September 30, 1954, NARA, RG 469, entry 1453, box 1.

53. Donald Sumner newsletter, June 29, 1959, IVS. For more information on IVS work with refugees, see Thomas, *The Vietnam Story of International Voluntary Services*.

54. See, e.g., Bui Van Luong to Ngo Dinh Diem, October 25, 1955, TTLT-II.

55. According to this plan, the refugee village administrative committees, composed of at least three residents who had been elected by their neighbors, had the authority to choose the firms and contractors and decide on other particular details of the projects for their villages. However, the committees were bound by their obligation to fulfill the fundamental aims of the given project, preserve all essential records, and submit regular reports to the Commissariat General for Refugees. This plan mirrored the basic decentralized structure of public administration in Vietnam at the time and conformed to existing patterns of local government in the provinces. For a description of the plan by GVN officials, see Tran Huu Phong to Ngo Dinh Diem, June 1, 1956, TTLT-II.

56. For a discussion of Diem's thinking on democracy, particularly with respect to his understanding of how Confucian teachings and personalist philosophy could direct political and administrative reforms, see Miller, *Misalliance*, 132–40.

57. The MSU team was particularly outspoken in its criticism of the village committees. MSU advisers considered the appointment of trained professionals a key antidote to the perennial problems of corruption and embezzlement that seemed to plague refugee assistance programs. In an attempt to address these problems, the MSU group advised the Refugee Commissariat to appoint provincial delegates to control expenditures and supervise the distribution of funds. According to its recommendations, these delegates would be licensed experts and accountable to the central government. MSU Vietnam Technical Assistance Project, "Review of Recommendations concerning Proposed Field Organization of the Commissariat for Refugees of September 20, 1955," June 29, 1956, TTLT-II.

58. For more on the conflict between expertise and local knowledge, see James

Scott, *Seeing Like a State: How Certain Schemes to Improve the Human Condition Have Failed* (New Haven, CT: Yale University Press, 1998).

59. MSU Vietnam Technical Assistance Project, "Review of Recommendations concerning Proposed Field Organization of the Commissariat for Refugees of September 20, 1955," June 29, 1956, TTLT-II. MSU advisers were dismayed at USOM's acquiescence. For their reaction, see Walter Mode to Wesley Fishel, September 14, 1956, box 675, folder 21, VPP.

60. MAAG, Coordinators Report of Operations, "Campaign for Freedom," August 8, 1954–September 30, 1954, NARA, RG 469, entry 1453, box 1.

61. Walter Mode, "Review of MSUG Field Administration Division Vietnam, July 1955–June 1957," box 1209, folder 21, VPP.

62. "Report of Division Chiefs Meeting," September 24, 1954, NARA, RG 469, entry 1453, box 1.

63. The fact that Bui Van Luong was later appointed commissioner for land development in South Vietnam demonstrates the links between refugee resettlement and other GVN development programs.

64. Of the 319 COMIGAL refugee villages, 288 were identified as primarily agricultural settlements, 26 were fishing villages, and 5 were established to house artisans and craftspeople. Wiesner, *Victims and Survivors,* 16.

65. "Report on Conference of Commissariat for Refugees," October 12, 1955, box 657, folder 24, VPP.

66. Ibid.

67. Evans to Hackett, November 2, 1956, box 674, folder 28, VPP.

68. Wiesner, *Victims and Survivors,* 15.

69. Can Tho Survey, n.d., box 675, folder 35, VPP.

70. MSU Vietnam Technical Assistance Project, "Review of Recommendations concerning Proposed Field Organization of the Commissariat for Refugees of September 20, 1955," June 29, 1956, TTLT-II.

71. Leland Barrows, "Statement before Vietnam's Committee on Foreign Aid," June 14, 1956, p. 14, box 649, folder 19, VPP.

72. "Project Agreement between the Foreign Operations Administration, an Agency of the Government of the United States of America, and the Committee for Foreign Aid, an Agency of the Government of Vietnam," project no. 30-82-075, January 1956, TTLT-II.

73. "Report on Conference of Commissariat for Refugees," October 12, 1955, box 657, folder 24, VPP.

74. Evans to Hackett, November 2, 1956, box 674, folder 28, VPP.

75. Barrows to Cardinaux, May 13, 1955, NARA, RG 469, entry 1453, box 1.

76. Briefing Book for Visit of John Hollister (Director of the International Cooperation Administration) Compiled by Raymond Miller, October 25, 1955, NARA, RG 469, entry 461, box 1.

77. John Prados, *The Hidden History of the Vietnam War* (Chicago: I. R. Dee, 1995), 20.

78. Herring, *America's Longest War,* 52.

79. Can Tho Survey, n.d., box 675, folder 35, VPP.

80. The Binh Xuyen was a criminal organization that operated in and around Saigon. For more on it, see Kahin, *Intervention;* and Chapman, "Staging Democracy."

81. Wiesner, *Victims and Survivors,* 13.

82. In 1954, 35.5 piasters equaled $1.00. Wiesner, *Victims and Survivors,* 7.

83. "Report of Division Chiefs' Meeting," September 24, 1954, NARA, RG 469, entry 1453, box 1.

84. Ernst, *Forging a Fateful Alliance,* 28.

85. Can Tho Survey, n.d., box 675, folder 35, VPP.

86. Ernst, *Forging a Fateful Alliance,* 28–29.

87. Robert Scigliano, *South Vietnam: Nation under Stress* (Boston: Houghton Mifflin, 1964), 54. Kahin provides a good description of Diem's decision to abolish elections for village councils in mid-1956 and allow the Interior Ministry to appoint northern transplants as local officials. See Kahin, *Intervention,* 98–101. Even at the national level, refugees enjoyed advantages in winning coveted positions in the government.

88. Carter, *Inventing Vietnam,* 59.

89. Can Tho Survey, n.d., box 675, folder 35, VPP.

90. Wiesner, *Victims and Survivors,* 9. Hansen's research also supports this claim. See Hansen, "Bac Di Cu," 193–201.

91. Catton, *Diem's Final Failure,* 61.

92. "Cai San Resettlement Plan," n.d., NARA, RG 469, entry 461, box 1. According to David Biggs, Diem had supported colonial land-reclamation and -resettlement projects since his time as a provincial chief in the 1920s. See David Biggs, *Quagmire: Nation Building and Nature in the Mekong Delta* (Seattle: University of Washington Press, 2012), 163. For a good overview of the colonial-era precedents and models for Cai San and similar projects, see ibid., 161–64.

93. MSU Vietnam Technical Assistance Project, "Review of Recommendations concerning Proposed Field Organization of the Commissariat for Refugees of September 20, 1955," June 29, 1956, TTLT-II.

94. Hickey, *Window on a War,* 26–27.

95. Wiesner, *Victims and Survivors,* 15.

96. "Cai San Resettlement Plan," n.d., NARA, RG 469, entry 461, box 1.

97. According to Biggs, only six hundred of the northerners who settled Cai San in 1956 were not Catholic. See Biggs, *Quagmire,* 164.

98. Gene Myers newsletter, October 21, 1957, IVS.

99. Wiesner, *Victims and Survivors,* 15.

100. *Vietnam Press* article, July 26, 1955, box 657, folder 72, VPP.

101. Leland Barrows, "Statement before Vietnam's Committee on Foreign Aid," June 14, 1956, p. 19, box 649, folder 19, VPP.

102. MSU Vietnam Technical Assistance Project, "Review of Recommendations concerning Proposed Field Organization of the Commissariat for Refugees of September 20, 1955," June 29, 1956, TTLT-II.

103. Catton demonstrates how the Ngo family saw refugee resettlement as part of a larger project of land development, and, in doing so, he illustrates many of the direct links between the refugee period and later policies, especially in the Mekong delta and the highlands. See Catton, *Diem's Final Failure*, 56–57. Miller also discusses connections between the Ngos' early resettlement schemes such as Cai San and later "population regroupment" plans, including land development and the agroville program. See Miller, *Misalliance*, 171–84.

104. Hickey, *Window on a War*, 26.

105. "Hostile activities" quote from Mike Adler, "Viet Minh Activity, Province of Gia Dinh," December 30, 1955, NARA, RG 469, entry 1455, box 1. See also R. A. Nichols to D. C. Lavergne, "Obstacles to Recovery in the Southern Provinces," September 12, 1956, NARA, RG 469, entry 1453, box 2; and D. C. Lavergne, "Special Projects," January 21, 1957, NARA, RG 469, entry 1453, box 5.

106. Barrows to Cardinaux, October 5, 1956, NARA, RG 469, entry 1453, box 2.

107. Lansdale to Barrows, "Incident Near Long Xuyen," October 4, 1956, NARA, RG 469, entry 1453, box 2.

108. Biggs, *Quagmire*, 162.

109. Ibid., 167.

110. Miller, *Misalliance*, 168. See also Fall, *Vietnam Witness*, 180; and Thomas, *The Vietnam Story of International Voluntary Services*, 119.

111. Biggs, *Quagmire*, 168–69.

112. Gene Myers newsletter, October 21, 1957, and Robert Yates newsletter, August 27, 1957, IVS.

113. Thomas, *The Vietnam Story of International Voluntary Services*, 119.

114. There were even tensions related to the issue of Catholic influence among American organizations working in Vietnam. A feud erupted between USOM and CRS in mid-1955, largely as a result of "differences of opinion, regarding refugee resettlement" between the US government aid workers and the Catholic volunteers and their leader, Monsignor Harnett. USOM officials criticized CRS management of a food-surplus project, and CRS leadership charged that "government aid to the refugees is ineffectual." See D. C. Lavergne to Gardner Palmer, April 16, 1956, Lavergne to Leland Barrows, April 15, 1956, and the Catholic Relief Services Monthly Narrative Report, March 1956, NARA, RG 469, entry 1453, box 2.

115. Leland Barrows, "Statement before Vietnam's Committee on Foreign Aid," June 14, 1956, box 649, folder 19, VPP.

116. Thomas, *The Vietnam Story of International Voluntary Services*, 112, 122.

117. Leland Barrows, "Statement before Vietnam's Committee on Foreign Aid," June 14, 1956, box 649, folder 19, VPP.

118. "John F. Kennedy's Remarks at the Conference on Vietnam at the Willard Hotel, Washington, DC," June 1, 1956, *Public Papers of the Presidents of the United States: John F. Kennedy, 1961* (Washington, DC: US Government Printing Office, 1962).

119. *The Pentagon Papers*, 1:248.

120. ICA [International Cooperation Administration] Briefing Materials, December 28, 1956, NARA, RG 469, entry 461, box 1.

## 2. Civil Servants and Cold Warriors

1. Guy Fox, "MSUG in Vietnam," June 16, 1960, box 657, folder 27, VPP.

2. Leland Barrows, "Statement before Vietnam's Committee on Foreign Aid," June 14, 1956, box 649, folder 19, VPP.

3. On intellectuals and modernization theory, see Gilman, "Modernization Theory." For universities' role in Cold War foreign policy and the military-industrial-academic complex, see Leslie, *The Cold War and American Science;* Lowen, *Creating the Cold War University;* and Olivier Zunz, *Why the American Century?* (Chicago: University of Chicago Press, 1998).

4. For useful analyses of the mid-twentieth-century alliance between the US government and intellectuals, see Latham, *Modernization as Ideology;* Richard Pells, *Not Like Us: How Europeans Have Loved, Hated, and Transformed American Culture since World War II* (New York: Basic, 1997); and Ron Robin, *The Making of the Cold War Enemy* (Princeton, NJ: Princeton University Press, 2001).

5. Mary Furner, *Advocacy and Objectivity: A Crisis in the Professionalization of American Social Science, 1865–1905* (Lexington: University Press of Kentucky, 1975), 147.

6. As the historians Alice O'Connor and Ron Robin show, by midcentury many prominent scholars in all fields subscribed to the belief that scientific knowledge of a particular variety should be applied to public policy issues. See Alice O'Connor, *Poverty Knowledge* (Princeton, NJ: Princeton University Press, 2001); and Robin, *The Making of the Cold War Enemy.*

7. O'Connor, *Poverty Knowledge,* 8.

8. Theodore Porter's *Trust in Numbers: The Pursuit of Objectivity in Science and Public Life* (Princeton, NJ: Princeton University Press, 1995) illustrates how empirical research based on quantitative methods assumed a central role in the work of social scientists working in academic departments and public institutions.

9. Robin, *The Making of the Cold War Enemy,* 13, 5.

10. Ralph Smuckler, interview with the author, Washington, DC, April 16, 2004. For a discussion of the land-grant philosophy and its relation to international projects, see Smuckler, *A University Turns to the World,* esp. chap. 1.

11. Stanley Sheinbaum, interview with the author, Los Angeles, March 15, 2004. Although initially on board with MSU's nation-building efforts, Sheinbaum came to oppose its involvement in Vietnam. He was so turned off by the Vietnam Project that he not only rejected the university's program but also left academic life entirely in 1959.

12. Scigliano and Fox, *Technical Assistance in Vietnam,* 30.

13. Ralph Smuckler, interview with the author, Washington, DC, April 16, 2004.

14. "Proposed Program for FY 1963, Vol. II," USAID.

15. O'Connor's claim that employing academic knowledge to inform policy

constitutes an "inescapably political act" applies also to policy makers' use of modernization theory, which at its heart obscured politics in favor of cultural or social analysis. See O'Connor, *Poverty Knowledge,* 12–15.

16. Richard Pells describes this dynamic, explaining that intellectuals viewed their involvement in government-sponsored projects as "politically necessary and morally ennobling" and derived power from having ideas that corresponded with those driving US policy. See Pells, *Not Like Us,* 73.

17. Ralph Smuckler, interview with the author, Washington, DC, April 16, 2004. For a description of the common pattern of ambitious universities accepting contracts from the US government to work abroad during the Cold War, see Lowen, *Creating the Cold War University.*

18. "Final Report for MSUG," June 1962, p. 3, box 658, folder 6, VPP.

19. Nghiem Dang, *Vietnam: Politics and Public Administration* (Honolulu: East West Center Press, 1966), 2.

20. Miller, *Misalliance,* 132–40.

21. Nghiem Dang, "The National Institute of Administration," in *Viet-Nam: The First Five Years: An International Symposium,* ed. Richard Lindholm (East Lansing: Michigan State University, 1959), 162–66.

22. Nguyen Duy Xuan, "Technical Assistance to a Public Administration Institute: The Vietnam Case," in *Development Administration in Asia,* ed. Edward Weidner (Durham, NC: Duke University Press, 1970), 366–88.

23. Ernst, *Forging a Fateful Alliance,* 42.

24. Xuan, "Technical Assistance to a Public Administration Institute," 370–71.

25. Xuan, "Technical Assistance to a Public Administration Institute," 372.

26. "Program Review for Public Admin Division Prepared for USOM Mission Director," February 28, 1958, box 674, folder 78, VPP.

27. Ernst, *Forging a Fateful Alliance,* 42.

28. "Program Review for Public Admin Division Prepared for USOM Mission Director," February 28, 1958, box 674, folder 78, VPP.

29. Xuan, "Technical Assistance to a Public Administration Institute," 375. For a complete discussion of the curriculum and course offerings, see Ernst, *Forging a Fateful Alliance,* 41–62.

30. "Public Admin Division Fact Sheet on Program Status," October 1, 1959, box 649, folder 23, VPP.

31. Xuan, "Technical Assistance to a Public Administration Institute," 375.

32. Scigliano and Fox, *Technical Assistance in Vietnam,* 23.

33. Vu Quoc Thong, the director of the NIA, vocalized this fear when he suggested that members of the MSU group not be allowed to participate in the NIA's academic leadership council. See Edward Weidner, "Monthly Report of MSUG," September 8, 1955, box 658, folder 13, VPP.

34. Dang, *Vietnam,* 345.

35. "Michigan State University Contract—Vietnam, Revised," June 18, 1957, box 649, folder 1, VPP.

36. See, e.g., Hickey, *Sons of the Mountains, Free in the Forest,* and *Window on a War.*

37. Robert Scigliano to John Dorsey, "MSUG Research Program," November 1958, box 666, folder 51, VPP.

38. Wesley Fishel to Vu Quoc Thong, 1957, box 666, folder 51, VPP.

39. "Research Proposals," box 666, folder 50, VPP.

40. Robert Scigliano to John Dorsey, "MSUG Research Program," November 1958, box 666, folder 51, VPP.

41. Scigliano and Fox, *Technical Assistance in Vietnam,* 33.

42. See, e.g., Gerald Hickey and Vo Hong Phuoc, *Report on the Organization of the Department of Education* (Saigon: Michigan State University Advisory Group, 1957); and Gerald Hickey, "Research Report to the Department of Education," March 1957, box 658, folder 79, VPP. Smuckler identifies seven books, twenty-five published monographs, and at least thirty mimeographed studies and surveys produced by the Vietnam Project during its tenure. See Ralph Smuckler, "Report on the MSU–Vietnam Project," April 1966, box 658, folder 79, VPP.

43. Ralph Smuckler, interview with the author, Washington, DC, April 16, 2004.

44. See, e.g., Hickey and Phuoc, *Report on the Organization of the Department of Education;* and John Donoghue and Vo Hong Phuoc, *My Thuan: A Study of a Delta Village in South Vietnam* (Saigon: Michigan State University Advisory Group, 1961).

45. Robert Scigliano to John Dorsey, "MSUG Research Program," November 1958, box 666, folder 51, VPP.

46. Dang, *Vietnam,* 344.

47. Scigliano and Fox, *Technical Assistance in Vietnam,* 37.

48. Xuan, "Technical Assistance to a Public Administration Institute," 384.

49. Scigliano and Fox, *Technical Assistance in Vietnam,* 35.

50. Edward Weidner, "Monthly Report of MSUG," September 8, 1955, box 658, folder 13, VPP.

51. Xuan, "Technical Assistance to a Public Administration Institute," 376; Ernst, *Forging a Fateful Alliance,* 51–54; Scigliano and Fox, *Technical Assistance in Vietnam,* 37.

52. Scigliano and Fox, *Technical Assistance in Vietnam,* 35 (quote), 37.

53. Edward Weidner, "Monthly Report of MSUG," September 8, 1955, box 658, folder 13, VPP.

54. Ernst, *Forging a Fateful Alliance,* 49–50.

55. Edward Weidner, "Monthly Report of MSUG," September 8, 1955, box 658, folder 13, VPP.

56. For more detail on the in-service training program, see Ernst, *Forging a Fateful Alliance,* 53–54; and Xuan, "Technical Assistance to a Public Administration Institute," 377–80. During the MSU group's tenure in Vietnam, the NIA published a public administration journal, *Progress.* However, the end of the group's contract in 1962 signaled the termination of the journal, as the institute no longer had enough funding to cover the costs of publication.

57. Frederic Wickert to Wesley Fishel, "Proposals for the Series of Lectures for High and Middle-Level Executives of the Government of Vietnam," March 29, 1956, box 629, folder 38, VPP. The other six lecture topics were "The Role of Middle Management," "The Art of Leadership," "Staff Work," "Organization and Methods Work," "Some Aspects of Modern Budget Administration," and "The Executive and Personnel System." All ten lectures have been published in English and Vietnamese as *Aspects of Modern Public Administration* (Saigon: National Institute of Administration, 1956).

58. Frederic Wickert to Wesley Fishel, "Proposals for the Series of Lectures for High and Middle-Level Executives of the Government of Vietnam," March 29, 1956, p. 2, box 629, folder 38, VPP.

59. The lectures offered not just general advice but also specific suggestions. For example, when discussing executive development, Frederic Wickert, the coordinator of the NIA's in-service training program, presented examples of particular methods for preparing new administrators, such as having an inexperienced official shadow a more senior bureaucrat. Smuckler discussed established methods of instilling the need for responsibility and accountability, including hierarchical organization, budget control, and membership in professional associations. See Frederic Wickert, "How to Develop Executives," in *Aspects of Modern Public Administration,* 43–60, 45–46; and Ralph Smuckler, "Responsibility and Accountability in Public Service," in ibid., 139–49, 142–44.

60. Wickert, "How to Develop Executives," 43; Gene Adrian Gregory, "Service to the Public," in *Aspects of Modern Public Administration,* 87–110, 87, 89, 94.

61. Smuckler, "Responsibility and Accountability in Public Service," 140.

62. The Vietnam Project included a "Participant Program," in which MSU sent Vietnamese students to the United States or some other foreign country. Between 1955 and 1961, the university sponsored 179 Vietnamese students for foreign study, and 116 of those participants studied in the United States. However, at the time of the Presidential Lecture Series, only a handful of Vietnamese civil servants had participated in study or observation tours in the United States, and none who had done so had returned to Vietnam yet. In November 1955, the first group of program participants—ten Vietnamese civil servants—arrived in East Lansing for nine months of instruction in public administration, economics, and police administration. "Final Report for MSUG," June 1962, box 658, folder 6, VPP.

63. Gregory, "Service to the Public."

64. Ibid., 106.

65. For a discussion of GVN leaders' political philosophy, see Catton, *Diem's Final Failure;* and Miller, *Misalliance.* Miller argues that the doctrine of personalism "served as the government's official ideology." Miller, *Misalliance,* 138. He also explores in significant detail Diem's ideas about democracy, which differed fundamentally from most Americans' understanding. Ibid., 132–40.

66. Wickert, "How to Develop Executives," 54.

67. See, e.g., Vu Quoc Thong to Minister of the Interior, January 27, 1959, TTLT-

II, in which Thong asked for permission to delay John Montgomery's research trip to Khanh Hoa Province to study the Ha Lien Dam. See also Thong to Presidential Palace, March 6, 1959, TTLT-II, in which Thong requested permission for four professors to study the "problem of dividing land for established residents" in Binh Tuy. See also Thong to Presidential Palace, April 18, 1959, TTLT-II, in which Thong informed the palace that Lloyd Woodruff and John Dorsey requested permission to study local administration in Nha Trang, Quang Ngai, and Hue.

68. "Status of Research at MSUG," n.d., box 666, folder 52, VPP.

69. Scigliano and Fox, *Technical Assistance in Vietnam*, 51.

70. Ibid., 53.

71. John T. Dorsey, "South Vietnam in Perspective," *Far Eastern Survey* 27, no. 12 (December 1958): 177–82, 179, 182.

72. Elizabeth Jorzick (DOS [Department of State]) to S. M. Fine, February 10, 1959 (internal DOS/ICA memo on Dorsey article), NARA, RG 469, entry 461, box 2. According to this memo, Dorsey's statements may be "dangerous" if taken out of context.

73. ICA/Washington to USOM, January 15, 1959, NARA, RG 469, entry 461, box 2.

74. Barrows to ICA (confidential), August 12, 1958, NARA, RG 469, entry 461, box 2.

75. Miller, *Misalliance*, 211.

76. Muslof to Austin, November 16, 1960, box 677, folder 26, VPP.

77. For a discussion of the coup and Diem's response to it, see Miller, *Misalliance*, 202–13. For an earlier scholarly analysis, see Kahin, *Intervention*, 123–26.

78. Austin to Muslof, November 23, 1960, box 677, folder 26, VPP.

79. Muslof to Austin, December 15, 1960, box 677, folder 26, VPP.

80. Scigliano and Fox, *Technical Assistance in Vietnam*, 52–53 (referencing Donoghue and Phuoc, *My Thuan;* and Frank Child, "Essays on Economic Growth, Capital Formation, and Public Policy in Vietnam" [Saigon: Michigan State University/Viet-Nam Advisory Group, 1961]).

81. Donoghue and Phuoc, *My Thuan*, 30 (quote), 43.

82. "Final Report for MSUG," June 1962, box 658, folder 6, VPP.

83. Scigliano and Fox, *Technical Assistance in Vietnam*, 47.

84. Stoneman to Furst and Kirch (US State Department), November 19, 1963, NARA, RG 286, entry 450, box 244.

85. Scigliano and Fox, *Technical Assistance in Vietnam*, 48–49.

86. This course provided instruction in many areas, including the organizational structure of a customs house, transportation and warehousing of goods subject to customs, declaration and payment of duties, inspection on the high seas, litigation of customs matters, and methods for combating smuggling. Memo by Arthur Gardiner, USOM/Saigon, to ICA/Washington, September 3, 1959, NARA, RG 286, entry 449, box 236. Gardiner's memo also contains descriptions of other training courses that USOM offered to Vietnamese working in finance.

87. Memo by Arthur Gardiner, USOM/Saigon, to ICA/Washington, April 8, 1961, NARA, RG 286, entry 449, box 237.

88. Kalman Dienes, Chief PAD, to Education, Health and Sanitation, Public Safety, Agriculture, T.C.P., and Industry Divisions of USOM, June 27, 1960, NARA, RG 286, entry 449, box 237.

89. USOM PAD Quarterly Report, July 20, 1962, NARA, RG 286, entry 451, box 250.

90. Gustav Hertz to Joseph Brent, "Monthly Division Operational Report for November 1963," December 5, 1963, NARA, RG 286, entry 450, box 245. In addition to lack of security and poor civil administrative performance by military personnel, respondents also mentioned arbitrary arrests and imprisonment, forced labor, unfair collection of taxes, and persecution of certain religious groups as the most important reasons they lacked confidence in the GVN.

91. Gustav Hertz to Joseph Brent, "Monthly Division Operational Report for January 1964," February 7, 1964, NARA, RG 286, entry 450, box 245.

92. Henry Bush, PAD, to Gustav Hertz, "Report on the Province of Tay Ninh," October 11, 1963, NARA, RG 286, entry 450, box 245.

93. Gustave Hertz to Joseph Brent, "Monthly Division Operational Report for October 1963," November 5, 1963, NARA, RG 286, entry 450, box 245.

94. Gustav Hertz to Joseph Brent, "Monthly Division Operational Report for January 1964," February 7, 1964, NARA, RG 286, entry 450, box 245.

95. Gustav Hertz to Joseph Brent, "Monthly Division Operational Report for October 1963," November 5, 1963, NARA, RG 286, entry 450, box 245.

96. Gustav Hertz to Joseph Brent, "Meeting with Secretary of State for Interior," September 4, 1963, NARA, RG 286, entry 450, box 244.

97. Henry Bush to Gustav Hertz, "Report on Province of Binh Duong," September 26, 1963, NARA, RG 286, entry 450, box 245.

98. Henry Bush to Gustav Hertz, "Report on the Province of Binh Duong," September 26, 1963, and Bush to Hertz, "Report on the Province of Phuoc Long," October 3, 1963, NARA, RG 286, entry 450, box 245. See also Gustav Hertz, "Report on Trip to Dalat," July 5, 1963, NARA, RG 286, entry 450, box 245.

99. Henry Bush to Gustav Hertz, "Report on the Province of Phuoc Long," October 3, 1963, NARA, RG 286, entry 450, box 245.

100. Gustav Hertz to Joseph Brent, "Monthly Division Operational Report for September 1963," October 7, 1963, NARA, RG 286, entry 450, box 245.

101. USOM, "Public Administration Bulletin," December 9, 1963, NARA, RG 286, entry 450, box 245.

102. Gustav Hertz to Joseph Brent, "Monthly Division Operational Report for December 1963," January 6, 1964, NARA, RG 286, entry 450, box 245.

103. Gustav Hertz to Joseph Brent, "Monthly Division Operational Report for February 1964," March 6, 1964, NARA, RG 286, entry 450, box 244.

104. USOM, "Public Administration Bulletin," May 25, 1964, NARA, RG 286, entry 450, box 245.

105. Gustav Hertz to Joseph Brent, "Monthly Division Operational Report for December 1963," January 6, 1964, NARA, RG 286, entry 450, box 245.

106. Gustav Hertz to Joseph Brent, "Monthly Division Operational Report for February 1964," March 6, 1964, NARA, RG 286, entry 450, box 244.

107. In May 1964, the PAD stressed the "role of the military vis a vis the civilian aspects of the government in the present situation." USOM, "Public Administration Bulletin," May 25, 1964, NARA, RG 286, entry 450, box 245.

108. Ibid.

109. A number of USOM documents refer to the NLF's shadow government and its policy of collecting taxes from the rural population, sometimes forcibly. See, e.g., Quentin Verdier, "Report on Trip to Long-An Province," January 25, 1964, and J. L. Ouellette, "Report of Visit to Darlac Province," January 29, 1964, NARA, RG 286, entry 450, box 245.

### 3. Sowing the Seeds of Discontent

1. Cullather, *The Hungry World,* 70.

2. Biggs, *Quagmire,* 141.

3. Anderson, *Trapped by Success,* 140.

4. Gareth Porter, *The Myth of the Bloodbath: North Vietnam's Land Reform Reconsidered* (Ithaca, NY: International Relations of East Asia Project, Cornell University, 1972), 10.

5. Anderson, *Trapped by Success,* 153.

6. Biggs, *Quagmire,* 141–45. See also Kahin, *Intervention,* 98–99.

7. For a good overview and comparative discussion of land-reform efforts, see Edwin Moise, *Land Reform in China and North Vietnam: Consolidating the Revolution at the Village Level* (Chapel Hill: University of North Carolina Press, 1983). Many early American accounts were overwhelmingly critical of the DRV land reform, commonly portraying it as a *bloodbath.* See, e.g., P. J. Honey, *Genesis of a Tragedy: The Historical Background to the Vietnam War* (London: Benn, 1968); Joseph Buttinger, *A Dragon Defiant: A Short History of Vietnam* (New York: Praeger, 1972), and *Vietnam: A Political History* (New York: Praeger, 1968); and Fall, *The Two Vietnams,* and *Vietnam Witness.* For a more balanced view, one that relies on North Vietnamese sources, see Moise, *Land Reform in China;* Porter, *The Myth of the Bloodbath;* and Christine White, *Land Reform in North Vietnam* (Washington, DC: US Agency for International Development, 1970). Porter in particular attempts to dispel what he calls "the myth of the bloodbath." He argues that, despite the negative short-term consequences, DRV land reform had the long-term benefits of "improved social and political status in the villages . . . and bringing the peasants into the political process." Porter, *The Myth of the Bloodbath,* 22, 57–58.

8. Asselin, *Hanoi's Road to the Vietnam War,* 38.

9. Porter claims that this slogan did not accurately portray actual DRV policy. See Porter, *The Myth of the Bloodbath,* 20–21. For a more recent discussion of DRV land reform, see Duiker, *Ho Chi Minh,* 476–81.

10. Kahin, *Intervention,* 98–99.

11. Jeffrey Race, *War Comes to Long An: Revolutionary Conflict in a Vietnamese Province* (Berkeley and Los Angeles: University of California Press, 1972), 55–61.

12. Miller, *Misalliance,* 159. According to Miller, the percentage of farmland in the Mekong delta cultivated by tenant farmers (about 80 percent) was virtually unchanged from 1954 to 1968.

13. Both Edward Miller and Philip Catton discuss these disagreements in detail. See Miller, *Misalliance,* 158–84; and Catton, *Diem's Final Failure,* 51–72.

14. For a discussion of the significance of the village in Cold War–era development schemes, see Sackley, "The Village as Cold War Site." According to Sackley: "'The village' contained all of the dangers and possibilities that development experts saw in 'Third World' people." Ibid., 482.

15. As of June 1957, 17 percent of all foreign aid money administered by the International Cooperation Agency went to Vietnam. The only nation to obtain more US funding for military, economic, and technical assistance was South Korea, which received 20 percent of the US foreign aid budget. "International Cooperation Administration Operations Report," June 30, 1957, p. 5, USAID.

16. "Mutual Security Program, Fiscal Year 1958 Estimates for the Far East and Pacific," p. 126, USAID.

17. "Mutual Security Program, Fiscal Year 1961 Estimates, Vol. II: Far East, Latin America and Non-Regional," p. 66, USAID.

18. "Mutual Security Program, Fiscal Year 1958 Estimates for the Far East and Pacific," p. 3, USAID.

19. Deborah Fitzgerald, *Every Farm a Factory: The Industrial Ideal in American Agriculture* (New Haven, CT: Yale University Press, 2003), 3–12.

20. Ibid., 181.

21. Most of the Americans returned from the Soviet Union feeling as if they had accomplished very little. They reported that Soviet farmworkers had rejected their suggestions and that widespread resentment of the United States had made it difficult to introduce industrial methods to the Soviet farms. Ibid., 174–80.

22. Cullather, *The Hungry World,* 42.

23. Fitzgerald discusses the intersection between land-grant colleges and the applied science of farming as well as the professionalization of agriculture. See Fitzgerald, *Every Farm a Factory,* 22–23. Ralph Smuckler highlights the connections between land-grant institutions and public service. See Smuckler, *A University Turns to the World,* 4–6. For a discussion of the land-grant college movement as well as the introduction of agricultural experiment stations to universities during the late nineteenth century and the early twentieth, see Roger Williams, *The Origins of Federal Support for Higher Education: George W. Atherton and the Land-Grant College Movement* (University Park: Pennsylvania State University Press, 1991).

24. Fitzgerald, *Every Farm a Factory,* 182.

25. Don Schmidt newsletter, November 12, 1960, IVS.

26. Leslie Small newsletter, July 26, 1964, IVS.

27. In theory, USOM was not supposed to develop agricultural programs of its own; instead, the agency was charged with providing aid to GVN programs that the US government agreed to support. "USOM Agriculture Vietnam," July 1, 1963, NARA, RG 286 (US Agency for International Development), entry 449, box 240.

28. Lawrence Doran, "End of Tour Report," April 14, 1964, NARA, RG 286, entry 449, box 240. In 1955, the GVN created the National Directorate of Agriculture to administer the extension service. Doran and other aid workers from USOM worked closely with this service.

29. For details of USOM activities, see the divisions' monthly reports, such as "USOM Agricultural Monthly Report, August 1963," NARA, RG 286, entry 449, box 240. See also "USOM Agriculture Vietnam," July 1, 1963, NARA, RG 286, entry 449, box 240.

30. For example, during the three-and-a-half-year tenure of one USOM aid worker, one Vietnamese staff member spent eighteen months in the United States and earned a BS in agricultural economics. Fifteen other Vietnamese employees participated in a one-month training course in Taiwan. Richard Pringle, "End of Tour Report," May 22, 1964, NARA, RG 286, entry 449, box 240. Between 1962 and 1964, over twelve thousand "farm leaders" participated in a four-day training program in Vietnam and were then sent home to apply what they had learned. Lawrence Doran, "End of Tour Report," April 14, 1964, NARA, RG 286, entry 449, box 240.

31. Lawrence Doran, "End of Tour Report," April 14, 1964, NARA, RG 286, entry 449, box 240.

32. "USOM Agriculture Vietnam," July 1, 1963, NARA, RG 286, entry 449, box 240.

33. The first 4-T club was established in November 1955 in a village near Thu-Dau-Mot. As a USOM report explains, "by happy coincidence" the four Ts correspond with their counterparts in English. The mission of 4-H clubs is to develop the head (in Vietnamese, *tri oc*), the heart (*tam long*), the hand (*tay chan*), and the health (*than the*) of its young, rural members. "USOM Agriculture Vietnam," July 1, 1963, NARA, RG 286, entry 449, box 240.

34. Lawrence Doran, "End of Tour Report," April 14, 1964, NARA, RG 286, entry 449, box 240.

35. Founded in 1953, IVS was a private, nonprofit organization created to provide "person-to-person" assistance to developing countries. Although the organization had no explicit religious affiliation, many of its private donations came from church groups, some of its early leaders had connections with the Mennonite Central Committee, and many of its young volunteers were motivated by an evangelical sense of mission. IVS introduced a mission to Vietnam in 1956. For the first five years of its presence in the country, the organization supported only a relatively small group of male volunteers who worked on agricultural development. However, in 1961, it added programs in education and public health, and these later programs included female volunteers.

36. Thomas, *The Vietnam Story of International Voluntary Services* (Washington, DC: IVS, 1972), 109.

37. Richard Peters, interview with the author, San Jose, CA, November 28, 2003.

38. Burr Frutchey newsletter, December 11, 1960, IVS.

39. Elsewhere, IVS teams depended on some financial assistance from the government but relied primarily on private donations. Although, as noted, IVS had no particular religious affiliation, contributions from religious organizations constituted the largest source of private funding for its missions. However, the IVS mission in Vietnam differed from other programs owing to its complete dependence on public funds.

40. IVS volunteers served in Vietnam on two-year tours. All were college graduates, and most volunteered for IVS immediately following graduation. For more information on IVS activities in Vietnam, see Thomas, *The Vietnam Story of International Voluntary Services*.

41. Volunteers' acceptance of their position vis-à-vis the US government changed dramatically in later years, especially after the US ground war began. The most public display of criticism of and desire to break from US policies came in 1967, when a group of IVSers signed a petition opposing the war. For the text of the petition letter, see Don Luce and John Sommer, *Vietnam: The Unheard Voices* (Ithaca, NY: Cornell University Press, 1969), 315–21. For the IVSers' general discontent, see Thomas, *The Vietnam Story of International Voluntary Services*, 33–39.

42. Thomas, *The Vietnam Story of International Voluntary Services*, 8, 91.

43. See, e.g., "USOM Agriculture Vietnam," July 1, 1963, NARA, RG 286, entry 449, box 240. At the time this report was issued, USOM had twenty-two staff members working on agricultural development, and the agency received contract services from thirty IVS volunteers.

44. Thomas, *The Vietnam Story of International Voluntary Services*, 64.

45. Mike Chilton newsletter, September 20, 1960, IVS.

46. Rufus Philips, interview with the author, McLean, VA, April 14, 2004.

47. Ladejinsky had been one of the architects of Japan's land-reform program and was a vocal advocate for the political and strategic implications of land reform. As Cullather explains, he saw land reform as a way to spark democratic revolutions and provide peasants with a "stake in a capitalist future." Cullather, *The Hungry World*, 97–98.

48. Wolf Ladejinsky, "South Vietnam Revisited," July 16, 1955, NARA, RG 469 (USAID Predecessor agencies), entry 461, box 4.

49. Richard Pringle, "End of Tour Report," May 22, 1964, NARA, RG 286, entry 449, box 240.

50. Wolf Ladejinsky, "South Vietnam Revisited," July 16, 1955, NARA, RG 469, entry 461, box 4.

51. See "Economic Aid to Vietnam, Second through Fourth Meetings," May 7, 1957, NARA, RG 469, entry 461, box 7.

52. Wolf Ladejinsky, "South Vietnam Revisited," July 16, 1955, NARA, RG 469, entry 461, box 4.

53. Vietnamese peasants' focus on subsistence farming and their tendency to avoid unnecessary risks support the arguments made by James Scott and others about the nature of rural Southeast Asians. Scott, e.g., argues that rural inhabitants throughout Southeast Asia have historically exhibited an aversion to risk taking and have made choices based on their perceived survival needs and village relationships, according to what he calls the "safety first principle." Scott's argument figures as part of a larger scholarly debate about what factors have informed the decision-making processes of peasants and the basic social structures in rural Southeast Asia. See James Scott, *The Moral Economy of the Peasant: Rebellion and Subsistence in Southeast Asia* (New Haven, CT: Yale University Press, 1976). For a response to Scott, see Samuel Popkin, *The Rational Peasant: The Political Economy of Rural Society in Vietnam* (Berkeley and Los Angeles: University of California Press, 1979), in which it is contended that farmers make decisions with the conscious objective of maximizing their profits. According to Popkin, peasants' decisions are often based on individual motivations that are not driven by subsistence requirements or concerns about maintaining a social balance within the village. More recent scholarship has depicted the behavior of most peasants (and, of course, the term *peasants* describes an incredibly diverse range of people throughout Southeast Asia) as somewhere in the middle of either extreme. Although I generally agree with the more nuanced arguments regarding peasant behavior, I have found that American aid workers from USOM and IVS observed many cases in which Vietnamese farmers displayed an unwillingness to take economic risks or adopt new methods, thus conforming with some aspects of Scott's thesis.

54. Alan Berlet newsletter, January 29, 1963, IVS.

55. Bob McNeff newsletter, May 24, 1962, IVS.

56. Recent work by David Biggs and David Hunt suggests that rural populations in Vietnam were not as conservative as earlier observers and scholars assumed. See Biggs, *Quagmire;* and Hunt, *Vietnam's Southern Revolution.* However, the contemporary accounts of IVS and USOM personnel are nearly uniform in their description of the conservative and cautious nature of most peasants in Vietnam.

57. See Fitzgerald, *Every Farm a Factory,* 174–82.

58. Thomas, *The Vietnam Story of International Voluntary Services,* 91–92. See also USOM Agriculture Division Monthly Reports, NARA, RG 286, entry 450, box 246.

59. Everett La Rue newsletter, July 29, 1961, May 24, 1962, IVS. Fitzgerald also argues that the costs associated with adopting new farm techniques often outweigh the perceived benefits from the point of view of farmers. See Fitzgerald, *Every Farm a Factory,* 106–28.

60. Don Schmidt newsletter, February 14, 1961, IVS.

61. Larry Laverentz newsletter, July 23, 1961, IVS.

62. Harvey Neese newsletter, August 15, 1959, IVS.

63. David DePuy newsletter, October 1, 1964, IVS.

64. David DePuy newsletter, November 1, 1964, IVS.

65. Bob McNeff newsletter, November 24, 1963, IVS.

66. This assumption, which GVN and US officials shared, manifested itself most clearly in the agroville and strategic hamlet programs, both of which are discussed in detail in chapter 5 below.

67. David DePuy newsletter, February 15, 1965, IVS. DePuy's observations dovetail with the historian Richard Pells's arguments that cultural diplomacy and foreign assistance have been most successful when allowed to take their own course and aid recipients can employ ideas or resources according to their own needs. See Pells, *Not Like Us.*

68. Mike Chilton newsletter, January 20, 1961, IVS.

69. David Nuttle newsletter, March 5, 1960, IVS.

70. Everett La Rue newsletter, July 21, 1961, IVS.

71. Theodore Heavner, "Peasant Attitudes toward the GVN," June 16, 1960, NARA, RG 469, entry 461, box 8.

72. For an example of this approach and such policies, see "Tren Dia-hat Hanh-chanh" (In the realm of administration), n.d., TTLT-II. See also Hickey, *Sons of the Mountains,* chap. 5.

73. Gerald Hickey, an anthropologist and former participant in the Michigan State University Vietnam Project, wrote two of the most comprehensive accounts of ethnic minority groups in Vietnam. His *Sons of the Mountains* explores minority societies from the prehistoric period through 1954. His *Free in the Forest: Ethnohistory of the Vietnamese Central Highlands, 1954–1976* (New Haven, CT: Yale University Press, 1982) covers the ethnic minorities during the following two decades. According to Hickey, Vietnam's minorities spoke a variety of languages that can be traced to the Austronesian or Mon Khmer linguistic families.

74. Two important exceptions were the Khmer, who lived in the Mekong delta and close to the Cambodian border, and some of the remaining Cham communities. Before the Vietnamese conquered their lands in the fifteenth century, the Cham had historically occupied the central coast, living at or near what are now the cities of Hoi An, Da Nang, and Nha Trang. The Cham controlled the rivers and seaports in these areas, and they participated in maritime commercial activities with Chinese and other Southeast Asian traders. After the final defeat of their kingdom in 1471, many Cham fled to the highlands or neighboring states such as Cambodia. See Hickey, *Sons of the Mountains.*

75. Swidden agriculture consists of burning foliage to clear an area and add nitrogen to the soil. Afterward, ethnic minorities cultivated the cleared land for one or more seasons, until the soil lost its nutrients, and then moved on to another area, where they would begin the cycle anew. For a more detailed description of swidden agriculture as well as the social, political, and cultural implications arising from this system, see Hickey, *Sons of the Mountains,* 19–28, 412; and Mary Somers-Heidhues, *Southeast Asia: A Concise History* (New York: Thames & Hudson, 2000).

76. Anderson, *The Spectre of Comparisons,* 320–23; Hickey, *Sons of the Mountains,* 385.

77. "Tren Dia-hat Hanh-chanh" (In the realm of administration), n.d., TTLT-II. For more on GVN resettlement schemes and policies toward ethnic minorities, see also Catton, *Diem's Final Failure,* 56–62.

78. Hickey, *Sons of the Mountains,* 412.

79. Quoted in ibid., 411.

80. Ibid., 412.

81. Ted Lingren newsletter, September 26, 1961, IVS.

82. Bob Knoerschild newsletter, November 25, 1962, IVS.

83. Ray Borton recently recalled having many conversations with Vietnamese peasants who expressed their sense that the prospects of Diem's regime lasting several years seemed slim. Ray Borton, interview with the author, Davis, CA, August 2, 2004.

84. Bui Duong Chi to Don Schmidt, n.d., in Don Schmidt newsletter, July 16, 1961, IVS.

85. Ibid.

86. Ibid.

87. Ibid.; Don Schmidt newsletter, July 16, 1961, IVS.

88. Contributors to *Phong Thuong Mai* (which translates literally as *Chamber of Commerce*) wrote primarily about economic, financial, and trade issues facing the RVN. The Southeast Asian collection at the US Library of Congress contains many relevant issues of *Phong Thuong Mai.*

89. Ky Tam, "Van de Vien-tro doi voi nen Kinh-te Doc-lap" (The problem of foreign aid with respect to economic independence), *Phong Thuong Mai,* June 13, 1957.

90. Ibid.

91. Nhut Moc, "Bien Chuyen se Den Trong nen Kinh-te Nuoc ta" (Change will come to our economy), *Phong Thuong Mai,* October 17, 1957.

92. See in particular Kahin, *Intervention;* and Fall, *Vietnam Witness.*

93. Moc, "Bien Chuyen."

94. Through the CIP, the United States provided goods to Vietnamese importers for local currency. Rather than keep the payment for these goods, the United States required the importers to give it to the South Vietnamese government. The GVN then deposited the currency in Vietnamese banks and used these funds for local development projects. Most scholars have been highly critical of the effects of the CIP. For example, Fall argues that the low prices particular importers paid for American goods competed with local industries and prevented Vietnamese manufacturers from being able to sell their goods. See Fall, *Vietnam Witness,* 174–75. Kahin claims that the CIP resulted in an influx of luxury items that encouraged unsustainable lifestyles among Saigon's small elite class. See Kahin, *Intervention,* 84–88. Dacy contends that the basic US rationale behind the program—that the availability of consumer goods would contribute to popular support for the GVN—was flawed. See Dacy, *Foreign Aid, War, and Economic Development,* 27.

95. Kahin, *Intervention,* 85.

96. Letters written at the time by IVSers contain many examples of the volun-

teers' criticism that aid programs often failed to reach the populations most in need. See, e.g., Charles Fields Jr. newsletter, May 18, 1962, and Jim Green newsletter, April 18, 1961, IVS.

97. Mike Chilton newsletter, January 20, 1961, IVS.

98. Theodore Heavner, "Peasant Attitudes toward the GVN," June 16, 1960, NARA, RG 469, entry 461, box 8.

99. "Restive Political Situation in South Vietnam" (Department of State Intelligence Report), August 29, 1960, NARA, RG 469, entry 461, box 8.

100. Miller, *Misalliance,* 173–77.

101. Richard Pringle, "End of Tour Report," May 22, 1964, NARA, RG 286, entry 449, box 240. Nicole Sackley argues that many US policy makers at the time took the opposite view—they valued rural development over urban issues, such as poverty, etc. See Sackley, "The Village as Cold War Site."

102. Ray Borton, interview with the author, Davis, CA, August 2, 2004.

103. Ibid.

104. Donald Fortner newsletter, November 20, 1961, IVS.

105. Harvey Neese newsletter, July 10, 1959, IVS.

106. Charles Francis Lay newsletter, August 8, 1961, IVS. If sharing a house with the American military advisers was not bad enough, the MAAG installment at Ban Me Thuot occupied one of Bao Dai's former hunting lodges. In the minds of many IVSers, including Lay, living in one of the former emperor's residences would serve only to alienate further the volunteers from the people they were trying to assist.

107. Luce and Sommer, *Vietnam: The Unheard Voices,* 17, 12–13. "Caught in the Middle" is the title of the first chapter of *Vietnam: The Unheard Voices.*

108. For an excellent examination of the southern insurgency, see Hunt, *Vietnam's Southern Revolution.* Brigham's *Guerilla Diplomacy* provides a comprehensive account of the creation of the NLF and the role of the organization in the war. Chapman's *Cauldron of Resistance* examines opposition to the GVN within South Vietnam, focusing on non-Communist organizations in particular.

109. There is a fairly substantial body of literature that deals with this topic. Scholars in the United States and Vietnam have examined Le Duan's Southern Movement, and Americans who lived in Vietnam at the time have written about their experiences. See in particular Brigham, *Guerilla Diplomacy;* and Duiker, *The Communist Road to Power.* Race's *War Comes to Long An* describes the journalist author's experiences in the Mekong delta as that region became a bastion for anti-government and Communist activity. For more recent accounts of Le Duan's background, position, and influence within the VWP, see Asselin, *Hanoi's Road to the Vietnam War;* and Nguyen, *Hanoi's War.*

110. See in particular *The Pentagon Papers;* Herring, *America's Longest War;* and Kahin, *Intervention.*

111. Don Luce and John Sommer write about this early period with a tone of nostalgia for an almost romantic time in US-Vietnam relations. See Luce and Sommer, *Vietnam: The Unheard Voices.*

112. See Miller, *Misalliance,* 200–202 (on Law 10/59), 177–84 (on the agroville program). For an earlier discussion of these policies, see Lacouture, *Vietnam between Two Truces,* 29–31; and Kahin, *Intervention,* 98. On Law 10/59, see also *The Pentagon Papers,* 1:311.

113. For more on the creation and platform of the NLF, see Brigham, *Guerilla Diplomacy,* 1–19. See also Kahin, *Intervention,* 115–20.

114. Milton Esman to Leland Barrows, September 24, 1957, NARA, RG 469, entry 461, box 8.

115. "Restive Political Situation in South Vietnam," August 29, 1960, NARA, RG 469, entry 461, box 8.

116. "USOM Agriculture Monthly Report," August 1963, NARA, RG 286, entry 449, box 240. Ba Xuyen Province has been renamed and is now known as Soc Trang Province.

117. Verle Lanier newsletter, January 17, February 17, April 17, July 17, September 17, 1960, and January 17, 1961, IVS.

118. Thomas Beard newsletter, May 15, 1961, IVS.

119. Charles Francis Lay newsletter, August 8, 1961, IVS.

120. Bob Knoernschild newsletter, November 25, 1962, IVS.

121. Alan Berlet newsletter, April 3, 1962, IVS.

122. USAID Bureau for Far East Report, "Priority of Vietnam Program for AID Bureau for Far East," March 8, 1962, NARA, RG 286, entry 639, box 331.

123. "USOM Summary of U.S. Aid to Vietnam," March 6, 1964, NARA, RG 286, entry 450, box 244.

124. USOM to AID Offices in Asia, "Technical Service Report," February 19, 1963, NARA, RG 286, entry 450, box 246.

## 4. Policing the Insurgency

1. Ton That Trach, Director General of the Civil Guard, to the Head of the GVN Ministries, December 29, 1955, TTLT-II.

2. For a breakdown of US foreign aid to Vietnam in mid-1957, see "Technical Cooperation Program Summaries," June 1957, pp. 115–16, USAID. See also "Mutual Security Programs Fiscal Year Projects for Vietnam," May 21, 1957, April 1, 1958, and November 28, 1959, USAID. According to the US Defense Department's estimates, 80 percent of American aid money for South Vietnam was specifically earmarked for security projects. See *The Pentagon Papers,* 1:268.

3. In April 1955, MSU reached a joint agreement with the US government and the South Vietnamese government to provide Diem's regime with technical assistance in public and police administration. The MSU project received its funding from and operated under the auspices of the International Cooperation Administration, the US government agency responsible for foreign aid. For more detail, see "Agreement between the Government of the United States, Represented by the Foreign Operations Administration, and Michigan State University," April 19, 1955, box 627, folder 80, VPP.

4. As Jessica Chapman has shown, opposition from these opposition groups, especially the Hoa Hao and Cao Dai, continued to plague the GVN even after the crisis Vietnamese and American policy makers considered to have been resolved. She discusses the contributions and participation of these groups in the formation of the National Liberation Front at the end of the decade. See Chapman, *Cauldron of Resistance.* For earlier interpretations of the sect crisis and Diem's handling of it, see Anderson, *Trapped by Success,* 121–33; and Kahin, *Intervention,* 95–98. See also William Henderson and Wesley Fishel, "The Foreign Policy of Ngo Dinh Diem," in *Vietnam: Anatomy of a Conflict,* ed. Wesley Fishel (Itasca, IL: F. E. Peacock, 1968), 192–219, 201–2.

5. Although it is difficult to determine the extent of political violence in South Vietnam during the late 1950s, most scholars divide the period into three distinct phases when describing the insurgency. Most agree that the anti-GVN insurgency operated in a limited and unorganized fashion between 1955 and 1957, that violence escalated but was characterized by an indigenous South Vietnamese movement between 1957 and 1959, and that 1959 marked the beginning of an organized insurgency backed by the government in Hanoi. For one of the best recent accounts of the southern insurgency, see Hunt, *Vietnam's Southern Revolution.* However, it is important to note that US and GVN intelligence estimates for this period were not comprehensive. In fact, the US government did not produce a national intelligence estimate for South Vietnam between 1956 and 1959. According to *The Pentagon Papers,* intelligence on the security situation from 1954 to 1960 depended on "a narrow and less reliable range of sources" than in later years, especially after 1963. See *The Pentagon Papers,* 1:258.

6. Catton, *Diem's Final Failure,* 14. For more on the creation and early activities of the Can Lao, see Miller, *Misalliance,* 46–48. See also Lacouture, *Vietnam between Two Truces,* 28–31, 52; and *The Pentagon Papers,* 1:302.

7. For an overview of infrastructure projects from 1958 to 1960, see Carter, *Inventing Vietnam,* 88–91.

8. Weidner to Barrows, "Recommendations for American and Vietnamese Action re Civil Security," October 11, 1955, box 683, folder 89, VPP.

9. Weidner to Barrows, "Recommendations for American and Vietnamese Action re Civil Security," October 11, 1955, box 683, folder 89, VPP.

10. Although Brandstatter was based in East Lansing during the Vietnam Project's tenure, he was one of four members of the MSU team that traveled to Saigon in 1955 and was responsible for securing a contract with the GVN.

11. Ernst, *Forging a Fateful Alliance,* 64. Although the MSU police group, including the entrenched CIA unit, shared its Saigon headquarters with the university's public administration team, many of them spent more time in the field than did their colleagues in public administration. Given the nature of their work, which included providing training and supplying equipment for local security organizations, they frequently interacted with leaders at the provincial and village levels as well as with police officers living throughout South Vietnam.

12. Ralph Smuckler, interview with the author, Washington, DC, April 16, 2004. See also Ernst, *Forging a Fateful Alliance*, 82–83.

13. Michael McClintock, *Instruments of Statecraft: US Guerilla Warfare, Counterinsurgency, and Counter-Terrorism, 1940–1990* (New York: Pantheon, 1992), 191.

14. For example, the MSU group recommended developing South Vietnam's civil guard into a force that would operate at the provincial level and be closely modeled on US state police agencies. Similarly, it oversaw the creation of the Vietnamese Bureau of Investigation—patterned after the FBI—which sought to employ modern, scientific techniques in its investigations of criminals and political subversives.

15. Confidential Memo in USOM Program File for FY 1957, n.d., NARA, RG 469, entry 461, box 8.

16. Frank Walton, "National Police Plan for Vietnam, March 1964," pp. 10, 14, NARA, RG 286, entry 32, box 67, folder 24.

17. As one American in Vietnam at the time reported in a secret memo: "Diem will not tolerate any opposition whatsoever." William Ellis, "Vietnam Report," August 15, 1960, p. 2, NARA, RG 469, entry 461, box 14.

18. In *Guerilla Diplomacy*, Brigham argues that the National Liberation Front (NLF) had distinct demands, interests, and policies from the Democratic Republic of Vietnam. Pierre Asselin also describes tension and disagreements between the Vietnamese Workers' Party in Hanoi and the leadership of the NLF in the South. See Asselin, *Hanoi's Road to the Vietnam War*.

19. William Ellis, "Vietnam Report," August 15, 1960, p. 7, NARA, RG 469, entry 461, box 14.

20. Lansdale, *In the Midst of Wars*, 353.

21. William Ellis, "Vietnam Report," August 15, 1960, pp. 5–6, NARA, RG 469, entry 461, box 14.

22. Sloane to Howard Hoyt, "Survey of Police Organization Central Vietnam and City of Hue," March 1, 1956, box 682, folder 42, VPP.

23. Rumpf to Hoyt, "Field Survey Trip to Phan Thiet," December 12, 1957, box 682, folder 42, VPP.

24. The funding for such material aid was provided by the US government, via USOM, and the MSU group was charged with identifying, purchasing, and distributing the necessary equipment. "International Cooperation Administration Subproject Agreement 1 for Project 30-79-120," June 21, 1956, TTLT-II. This agreement was signed by Leland Barrows (USOM director for Vietnam), Vu Van Thai (GVN's director of foreign aid), R. W. Rogers (MSU police adviser), and Ton That Trach (director general of the civil guard). See also Trach to Head of GVN's Ministries, July 12, 1956, TTLT-II.

25. "Report of Visit to Nha Trang," September 23, 1959, box 682, folder 44, VPP.

26. The minimum prerequisites for the Central Vietnam municipal police required that officers be between the ages of eighteen and forty-five, be at least five-foot-one tall, and have completed elementary education through the seventh year.

Sloane to Hoyt, "Survey of Police Organization Central Vietnam and City of Hue," March 1, 1956, box 682, folder 42, VPP.

27. Students at the Hue police school participated in courses on judo, gymnastics, law, rules and regulations, and criminal investigation. They lived at the school during their period of enrollment, and the cost of their training was deducted from their paychecks after their graduation. Sloane to Hoyt, "Survey of Police Organization Central Vietnam and City of Hue," March 1, 1956, box 682, folder 42, VPP.

28. Rumpf to Hoyt, "Field Survey Trip to Phan Thiet," December 12, 1957, box 682, folder 42, VPP.

29. Police Administration Division, Semi-Annual Report, June 1957, box 683, folder 56, VPP.

30. G. Shelby, "Technical Training," n.d., box 680, folder 36, VPP.

31. MSU Vietnam Advisory Group, "Police Lectures Developed in Vietnam," November 1958, box 686, folder 30, VPP. This document provides a complete list of the lectures delivered by the police team.

32. Hoyt to Le, November 28, 1955, box 690, folder 45, VPP. Hoyt's letter includes an enclosure with specific comments from the English instructors about the nine students who were "not taking full advantage of their opportunity to learn" and the student who dropped out of the program.

33. Ibid.

34. Rosenau, *U.S. Internal Security Assistance,* 37.

35. Ryan to Hoyt, "Brief History of the Surete in Indo-China," January 10, 1956, box 682, folder 9, VPP. Ryan's report was based on his conversations with Charles Le Can, a Vietnamese commissaire of the Sûreté. For a description of other law enforcement agencies operating in Vietnam prior to MSU's arrival, see also Weidner to Barrows, "Recommendations for American and Vietnamese Action re Civil Security," October 11, 1955, box 683, folder 89, VPP. William Rosenau also provides a good discussion of the existing security forces, and especially the Sûreté. See Rosenau, *U.S. Internal Security Assistance,* 52–57.

36. Police Administration Division, Semi-Annual Report, June 1957, box 683, folder 56, VPP.

37. Jack Ryan to Wesley Fishel, "Progress of the Police Program," June 20, 1957, box 690, folder 44, VPP.

38. According to the MSU plan, the VBI would assume and expand on the responsibilities formerly assigned to the Sûreté, thus replacing an agency that had been established by the French.

39. The MSU team proposed that the imperial gendarmerie be incorporated into the civil guard and that American agencies refuse to train or equip either village law enforcement organizations or rural militias. Weidner to Barrows, "Recommendations for American and Vietnamese Action re Civil Security," October 11, 1955, box 683, folder 89, VPP.

40. Ibid.

41. Ibid.

42. Jack Ryan to Wesley Fishel, "Progress of the Police Program," June 20, 1957, box 690, folder 44, VPP.

43. Ralph Turner, the chief adviser of MSU's police team, recommended in July 1956 that all Vietnamese police officers use the Henry system and that all fingerprints be stored at a central archive in Camp des Mares. Turner Memo, July 20, 1956, TTLT-II. For a good description of the problems arising from South Vietnam's police forces using several different fingerprinting systems and an explanation of the origins of the Henry system, see Ernst, *Forging a Fateful Alliance,* 70–71.

44. Jack Ryan to Wesley Fishel, "Progress of the Police Program," June 20, 1957, box 690, folder 44, VPP.

45. According to James Scott, by standardizing and simplifying the state can transform "complex, illegible, local social practices" into a society "seen" and manipulated from the top and center. See Scott, *Seeing Like a State,* 2.

46. John Ernst, interview with Ralph Turner, March 16, 1994, quoted in Ernst, *Forging a Fateful Alliance,* 72.

47. Newman to Ryan, "Semi-Annual Report for January to June 1958," June 24, 1958, box 686, folder 22, VPP.

48. Turner Memo, July 20, 1956, TTLT-II; Jack Ryan to Wesley Fishel, "Progress of the Police Program," June 20, 1957, box 690, folder 44, VPP.

49. Jack Ryan to Wesley Fishel, "Progress of the Police Program," June 20, 1957, box 690, folder 44, VPP.

50. Police Administration Division, Semi-Annual Report, June 1960, box 683, folder 59, VPP.

51. The identification program was reactivated in early June 1960. When the MSU group issued a report at the end of that month, the VBI had issued 13,600 ID cards to residents of Saigon-Cholon since early June. Police Administration Division, Semi-Annual Report, June 1960, box 683, folder 59, VPP.

52. *The Pentagon Papers,* 1:333–36 (for Fall's estimate), 334 (for Carver quote). *The Pentagon Papers* contains details from US, GVN, and international reports about terrorist attacks and violence during this period.

53. Ibid., 133–36.

54. Ibid.

55. Hoyt to Gardiner, "Discussion of Internal Security Conditions in Vietnam," May 26, 1959, box 683, folder 89, VPP.

56. Jack Ryan to Wesley Fishel, "Progress of the Police Program," June 20, 1957, box 690, folder 44, VPP.

57. Hoyt to Gardiner, "Discussion of Internal Security Conditions in Vietnam," May 26, 1959, box 683, folder 89, VPP.

58. See, e.g., Weidner to Barrows, "Recommendations for American and Vietnamese Action re Civil Security," October 11, 1955, box 683, folder 89, and Jack Ryan to Wesley Fishel, "Progress of the Police Program," June 20, 1957, box 690, folder 44, VPP.

59. Rosenau, *U.S. Internal Security Assistance,* 62.

60. Obst to Barrows, secret, July 3, 1958, NARA, RG 469, entry 461, box 7.

61. Hoyt to Gardiner, "Discussion of Internal Security Conditions in Vietnam," May 26, 1959, box 683, folder 89, VPP.

62. *The Pentagon Papers,* 1:257.

63. Rosenau, *U.S. Internal Security Assistance,* 65.

64. Spector, *Advice and Support,* 321–22.

65. Miller, *Misalliance,* 172–73.

66. Hoyt to Gardiner, "Discussion of Internal Security Conditions in Vietnam," May 26, 1959, box 683, folder 89, VPP.

67. Sloane to Hoyt, "Survey of Police Organization Central Vietnam and City of Hue," March 1, 1956, box 682, folder 42, VPP.

68. For example, when asked about a hypothetical political assassination, Diem explained that members of the civil guard would apprehend the suspects, the Sûreté's imperial gendarmerie would determine whether the offenders belonged to one of the illegal sects or were "ordinary criminals," and then the army would prosecute the suspects in the military court system. Hoyt, "Memorandum for the Record," November 20, 1956, box 690, folder 44, VPP.

69. Rosenau, *U.S. Internal Security Assistance,* 68–69.

70. MAAG to Commander-in-Chief-Pacific (CINPAC) Pearl Harbor (Army internal communications), secret, February 18, 1957, NARA, RG 469, entry 461, box 13.

71. Memo of Conversation between Durbrow and Diem, January 14, 1958, NARA, RG 469, entry 461, box 8.

72. MAAG to CINPAC Pearl Harbor (Army internal communications), secret, February 18, 1957, NARA, RG 469, entry 461, box 13.

73. Lansdale, *In the Midst of Wars,* 352, 353.

74. Raymond Moyer to Frederick Bunting, Cable on the Guard Civile, secret, May 7, 1958, NARA, RG 469, entry 461, box 11.

75. Ernst, *Forging a Fateful Alliance,* 78–79.

76. Spector, *Advice and Support,* 322.

77. Lansdale, *In the Midst of Wars,* 353.

78. Scigliano and Fox, *Technical Assistance in Vietnam,* 22. See also Ernst, *Forging a Fateful Alliance,* 79.

79. Hoyt and Ryan to Arthur Brandstatter, "Communications Program for Vietnam," February 9, 1960, NARA, RG 286, box 93, entry 32.

80. Smuckler to USOM and MSU, "Monthly Report of the MSU Group, May 1958," June 6, 1958, box 658, folder 41, VPP.

81. "Final Report for MSUG," June 1962, box 658, folder 6, VPP. Jack Ryan, who had served as both the deputy and later the chief adviser for the MSU police program, eventually resigned from the Vietnam Project and took a position with USOM so that he could continue working on police administration. Smuckler, *A University Turns to the World,* 36.

82. Mary Joan Fox (USOM/VN) to Alvin Roseman (ICA/W), November 27, 1959, NARA, RG 286, entry 461, box 1.

83. USOM, "Report on Status of Civil Guard," July 20, 1959, NARA, RG 469, entry 461, box 13.

84. Arthur Gardiner (Director of USOM) to Lam Le Trinh (GVN Minister of the Interior), February 16, 1959, TTLT-II.

85. US Information Service Presentation to General Wheeler, January 22, 1963, NARA, RG 286, entry 450, box 245.

86. Charles Sloane, "Field Trip to North Central Lowlands Region, Hue: 5 to 9 November, 1962," November 20, 1962, NARA, RG 286, entry 451, box 250.

87. M. M. Fruit, Acting Chief Public Safety Division, "Report of Status of Civil Guard," July 20, 1959, NARA, RG 469, entry 461, box 13.

88. See, e.g., "Assessment of USOM's Projects," March 1, 1960, NARA, RG 469, entry 461, box 1; and USOM, "Comprehensive Police Plan for 1963," May 20, 1963, NARA, RG 286, entry 32, box 66.

89. Brooks D. Anderson, "End of Tour Report," July 1964, NARA, RG 286, entry 449, box 242.

90. Strecher to Musolf, March 7, 1960, box 686, folder 45, VPP.

91. Ibid.

92. Smuckler, *A University Turns to the World*, 28.

93. Smuckler's book demonstrates this point. Immediately after posing several questions about the implications of the police team's work, Smuckler discusses the reasons for MSU involvement in this field—the security realities and needs of Vietnam, the reputation of MSU's Police Administration School, and the request for assistance from both the US government and GVN—and argues for the importance of the assignment. See Smuckler, *A University Turns to the World*, 28–29.

94. Stanley Sheinbaum, interview with the author, Los Angeles, March 15, 2004. See also Ernst, *Forging a Fateful Alliance*, 93–97.

95. The Office of Strategic Services, the forerunner to the CIA, first became involved in Vietnam during World War II, when its operatives provided weapons to the Viet Minh in exchange for information about Japanese troop movement in southern China. In the early 1950s, the agency began aiding French colonial forces in their efforts to crush the Viet Minh. In early 1954, the CIA established the Saigon Military Mission (SMM), which functioned under the agency's auspices and Lansdale's direction. The CIA charged the SMM with conducting unconventional warfare and political-psychological operations in Vietnam and neighboring Laos and Cambodia. For a discussion of the CIA and the SMM in Vietnam, see McClintock, *Instruments of Statecraft*, 126–32.

96. Stanley Sheinbaum, interview with the author, Los Angeles, March 15, 2004.

97. Ibid.

98. Ibid.

99. Ernst, *Forging a Fateful Alliance*, 123.

100. Smuckler, *A University Turns to the World*, 41.

101. Scigliano and Fox describe MSU's "somewhat forced hospitality as organization cover for certain intelligence functions of the US government until mid-1959."

They argue: "The cover was quite transparent." Scigliano and Fox, *Technical Assistance in Vietnam,* 60.

102. Ralph Smuckler, interview with the author, Washington, DC, April 16, 2004; Ernst, *Forging a Fateful Alliance,* 82–83.

103. Jack Ryan wrote a letter to Art Brandstatter, the head of the Police Administration Department on campus, referring to the CIA agents in early 1956. See Ryan to Brandstatter, January 11, 1956, box 680, folder 2, VPP.

104. McClintock, *Instruments of Statecraft,* 131.

105. Ibid., 132.

106. John Ernst, interview with Ralph Smuckler, quoted in Ernst, *Forging a Fateful Alliance,* 83. See also Anderson, *Trapped by Success,* 144–45.

107. Hinckle, Scheer, and Stern, "The University on the Make."

108. Phon Anh to Wesley Fishel, July 24, 1957, box 1209, folder 24, WFP.

109. "Transcript to Discuss MSUG in the Eyes of the GVN," July 17, 1957, box 1209, folder 24, WFP.

110. Ibid.

111. Although Fishel commissioned this guide (see ibid.), neither the Vietnam Project archives nor Fishel's own personal papers contain evidence that any such manual was ever completed.

112. Ibid.

113. Phon Anh to Wesley Fishel, July 24, 1957, box 1209, folder 24, WFP.

114. Ibid.

115. Gollings to Hoyt, "Field Survey Problem," October 15, 1957, box 680, folder 39, VPP.

116. Central Vietnam Field Trip Report, "Observations" section, January 20, 1958–February 1, 1958, box 682, folder 44, VPP.

117. Ralph Smuckler, interview with the author, Washington, DC, April 16, 2004.

118. Ernst, *Forging a Fateful Alliance,* 76–77.

119. Jack Ryan to Wesley Fishel, "Progress of the Police Program," June 20, 1957, box 690, folder 44, VPP.

120. Howard Hoyt newsletter no. 3, October 20, 1957, and no. 8, September 28, 1958, box 695, folder 5, VPP.

121. Fishel to Diem, April 30, 1960, box 1184, folder 33, WFP. Fishel gave an example of the "brutal activities of the Vietnamese marines" to illustrate his argument about Diem's dependence on repressive tactics. He pointed to criticism within the US State Department over the marines' actions and behavior and argued that, if Diem did not address such concerns, he might lose the support of the State Department and other US agencies.

122. Fishel to Diem, November 19, 1960, box 1184, folder 33, WFP.

123. Ralph Smuckler, interview with the author, Washington, DC, April 16, 2004. Smuckler described how many officials at the US embassy and USOM, especially those "not well established in their careers," suspected Fishel's motives and worried about his influence over Diem.

124. Fishel to Diem, March 28, 1962, box 1184, folder 33, WFP.

125. Fishel to Hannah, February 17, 1962, box 1184, folder 27, WFP.

126. Hannah forwarded Fishel's letter to the White House, and McGeorge Bundy distributed copies to Kennedy and "those officers on the President's staff who are following the situation in Vietnam." Hannah to Kennedy, February 26, 1962, and McGeorge Bundy to Hannah, March 26, 1962, box 1184, folder 27, WFP.

127. "Final Report for MSUG," June 1962, box 658, folder 6, VPP.

## 5. Teaching Loyalty

1. Thomas, *The Vietnam Story of International Voluntary Services*, 4.

2. US Operations Mission/Vietnam to International Cooperation Agency/Washington, "Coordination of Foreign Assistance to Technical-Vocational Education in Vietnam," June 6, 1961, NARA, RG 286 (USAID), entry 639, box 331.

3. In 1960, there were 1,322,322 children attending elementary schools and 24,486 teachers. USOM Education Division Report, "What Is ICA Doing in Education in Viet-Nam?" June 22, 1961, NARA, RG 286, entry 639, box 331.

4. In 1955, South Vietnam's elementary schools had 13,027 classrooms and its high schools 1,132 classrooms. By 1960, there were 28,020 elementary and 3,331 high school classrooms. Ibid.

5. In 1961, approximately thirteen hundred teachers were enrolled in South Vietnam's normal schools. The training program at those schools typically took three years to complete, though some normal schools offered an accelerated, one-year-long program of study. USOM set a target of fifteen hundred teachers graduating annually from normal schools by 1965. Secondary teachers in Vietnam received their training at the University of Saigon or the University of Hue. Ibid.

6. Ibid., p. 3.

7. According to a USOM report: "There has been great interest shown by some DNE officials in the concept of a modern, comprehensive high school, and the expected 7-man contract team (Ohio University) will be able to influence materially the administration and over-all program of this important type of school." Ibid., p. 6.

8. Herbert Walther to Arthur Gardiner, "Needed Secondary School Teachers of English," November 16, 1961, NARA, RG 286, entry 639, box 331.

9. Thomas, *The Vietnam Story of International Voluntary Services*, 176, 185.

10. *Public Papers of . . . Harry S. Truman, 1949*, 112–16.

11. *Public Papers of . . . John F. Kennedy, 1961*, 3.

12. John Sommer newsletter, September 1964, IVS. For the original Inaugural Address passage, see *Public Papers of . . . John F. Kennedy, 1961*, 2.

13. At the time of IVS involvement in Vietnam, Indian boarding schools continued to serve as a central element of official US Indian policy. The Bureau of Indian Affairs did not terminate the program until the 1970s. For more on Indian boarding schools, see Brenda Child, *Boarding School Seasons: American Indian Families, 1900–1940* (Lincoln: University of Nebraska Press, 1998).

14. On US colonialism in the Philippines, see Meg Wesling, *Empire's Proxy, American Literature and U.S. Imperialism in the Philippines* (New York: New York University Press, 2011); Alfred McCoy, *Philippine Social History: Global Trade and Local Transformations* (Quezon City: Manila University Press, 1982); David Steinberg, *The Philippines: A Singular and a Plural Place* (Boulder, CO: Westview, 1982); and D. G. E. Hall, *A History of Southeast Asia* (New York: St. Martin's, 1955).

15. Rodell, "John F. Noffsinger."

16. See, e.g., David DePuy newsletter, October 1, 1964, Charles Fields Jr. newsletter, November 22, 1962, Jim Green newsletter, January 1, 1962, and Bob McNeff newsletter, May 24, 1962, IVS. See also Thomas, *The Vietnam Story of International Voluntary Services*, 101.

17. Thomas, *The Vietnam Story of International Voluntary Services*, 26, 103, 102.

18. *IVS Reporter,* December 1964, IVS.

19. In addition to the education team, IVS introduced a small public health team to Vietnam in 1962. These volunteers primarily focused on eradicating malaria by treating patients, spraying homes and villages with pesticides, and conducting outreach programs to inform the population about how to prevent the spread of the disease. They also distributed basic medical supplies and first-aid kits. See, e.g., Neal Spencer newsletter, April 1959, June 6, 1959, May 24, 1960, May 31, 1960, October 18, 1960, and January 1, 1961, and James Rothschild newsletter, March 13, 1963, April 5, 1963, May 20, 1963, July 5, 1963, and April 1964, IVS.

20. Thomas, *The Vietnam Story of International Voluntary Services*, 101.

21. For full descriptions of IVSers' vacation activities, see USOM Report, "Summer Programs for IVS Education Personnel," 1963, NARA, RG 286, entry 450, box 246.

22. William Forest Gerdes newsletter, September 1963, IVS.

23. Gloria Johnson newsletter, December 18, 1964, IVS

24. Terence Murphy newsletter, September 27, 1964, IVS.

25. Ibid.

26. USAID Bureau for Far East Report, "Priority of Vietnam Program for AID Bureau for Far East," March 8, 1962, NARA, RG 286, entry 639, box 331. This memo also ranked the priorities of American aid activities, with "Construction of Educational Facilities (village elementary schools only—plus directly supporting short-term teacher training and educational materials)" falling under the highest-priority category. Expansion of technical-vocational education, teacher training, and higher education as well as the development of instructional materials and establishment of regional facilities for English-language training all fell under the third-priority category. USAID defined this category as "long-term economic and social development (and terminating projects) which, although important, are not apt to contribute directly to the short-run counter-insurgency effort."

27. "USOM Summary of U.S. Aid to Vietnam," March 6, 1964, NARA, RG 286, entry 450, box 244. The authors of this report recognized the fundamental tension between counterinsurgency and economic- and social-development programs,

including education programs. The report concludes with a comment on the category of economic and social development: "Whereas CI [counterinsurgency] is directed at winning a war, the activities grouped within this category are directed at building a nation. In a very real sense our CI programs exist to the end that the activities under this heading [economic and social development] may one day, rather sooner than later, realize in the full objectives."

28. For detailed discussions of the origins and implementation of the strategic hamlet program, see Catton, *Diem's Final Failure*, 73–98; and Miller, *Misalliance*, 232–33. Miller argues that Ngo Dinh Nhu, the primary architect of the program, rejected British and American models from Malaysia and the Philippines, respectively, and was most heavily influenced by the writings of Roger Trinquier, a French counterinsurgency specialist.

29. For more on how governments attempt to make their societies more legible, including in less dramatic fashion than the strategic hamlet program, see Scott, *Seeing Like a State*.

30. Miller, *Misalliance*, 237.

31. "Tren Dia-hat Hanh-chanh" (In the realm of administration), n.d., TTLT-II. This report explains that, in the wake of the disorder and division caused by the 1954 Geneva Accords, the new government sought to unify the diverse regions of South Vietnam and improve administrative efficiency throughout the countryside. Diem's regime explicitly linked the abolition of regional autonomy and the consolidation of the central government with South Vietnam's ability to succeed in the revolution.

32. For a good discussion of the agroville program, see Miller, *Misalliance*, 177–84. See also Kahin, *Intervention*, 100, 122; Herring, *America's Longest War*, 68–69; and *The Pentagon Papers*, 1:256.

33. For a discussion of the shortcomings of the agroville program and Vietnamese peasants' largely negative responses to it, see Catton, *Diem's Final Failure*, 51–72. See also Kahin, *Intervention*, 100, 122; and Herring, *America's Longest War*, 68–69.

34. Kahin, *Intervention*, 100.

35. Karnow, *Vietnam*, 231.

36. Miller describes Nhu's vision of the strategic hamlet program as an "important departure" from the palace's earlier counterinsurgency efforts, including the agroville program. See Miller, *Misalliance*, 234. However, Miller's claim is only somewhat convincing, given the similarities between both the goals—military, social, and political—and the implementation of the two projects.

37. During the 1950s, the CIA and the US military attempted to put down the Huk Rebellion in central Luzon. What had begun in the early 1940s as a peasant movement to resist Japanese occupation of the Philippines materialized a decade later as the Hukbalahap, a military and political organization that used conventional and guerilla tactics in its efforts to restore control of agrarian policies and local politics to the Filipino peasantry. Edward Lansdale, a CIA agent who had directed US intelligence on the Philippines between 1945 and 1948, led the efforts. Lansdale

believed that the United States could defeat the Huks through a program of psychological warfare based on winning public support for a pro-US regime while simultaneously annihilating the Huk guerilla fighters. As he explained in his memoir years later, he assumed that "socio-economic ills caused people to join the Huk ranks." He believed that the United States could weaken the popular appeal of the Huks by attracting peasants and inducing Huk insurgents to surrender with the promise of economic assistance. On the basis of this assumption, Lansdale and his colleagues developed the Economic Development Corps (EDCOR) program, which created protected farms with basic amenities for government sympathizers and Huk defectors. The EDCOR farms served as one of the central models for the strategic hamlets in Vietnam. See Lansdale, *In the Midst of Wars,* 50–59 (quote 51). For a discussion of the Huk Rebellion, see McClintock, *Instruments of Statecraft,* 85–91. For more on Lansdale's work in the Philippines and EDCOR, see McClintock, *Instruments of Statecraft,* 107, 112–15.

38. Latham, *Modernization as Ideology,* 153.

39. According to Miller: "The [Ngo] brothers pointedly rejected key parts of the British model as inappropriate for Vietnam." Miller, *Misalliance,* 232. In early 1962, William Colby, the CIA station chief in South Vietnam, recommended that President Diem and his brother Nhu meet with Robert Thompson, who had engineered a program similar to Lansdale's EDCOR in Malaya in order to defeat Chinese and Communist insurgents. On the basis of his experiences working for the British Colonial Services, Thompson recommended isolating insurgent groups and then saturating them with military and police force. The central element of his strategy was the complete political and physical separation of the guerillas and the population. Writing to W. Averell Harriman, assistant secretary of state for Far Eastern affairs, Sterling Cottrell, the director of the Vietnam Task Force, explained Thompson's strategy as he presented it to GVN and US officials. See Cottrell to Harriman, April 6, 1962, *FRUS, 1961–63,* vol. 2, pp. 310–15.

40. The US Special Forces published an updated manual in 1960 titled "Counter-Insurgency Operations." These two manuals formed the intellectual and ideological basis in the United States of the "new doctrine of counterinsurgency" during the Cold War. See McClintock, *Instruments of Statecraft,* 214–18.

41. Ibid., 216, 297.

42. For an explanation of Nhu's triple revolution concept, see Miller, *Misalliance,* 235–37. For discussions of the Ngo brothers' ideas about personalism and its applicability in Vietnam, see ibid., 43–46; and Catton, *Diem's Final Failure,* 41–49.

43. Memorandum from Conversation at Gia Long Palace during Senator Mike Mansfield's Visit to Vietnam, December 1, 1962, *FRUS, 1961–63,* vol. 2, pp. 750–57.

44. See Catton, *Diem's Final Failure,* 66–70; and Miller, *Misalliance,* 177–84.

45. John F. Kennedy to Ngo Dinh Diem, October 24, 1962, and Ngo Dinh Diem to John F. Kennedy, November 15, 1962, *FRUS, 1961–63,* vol. 2, pp. 719, 731.

46. Report by the Deputy Director of the Vietnam Working Group (Theodore Heavner), December 11, 1962, ibid., 763–77.

47. This point is made in Theodore Heavener, the deputy director of the Vietnam Working Group, to Chalmers Wood, the group's director, August 3, 1962, ibid., 571–75.

48. Smith, *An International History of the Vietnam War: The Kennedy Strategy,* 59.

49. Karnow, *Vietnam,* 256.

50. Maxwell Taylor to Robert McNamara, November 17, 1962, *FRUS, 1961–63,* vol. 2, pp. 736–38. A report from one month later states that the GVN reported a total of thirty-five hundred hamlets already constructed and in use. Roger Hilsman to Averell Harriman, December 19, 1962, ibid., 789–92.

51. Maxwell Taylor to Robert McNamara, November 17, 1962, ibid., 736–38.

52. Roger Hilsman to Averell Harriman, December 19, 1962, ibid., 789–92.

53. Maxwell Taylor to Robert McNamara, November 17, 1962, ibid., 736–38.

54. Roger Hilsman to Averell Harriman, December 19, 1962, ibid., 789–92.

55. The DNE statistics are cited in USOM Quarterly Technical Service Report, Education for October 1 to December 31, 1962, February 1, 1963, NARA, RG 286, entry 450, box 246.

56. USOM Monthly Report, Education for July 1962, August 1, 1962, NARA, RG 286, entry 450, box 246.

57. USOM Quarterly Technical Service Report, Education for October 1 to December 31, 1962, February 1, 1963, NARA, RG 286, entry 450, box 246.

58. USOM Quarterly Service Report, Education for January 1, 1963–March 31, 1963, April 26, 1963, NARA, RG 286, entry 450, box 246.

59. G. S. Hammond (Chief Education Adviser) to Brent (USOM Director), "Monthly Report, Education for June 1963," July 8, 1963, NARA, RG 286, entry 450, box 246.

60. Walter Robertson newsletter, August 12, 1963, IVS.

61. Ibid.

62. Although in this discussion I focus only on the IVS education team's work in the hamlets, volunteers from the agriculture team were also involved, though to a lesser extent. For more on IVS's agricultural-development work in the strategic hamlets, see Thomas, *The Vietnam Story of International Voluntary Services,* 154–55.

63. Ibid., 158, 167 (quote).

64. Theodore Heavener to Chalmers Wood, August 3, 1962, *FRUS, 1961–63,* vol. 2, pp. 571–75.

65. Thomas, *The Vietnam Story of International Voluntary Services,* 167. In his description of how the hamlets were laid out, Thomas claims that each one had approximately twelve hundred people whose houses were clustered around the central buildings and facilities, which included a school, a well, and a fortified watchtower. Ibid., 169.

66. Ibid., 168.

67. The IVS final report includes a general description of the volunteers' activities within the hamlets. See ibid., 165–68.

68. Walter Robertson newsletter, August 12, 1963, IVS.

69. Ibid.

70. Willie Meyers newsletter, October 28, 1963, IVS.

71. Roger Hilsman to Averell Harriman, December 19, 1962, *FRUS, 1961–63,* vol. 2, pp. 789–92.

72. Quoted in Latham, *Modernization as Ideology,* 173.

73. Willie Meyers newsletter, October 28, 1963, IVS.

74. William Forest Gerdes newsletter, September 1963, IVS.

75. Many Americans and South Vietnamese borrowed the French term *Montagnards,* which translates as *mountaineers,* to describe the ethnic minorities. This label fails to differentiate among the many diverse groups that lived in the upland areas of Vietnam's Central Highlands.

76. Pierre Asselin discusses the deliberations among the leadership of the VWP, including the pivotal decision in early 1964 to authorize PAVN troop movement south in order to fight alongside NLF insurgents. See Asselin, *Hanoi's Road to the Vietnam War,* 162–73.

77. This argument is laid out in a report issued by Theodore Heavner, the deputy director of the US government's Vietnam Working Group, from late 1962. This report stated that the Vietnamese had grasped the importance of using minority groups against the Viet Cong insurgency. In the confident words of the author of this report: "We can choke off most infiltration via the high plateau." Report by Deputy Director of the Vietnam Working Group (Theodore Heavner), December 11, 1962, *FRUS, 1961–63,* vol. 2, pp. 763–77.

78. Benedict Anderson explores the attempts of European colonial powers to build coalitions with minority groups in Vietnam and elsewhere in Southeast Asia. He argues that colonial policies toward minorities shaped a "politics of ethnicity" in the region that pitted minorities against the majority group of each country. See Anderson, *The Spectre of Comparisons,* esp. 320–28.

79. Hickey, *Sons of the Mountains,* 412.

80. For a more detailed description of swidden agriculture as well as the social, political, and cultural implications arising from this system, see Hickey, *Sons of the Mountains,* 27–28, 412; and Somers-Heidhues, *Southeast Asia.*

81. Walter Robertson newsletter, August 12, 1963, IVS.

82. Gloria Johnson newsletter, November 1, 1963, IVS.

83. John Sommer newsletter, October 1, 1963, IVS. Despite the difficulty of traveling in certain "tricky" areas, Sommer explained that IVSers were "very little bothered by Viet Cong activities" because they did most of their long-distance traveling by plane.

84. John Sommer newsletter, November 20, 1963, IVS.

85. Ibid. Many IVSers used *Montagnard* to describe all minority people, which suggests their lack of appreciation for differences among the minority groups.

86. John Sommer newsletter, November 20, 1963, IVS. For more on the Vietnamese government's plan to modernize and civilize ethnic minority groups, see GVN documents such as "In the Realm of Public Administration," n.d., TTLT-II.

87. Gloria Johnson newsletter, November 1, 1963, IVS.

88. Ibid.

89. Gloria Johnson newsletter, December 18, 1964, IVS.

90. Ibid.

91. Ibid.

92. Gloria Johnson newsletter, April 7, 1965, IVS.

93. Gloria Johnson newsletter, December 12, 1966, IVS.

94. Robert Biggers to Dr. Russell Stevenson, October 1, 1963, IVS. At the time he wrote this letter, Biggers had been in Vietnam for three months. He stated that he would remain there until the end of the calendar year (which would mean a total of six months in the country) and then return to the United States unless he felt significantly better about the situation for IVSers in Vietnam.

95. Robert Biggers newsletter, March 1964, IVS. Biggers's file in the IVS documents contains both the original draft of his letter and the version that the organization sent out to his contact list, which appears on IVS letterhead. The letterhead version is identical to the original, except that the controversial sentence has been omitted.

96. Robert Biggers newsletter, February 1964, IVS.

### Conclusion

1. David Nuttle, "They Have Stone Ears, Don't They," n.d. (copy, ca. 1996), IVS. Although this document is not dated, Nuttle references Robert McNamara's *In Retrospect,* which was published in March 1996.

2. Ibid.

3. The full text of the letter to Johnson, which is dated September 19, 1967, can be found in Luce and Sommer, *Vietnam: The Unheard Voices,* 315–21.

4. Ibid., 320.

5. Michael Hunt and Steven Levine, *Arc of Empire: America's Wars in Asia from the Philippines to Vietnam* (Chapel Hill: University of North Carolina Press, 2012). Hunt and Levine consider Hawaii, where American policy makers, businessmen, and missionaries pursued various nation-building and modernizing projects, to be "the scene of the first overtly imperial exercise in the Pacific" by the United States. Ibid., 13.

6. Luce and Sommer, *Vietnam: The Unheard Voices,* 315–16, 321.

7. Ibid., 315.

8. Carter, *Inventing Vietnam,* 181–231.

9. Luce and Sommer, *Vietnam: The Unheard Voices,* xiii.

10. Quoted anonymously in Thomas, *The Vietnam Story of International Voluntary Services,* 249.

11. For example, in the presidential debate between George W. Bush and

Al Gore on October 11, 2000, Bush said: "I think what we need to do is convince people who live in the lands they live in to build the nations. . . . I mean we're going to have some kind of nation-building corps from America? Absolutely not." The full transcript of this presidential debate can be found on the Web site of the Commission on Presidential Debates, http://www.debates.org/index.php?page=october-11-2000-debate-transcript.

12. Bradley Simpson, *Economists with Guns: Authoritarian Development and U.S.-Indonesian Relations, 1960–1968* (Stanford, CA: Stanford University Press, 2008), 3.

13. For a compelling comparison between the wars in Vietnam and Iraq, see Robert Brigham, *Iraq, Vietnam, and the Limits of American Power* (New York: Public Affairs, 2008).

14. Greg Grandin, *Empire's Workshop* (New York: Holt, 2006), 15.

# Bibliography

## Archival Collections

Fishel, Wesley, Papers, Michigan State University Archives and Historical Collections, East Lansing.

International Voluntary Services (IVS) Collection, in the possession of Anne Shirk (former executive director of IVS), now housed at Goshen College, Goshen, IN.

Michigan State University Vietnam Project Papers, Michigan State University Archives and Historical Collections, East Lansing.

Phu Tong Thong De Nhat Cong Hoa, 1955–1963 Series (Papers of the President of the Republic of Vietnam), Trung Tam Luu Tru Quoc Gia II (National Archives Number II), Ho Chi Minh City.

Records of the US Agency for International Development (Record Group 286), National Archives and Records Administration, Archives II, College Park, MD.

Records of US Foreign Assistance Agencies, 1948–1961 (Record Group 469), National Archives and Records Administration, Archives II, College Park, MD.

US Agency for International Development Collection, US Agency for International Development Library and Historical Collections, Washington, DC.

## Interviews

Borton, Ray. Davis, CA, August 2, 2004.

Peters, Richard. San Jose, CA, November 28, 2003.

Philips, Rufus. McLean, VA, April 14, 2004.

Sheinbaum, Stanley. Los Angeles, CA, March 15, 2004.

Smuckler, Ralph. Washington, DC, April 16, 2004.

## Published Government Documents

US Department of Defense. *The Pentagon Papers: The Defense Department History of United States Decision-Making on Vietnam.* 4 vols. Boston: Beacon, 1972.

US Department of State. *Foreign Relations of the United States, 1952–1954.* Vol. 16, *The Geneva Conference.* Washington, DC: US Government Printing Office, 1981.

———. *Foreign Relations of the United States, 1961–1963.* Vol. 2, *Vietnam, 1962.* Washington, DC: US Government Printing Office, 1990.

*Public Papers of the Presidents of the United States: Harry S. Truman, 1949.* Washington, DC: US Government Printing Office, 1957.

*Public Papers of the Presidents of the United States: Dwight D. Eisenhower, 1953–1959.* Washington, DC: US Government Printing Office, 1958–1960.

*Public Papers of the Presidents of the United States: John F. Kennedy, 1961.* Washington, DC: US Government Printing Office, 1962.

### Secondary Sources

Adas, Michael. *Dominance by Design: Technological Imperatives and America's Civilizing Mission.* Cambridge, MA: Harvard University Press, 2009.

Anderson, Benedict. *The Spectre of Comparisons: Nationalism, Southeast Asia, and the World.* New York: Verso, 1998.

Anderson, David. *Trapped by Success: The Eisenhower Administration and Vietnam.* New York: Columbia University Press, 1991.

Asselin, Pierre. *Hanoi's Road to the Vietnam War, 1954–1965.* Berkeley and Los Angeles: University of California Press, 2013.

Berman, Larry. *Planning a Tragedy: The Americanization of the War in Vietnam.* New York: Norton, 1982.

———. *Lyndon Johnson's War: The Road to Stalemate in Vietnam.* New York: Norton, 1989.

Biggs, David. *Quagmire: Nation Building and Nature in the Mekong Delta.* Seattle: University of Washington Press, 2012.

Bon Tempo, Carl. *Americans at the Gate: The United States and Refugees during the Cold War.* Princeton, NJ: Princeton University Press, 2008.

Bradley, Mark. *Imagining Vietnam and America: The Making of Postcolonial Vietnam, 1919–1950.* Chapel Hill: University of North Carolina Press, 2000.

Brazinsky, Gregg. *Nation Building in South Korea: Koreans, Americans, and the Making of a Democracy.* Chapel Hill: University of North Carolina Press, 2009.

Brigham, Robert. *Guerilla Diplomacy: The NLF's Foreign Relations and the Vietnam War.* Ithaca, NY: Cornell University Press, 1998.

———. *Iraq, Vietnam, and the Limits of American Power.* New York: Public Affairs, 2008.

Buttinger, Joseph. *Vietnam: A Political History.* New York: Praeger, 1968.

———. *A Dragon Defiant: A Short History of Vietnam.* New York: Praeger, 1972.

Carter, James. *Inventing Vietnam: The United States and State Building, 1954–1968.* New York: Cambridge University Press, 2008.

Catton, Philip. *Diem's Final Failure: Prelude to America's War in Vietnam.* Lawrence: University of Kansas Press, 2002.

Chapman, Jessica. "Staging Democracy: South Vietnam's 1955 Referendum to Depose Bao Dai." *Diplomatic History* 30, no. 4 (September 2006): 671–703.

———. "The Sect Crisis of 1955 and American Commitment to Ngo Dinh Diem." *Journal of Vietnamese Studies* 5, no. 1 (Winter 2010): 37–85.

———. *Cauldron of Resistance: Ngo Dinh Diem, the United States, and 1950s Southern Vietnam.* Ithaca, NY: Cornell University Press, 2013.

Child, Brenda. *Boarding School Seasons: American Indian Families, 1900–1940.* Lincoln: University of Nebraska Press, 1998.

Chirot, Daniel, and Anthony Reid, eds. *Essential Outsiders: Chinese and Jews in the Modern Transformation of Southeast Asia and Central Europe.* Seattle: University of Washington Press, 1997.

Chomsky, Noam, ed. *The Cold War and the University: Toward an Intellectual History of the Post War Years.* New York: New Press, 1997.

Cullather, Nick. *The Hungry World: America's Cold War Battle against Poverty in Asia.* Cambridge, MA: Harvard University Press, 2010.

Dacy, Douglas. *Foreign Aid, War, and Economic Development: South Vietnam, 1955–1975.* Cambridge: Cambridge University Press, 1986.

Dang, Nghiem. *Vietnam: Politics and Public Administration.* Honolulu: East West Center Press, 1966.

Donoghue, John, and Vo Hong Phuoc. *My Thuan: A Study of a Delta Village in South Vietnam.* Saigon: Michigan State University Advisory Group, 1961.

Dooley, Tom. *Deliver Us from Evil: The Story of Vietnam's Flight to Freedom.* New York: Farrar, Straus, & Cudahy, 1956.

Dower, John. *Embracing Defeat: Japan in the Wake of World War II.* New York: Norton/New Press, 2000.

Duiker, William. *The Communist Road to Power in Vietnam.* Boulder, CO: Westview, 1981.

———. *Ho Chi Minh.* New York: Hyperion, 2000.

Ekbladh, David. *The Great American Mission: Modernization and the Construction of an American World Order.* Princeton, NJ: Princeton University Press, 2010.

Engerman, David, Nils Gilman, Mark Haefele, and Michael Latham, eds. *Staging Growth: Modernization, Development, and the Global Cold War.* Amherst: University of Massachusetts Press, 2003.

Ernst, John. *Forging a Fateful Alliance: Michigan State University and the Vietnam War.* East Lansing: Michigan State University Press, 1999.

Fall, Bernard. *Two Vietnams: A Political and Military Analysis.* New York: Praeger, 1963.

———. *Vietnam Witness, 1956–1963.* New York: Praeger, 1966.

Fishel, Wesley, ed. *Vietnam: Anatomy of a Conflict.* Itasca, IL: F. E. Peacock, 1968.

Fitzgerald, Deborah. *Every Farm a Factory: The Industrial Ideal in American Agriculture.* New Haven, CT: Yale University Press, 2003.

Forsythe, David. *Humanitarian Politics: The International Committee of the Red Cross.* Baltimore: Johns Hopkins University Press, 1977.

Fukuyama, Francis. *State Building: Governance and World Order in the 21st Century.* Ithaca, NY: Cornell University Press, 2004.

Furner, Mary. *Advocacy and Objectivity: A Crisis in the Professionalization of American Social Science, 1865–1905.* Lexington: University Press of Kentucky, 1975.

Furner, Mary, and Barry Supple, eds. *The State and Economic Knowledge: The American and British Experience.* Cambridge: Cambridge University Press, 1990.

Gardner, Lloyd, and Marilyn Young, eds. *The New American Empire: A 21st Century Teach-In on US Foreign Policy.* New York: New Press, 2005.

Grandin, Greg. *Empire's Workshop: Latin America, the United States, and the Rise of the New Imperialism.* New York: Holt, 2006.

Gurtov, Melvin. *The First Vietnam Crisis: Chinese Communist Strategy and United States Involvement.* New York: Columbia University Press, 1967.

Hall, D. G. E. *A History of Southeast Asia.* New York: St. Martin's, 1955.

Hannah, John A. *A Memoir.* East Lansing: Michigan State University Press, 1980.

Hansen, Peter. "Bac Di Cu: Catholic Refugees from the North of Vietnam, and Their Role in the Southern Republic, 1954–1959." *Journal of Vietnamese Studies* 4, no. 3 (2009): 173–211.

Herring, George. *America's Longest War: The United States and Vietnam, 1950–1975.* New York: Knopf, 1986.

Hickey, Gerald. *Free in the Forest: Ethnohistory of the Vietnamese Central Highlands, 1954–1976.* New Haven, CT: Yale University Press, 1982.

———. *Sons of the Mountains: Ethnohistory of the Vietnamese Central Highlands to 1954.* New Haven, CT: Yale University Press, 1982.

———. *Shattered World: Adaptation and Survival among Vietnam's Highland Peoples during the Vietnam War.* Philadelphia: University of Pennsylvania Press, 1993.

———. *Window on a War: An Anthropologist in the Vietnam Conflict.* Lubbock: Texas Tech University Press, 2002.

Hickey, Gerald, and Vo Hong Phuoc. *Report on the Organization of the Department of Education.* Saigon: Michigan State University Advisory Group, 1957.

Hinckle, Warren, Robert Scheer, and Sol Stern. "The University on the Make (or How MSU Helped Arm Madame Nhu)." *Ramparts Magazine* 4 (April 1966): 11–22.

Hogan, Michael. *The Marshall Plan: America, Britain and the Reconstruction of Europe, 1947–1952.* Cambridge: Cambridge University Press, 1987.

Honey, P. J. *Genesis of a Tragedy: The Historical Background to the Vietnam War.* London: Benn, 1968.

Hunt, David. *Vietnam's Southern Revolution: From Peasant Insurrection to Total War.* Amherst: University of Massachusetts Press, 2008.

Hunt, Michael. *Ideology and US Foreign Policy.* New Haven, CT: Yale University Press, 1987.

Hunt, Michael, and Steven Levine. *Arc of Empire: America's Wars in Asia from the Philippines to Vietnam.* Chapel Hill: University of North Carolina Press, 2012.

Immerwahr, Daniel. *Thinking Small: The United States and the Lure of Community Development.* Cambridge, MA: Harvard University Press, 2015.

Jackson, Curtis. *A History of the Bureau of Indian Affairs and Its Activities among Indians.* San Francisco: R&E Research Associates, 1977.

Jamieson, Neil. *Understanding Vietnam.* Berkeley and Los Angeles: University of California Press, 1993.

Kahin, George. *Intervention: How America Became Involved in Vietnam.* New York: Knopf, 1986.

Karnow, Stanley. *Vietnam: A History.* New York: Viking, 1983.

Lacouture, Jean. *Vietnam between Two Truces.* Translated by Konrad Kellen and Joel Carmichael. New York: Random House, 1966.

LaFeber, Walter. *The New Empire: An Interpretation of American Expansionism, 1860–1898.* Ithaca, NY: Cornell University Press, 1963.

Lake, Anthony, ed. *The Vietnam Legacy: The War, American Society, and the Future of American Foreign Policy.* New York: New York University Press, 1976.

Lansdale, Edward. *In the Midst of Wars: An American's Mission to Southeast Asia.* New York: Harper & Row, 1972.

Latham, Michael. *Modernization as Ideology: American Social Science and "Nation Building" in the Kennedy Era.* Chapel Hill: University of North Carolina Press, 2000.

———. *The Right Kind of Revolution: Modernization, Development and U.S. Foreign Policy from the Cold War to the Present.* Ithaca, NY: Cornell University Press, 2010.

Lawrence, Mark. *The Vietnam War: A Concise International History.* Oxford: Oxford University Press, 2010.

Leslie, Stuart. *The Cold War and American Science: The Military-Industrial Academic Complex at MIT and Stanford.* New York: Columbia University Press, 1993.

Lindholm, Richard, ed. *Viet-Nam: The First Five Years: An International Symposium.* East Lansing: Michigan State University, 1959.

Logevall, Fredrik. *Choosing War: The Lost Chance for Peace and the Escalation of War in Vietnam.* Berkeley and Los Angeles: University of California Press, 1999.

Lowen, Rebecca. *Creating the Cold War University: The Transformation of Stanford.* Berkeley and Los Angeles: University of California Press, 1997.

Luce, Don, and John Sommer. *Vietnam: The Unheard Voices.* Ithaca, NY: Cornell University Press, 1969.

Lundestad, Geir. *The United States and Western Europe since 1945: From "Empire" by Invitation to Transatlantic Drift.* Oxford: Oxford University Press, 2003.

Marr, David. *Vietnamese Anticolonialism, 1885–1925.* Berkeley and Los Angeles: University of California Press, 1971.

———. *Vietnamese Tradition on Trial, 1920–1945.* Berkeley and Los Angeles: University of California Press, 1981.

———. *Vietnam 1945: The Quest for Power.* Berkeley and Los Angeles: University of California Press, 1995.

Masur, Matthew. "Hearts and Minds: Cultural Nation Building in South Vietnam, 1954–1963." PhD diss., Ohio State University, 2004.

———. "Exhibiting Signs of Resistance: South Vietnam's Struggle for Legitimacy, 1954–1960." *Diplomatic History* 33, no. 2 (March 2009): 293–313.

McClintock, Michael. *Instruments of Statecraft: US Guerilla Warfare, Counterinsurgency, and Counter-Terrorism, 1940–1990.* New York: Pantheon, 1992.

McCormick, Thomas. *America's Half-Century: US Foreign Policy in the Cold War.* Baltimore: Johns Hopkins University Press, 1989.

McCoy, Alfred, ed. *Southeast Asia under Japanese Occupation.* Monograph Series no. 22. New Haven, CT: Yale University Southeast Asia Studies, 1980.

———. *Philippine Social History: Global Trade and Local Transformations.* Quezon City: Manila University Press, 1982.

McHale, Shawn. *Print and Power: Confucianism, Communism, and Buddhism in the Making of Modern Vietnam.* Honolulu: University of Hawaii Press, 2004.

McVety, Amanda. *Enlightened Aid: U.S. Development as Foreign Policy in Ethiopia.* New York: Oxford University Press, 2012.

Michigan State University Advisory Group. *Aspects of Modern Public Administration.* Saigon: National Institute of Administration, 1956.

Miller, Edward. "Grand Designs: Vision, Power and Nation Building in America's Alliance with Ngo Dinh Diem, 1954–1960." PhD diss., Harvard University, 2004.

———. *Misalliance: Ngo Dinh Diem, the United States, and the Fate of South Vietnam.* Cambridge, MA: Harvard University Press, 2013.

Millikan, Max F., and Walt W. Rostow. *A Proposal: Key to an Effective Foreign Policy.* New York: Harper & Bros., 1957.

Moc, Nhut. "Bien Chuyen se Den Trong nen Kinh-te Nuoc ta" (Change will come to our economy). *Phong Thuong Mai* (Chamber of Commerce), October 17, 1957.

Moise, Edwin. *Land Reform in China and North Vietnam: Consolidating the Revolution at the Village Level.* Chapel Hill: University of North Carolina Press, 1983.

Morgan, Joseph. *The Vietnam Lobby: The American Friends of Vietnam, 1955–1975.* Chapel Hill: University of North Carolina Press, 1997.

Nguyen, Lien-Hang. *Hanoi's War: An International History of the War for Peace in Vietnam.* Chapel Hill: University of North Carolina Press, 2012.

Ninkovich, Frank, and Liping Bu, eds. *The Cultural Turn: Essays in the History of US Foreign Relations.* Chicago: Imprint, 2001.

O'Connor, Alice. *Poverty Knowledge.* Princeton, NJ: Princeton University Press, 2001.

Osborne, John. "The Tough Miracle Man of Vietnam." *Life,* May 13, 1957, 156–76.

Packenham, Robert. *Liberal America and the Third World: Political Development Ideas in Foreign Aid and Social Science.* Princeton, NJ: Princeton University Press, 1973.

Pells, Richard. *Not Like Us: How Europeans Have Loved, Hated, and Transformed American Culture since World War II.* New York: Basic, 1997.

Plummer, Brenda Gayle. *Rising Wind: Black Americans and US Foreign Affairs, 1935–1960.* Chapel Hill: University of North Carolina Press, 1996.

Popkin, Samuel. *The Rational Peasant: The Political Economy of Rural Society in Vietnam.* Berkeley and Los Angeles: University of California Press, 1979.

Porter, Frank. *The Bureau of Indian Affairs.* New York: Chelsea House, 1988.

Porter, Gareth. *The Myth of the Bloodbath: North Vietnam's Land Reform Reconsidered.* Ithaca, NY: International Relations of East Asia Project, Cornell University, 1972.

Porter, Theodore. *Trust in Numbers: The Pursuit of Objectivity in Science and Public Life.* Princeton, NJ: Princeton University Press, 1995.

Prados, John. *The Hidden History of the Vietnam War.* Chicago: I. R. Dee, 1995.

Race, Jeffrey. *War Comes to Long An: Revolutionary Conflict in a Vietnamese Province.* Berkeley and Los Angeles: University of California Press, 1972.

Robin, Ron. *The Making of the Cold War Enemy.* Princeton, NJ: Princeton University Press, 2001.

Rodell, Paul. "The International Voluntary Services in Vietnam: War and the Birth of Activism, 1958–1967." *Peace and Change* 27, no. 2 (April 2002): 225–44.

Rosenau, William. *US Internal Security Assistance to South Vietnam: Insurgency, Subversion, and Public Order.* New York: Routledge, 2005.

Rosenberg, Emily. *Spreading the American Dream: American Economic and Cultural Expansion, 1890–1945.* New York: Hill & Wang, 1982.

Rostow, Walt. *Stages of Economic Growth: A Non-Communist Manifesto.* New York: Cambridge University Press, 1960.

Ryan, David, and Victor Pungong, eds. *The United States and Decolonization: Power and Freedom.* New York: St. Martin's, 2000.

Sackley, Nicole. "The Village as Cold War Site: Experts, Development, and the History of Rural Reconstruction." *Journal of Global History* 6, no. 3 (2011): 481–504.

Scigliano, Robert. *South Vietnam: Nation under Stress.* Boston: Houghton Mifflin, 1964.

Scigliano, Robert, and Guy Fox. *Technical Assistance in Vietnam: The Michigan State University Experience.* New York: Praeger, 1965.

Scott, James. *The Moral Economy of the Peasant: Rebellion and Subsistence in Southeast Asia.* New Haven, CT: Yale University Press, 1976.

———. *Seeing Like a State: How Certain Schemes to Improve the Human Condition Have Failed.* New Haven, CT: Yale University Press, 1998.

Shenin, Sergei. *The United States and the Third World: The Origins of Postwar Relations and the Point Four Program.* New York: Nova Science, 2000.

Simpson, Bradley. *Economists with Guns: Authoritarian Development and U.S.-Indonesian Relations, 1960–1968.* Stanford, CA: Stanford University Press, 2008.

Smith, R. B. *An International History of the Vietnam War: Revolution versus Containment, 1955–1961.* New York: St. Martin's, 1983.

———. *An International History of the Vietnam War: The Kennedy Strategy.* New York: St. Martin's, 1986.

Smuckler, Ralph. *A University Turns to the World.* East Lansing: Michigan State University Press, 2003.

So, Alvin. *Social Change and Development: Modernization, Dependency, and World System Theories.* London: Sage, 1990.

Somers-Heidhues, Mary. *Southeast Asia: A Concise History.* New York: Thames & Hudson, 2000.

Spector, Ronald. *Advice and Support: The Early Years of the United States Army in Vietnam, 1941–1960.* New York: Free Press, 1985.

Statler, Kathryn. *Replacing France: The Origins of American Intervention in Vietnam.* Lexington: University Press of Kentucky, 2007.

Steinberg, David. *The Philippines: A Singular and a Plural Place.* Boulder, CO: Westview, 1982.

Sullivan, Marianna. *France's Vietnam Policy.* Westport, CT: Greenwood, 1978.

Suri, Jeremi. *Liberty's Surest Guardian: Rebuilding Nations after War from the Founding to Obama.* New York: Free Press, 2011.

Tai, Hue-Tam Ho. *Radicalism and the Origins of the Vietnamese Revolution.* Cambridge, MA: Harvard University Press, 1992.

Tam, Ky. "Van de Vien-tro doi voi nen Kinh-te Doc-lap" (The problem of foreign aid with regard to economic independence). *Phong Thuong Mai* (Chamber of Commerce), June 13, 1957.

Thomas, Winburn. *The Vietnam Story of International Voluntary Services, Inc.* Washington, DC: International Voluntary Services, 1972.

Villareal, Corazon. *Back to the Future: Perspectives on the Thomasite Legacy to Philippine Education.* Quezon City: American Studies Association of the Philippines, 2003.

Von Eschen, Penny. *Race against Empire: Black Americans and Anticolonialism, 1937–1957.* Ithaca, NY: Cornell University Press, 1997.

Wagenleitner, Reinhold. *Coca-Colonization and the Cold War: The Cultural Mission of the United States in Austria after the Second World War.* Chapel Hill: University of North Carolina Press, 1994.

Weidner, Edward, ed. *Development Administration in Asia.* Durham, NC: Duke University Press, 1970.

Wesling, Meg. *Empire's Proxy, American Literature and U.S. Imperialism in the Philippines.* New York: New York University Press, 2011.

Westad, Odd Arne. *The Global Cold War: Third World Interventions and the Making of Our Times.* Cambridge: Cambridge University Press, 2007.

Wiesner, Louis. *Victims and Survivors: Displaced Persons and Other War Victims in Viet-Nam, 1954–1975.* New York: Greenwood, 1988.

White, Christine. *Land Reform in North Vietnam.* Washington, DC: US Agency for International Development, 1970.

Williams, Roger. *The Origins of Federal Support for Higher Education: George W. Atherton and the Land-Grant College Movement.* University Park: Pennsylvania State University Press, 1991.

Williams, William Appleman. *The Tragedy of American Diplomacy.* New York: Norton, 1959.

Young, Marilyn. *The Vietnam Wars.* New York: Harper Collins, 1991.

Zhai, Qiang. *China and the Vietnam Wars, 1950–1975.* Chapel Hill: University of North Carolina Press, 2000.

Zinoman, Peter. *Colonial Bastille: A History of Imprisonment in Vietnam, 1862–1940.* Berkeley and Los Angeles: University of California Press, 2001.

Zunz, Olivier. *Why the American Century?* Chicago: University of Chicago Press, 1998.

# Index

STUDIES IN CONFLICT, DIPLOMACY, AND PEACE

SERIES EDITORS: George C. Herring, Andrew L. Johns, and Kathryn C. Statler

This series focuses on key moments of conflict, diplomacy, and peace from the eighteenth century to the present to explore their wider significance in the development of US foreign relations. The series editors welcome new research in the form of original monographs, interpretive studies, biographies, and anthologies from historians, political scientists, journalists, and policy makers. A primary goal of the series is to examine the United States' engagement with the world, its evolving role in the international arena, and the ways in which the state, nonstate actors, individuals, and ideas have shaped and continue to influence history, both at home and abroad.

BOOKS IN THE SERIES

www.ingramcontent.com/pod-product-compliance
Lightning Source LLC
Chambersburg PA
CBHW030922150426
42812CB00046B/478